SCALLY

SCALLY

Confessions of a Category C Football Hooligan

Andy Nicholls

MILO BOOKS LTD

First published in October 2002 by Milo Books
This paperback edition published in June 2004

ISBN   1 903854 25 3

Typeset by e-type

Printed and bound in Great Britain by
Cox and Wyman Ltd, Reading, Berkshire

MILO BOOKS LTD
info@milobooks.com

scally *adj.* [1980s+] a hooligan youth [abbr. SCALLYWAG] coined in Liverpool, where it is tinged with a degree of admiration (*The Cassell Dictionary of Slang*)

CONTENTS

1 IF YOU KNOW YOUR HISTORY

THERE IS NOTHING more enjoyable these days than watching home and away fans mingling good-naturedly outside Goodison Park football ground in their team shirts, popping into the club shop to browse the souvenir merchandise or pondering which pub to visit for a bottle of alcopops, without a care in the world. Long may it continue. They are no threat to anybody, usually mind their own business and, except for the Geordies, are no bother to anyone.

Equally there is nothing worse – and it makes my blood simmer – than to see a mob of knobheads from some ten-bob club, dressed head-to-toe in so-called terrace designer gear, acting hard and thinking it was always this easy.

Well, it wasn't. Everton today is a doddle for the visiting hooligan and his cloned mates – unless we know you are coming and have a score to settle. It is nothing compared to the Seventies and Eighties when Liverpool 4, which includes Walton, Goodison Park and County Road, was one of the most evil places for a travelling football fan. It did not matter in those days how you came: coach, train, car or van, motorbike and sidecar. You may as well have come on a three-legged camel with a septic hump, you would be in for just as rough a ride. You needed safety in numbers, serious numbers, as we would have mobs of over 1,000 at every game and one in ten was a blade merchant. There cannot be a ground in the country that has seen as many cuttings as Goodison.

If you came on a coach, you were parked on Priory Road and had a ten-minute walk to the ground. If it was a big game and the away following was substantial, the parking spilled down into Pinehurst Avenue; that could add another fifteen minutes to your journey. Another fifteen minutes in hell if we didn't like you. There was no escort in the Seventies to and from the coaches. It was a free-for-all, a battle of the fittest, well, of the nastiest, really. Unless you stuck together like Superglue, we were amongst you; once you split up or started running, you were in trouble. I saw men crying and pleading for help from the local police in the old days. Sometimes they were lucky and were pointed in the direction of their coaches. The unlucky ones were given a slap with a thick leather glove or, worse still, a crack with a long, metal-tipped stick and told not to come again if you couldn't handle it. Even the bizzies were evil at Everton.

The train was the safest option, and as long as you knew where you were going, you stood a chance. Very few did, and the wheel of fortune was derailed if you were sussed at Lime Street. It is an hour's walk to the ground from there, along the notorious Scotland Road, a feared stretch that typified inner-city decay. You could be mugged or attacked walking on "Scotty" on a Tuesday morning in June, never mind on a Saturday in November when thugs from other areas of the city, some even rougher than Walton, were prowling on the lookout for a stray Cockney or Manc.

Cars and vans were not advisable if you were less than fifty years old. We served our apprenticeship prowling the back streets and pub car parks for strays who talked funny. It was a well respected job for the Urchins, as our young Scallies were known, and could also be a good earner.

"Mind yer car, mate?"

Unless you coughed up a few shillings and the answer of, "Yes mate," came back in a local twang, you were marked and your car or van was history. We used to nick chalk from school, on the odd days we went, and any away fans not wearing colours were discreetly marked on their backs so that the older lads could pick them off as they neared the ground. Years later, muggers would do it to people getting money from cash machines to indicate a well-off punter who was then robbed further up the road. We were doing that in 1972.

If you made it to the ground unscathed you had done well but could not relax; the day was young and there was two hours in the ground and the walk back to negotiate before you could even dream about getting home in one piece. Everton's ground was one of the best in the country in the Seventies. We had the first triple-decker stand in the world when the Main Stand was constructed in 1971. That was for the rich bastards though; we were always in the Park End or the Gwladys Street End, depending if there was going to be trouble or not. The Gwladys Street was the home end and was never taken. Only Millwall ever tried, and they paid dearly.

It was 3 February 1973, an FA Cup fourth-round tie, when the feared Millwall "F Troop" made their assault. They were not in our end for long. As the *Sunday Mirror* reported bluntly on its front page the next day: "SEVEN STABBED." Every one of them was a Cockney, including one bloke who tried to climb onto the pitch to escape and was pulled back in when a meat hook went into his back.

I always preferred the Park End and went in there until I was banned from Goodison for life. I still have four Executive Lounge tickets which I let the lads use while I wait for the ban to be rescinded (!) and have held a season ticket in there since I was thirteen. An Executive Lounge in the Park End, that makes me laugh. It is like building a convent where a brothel used to be. That lounge is half full of all the old lads. They do say, once a Park Ender …

Long before it was knocked down, it was made for disorder. There was no segregation, and underneath the wooden terrace were toilets and a refreshment area which, unless you had rampant dysentery or were dying of starvation, you were wise to avoid. It was mayhem down there and the police presence was minimal. There was often more blood in the pisspots than urine if any away fans were desperate enough to go in.

I loved queuing to enter the Park End. You could hear the noise of feet scampering across the wooden terrace from Priory Road as the lads already in there steamed through the thin blue line and waded into any away following that was brave enough to show. Not many were in the Seventies: Leeds, Wolves, the Geordies and Chelsea in the League, and Bolton and Derby in the Cup, were the only teams to have a go. Only Leeds did better than average.

When Liverpool and Manchester United came, they were given the whole Park End and we had to use our season tickets in the Street End. It was never the same watching from there. It contained a boys' pen that was a den of iniquity; they were for the dads to put their kids in while they watched the game in peace, and only Everton and Liverpool had them.

It was a mad idea. The place was full of thieves, bullies, vandals and pickpockets, and had to be the most dangerous place in the ground. It had its own tea bar and you had to be quick with the purchase of your Wagon Wheel or else it and your change would be gone. If you'd never smoked a fag before you went in the pen, you had when you came out, as the older lads made you take a drag then charged you the price of a full Woodbine. I went in there only once and it frightened me more than any ground I have since visited. Once was enough, and I always made sure I had enough money to avoid going in there again.

I went to my first football match when I was about seven. My sister had married a Kopite and he took me to Anfield. Liverpool beat Stoke 2–1, despite the brilliance of Gordon Banks in goal. My brother-in-law asked me what I thought of Liverpool, hoping I would be a Red, but I said I wanted Stoke to win. He never took me to Anfield again, and did me a favour, as when you are young you can easily be persuaded to make the wrong choice.

Most of my mates in school were Blue; the balance of power was just turning on Merseyside after a period of Evertonian ascendancy (League champions 1963 and 1970, FA Cup winners 1966) and, unlike today, most schoolkids were Everton fans. I was not a bad fighter for my age and never backed down when older lads tried to bully you for your prized Aztec bar. I wasn't particularly big but could hit hard and even in junior school was quick with my head. I was always in lumber, so it was no surprise when a few of the older lads asked me why I didn't go to the match with them.

I had heard all the stories the year before when Millwall had been stabbed and fancied going to Goodison for the crack more than the football. My dad was always working weekend overtime though – I never wanted for much when I was a kid thanks to his work ethic – and he was not into the football much. He just seemed to be in work all the time. He never went to the boozer and was a gentleman. I don't know what happened to me; like him I was always polite and showed respect to elderly people, but that is where it ended and I was a wicked kid in school. I had nobody else to take me to games, as my only other hope was my sister's fella and he was a Red, so in the end I blagged my mum that I was going with my mate and his uncle.

She fell for it, gave me the coin to go and I first set foot in Goodison Park on 19 January 1973. We played Leeds and the crowd was just under 56,000. I was just ten years old and the place seemed enormous. We went in the Street End and I spent the whole game looking up at how high the Main Stand was. All I remember about the match was that we drew 0–0, and a lad in front of me had the fur around his parka coat set on fire by a few Urchins who took a dislike to him. The lad who took me was called Dave Allan. Years later he was killed in the Piper Alpha oil rig disaster. He was a sound lad, a few years older than me, and when his wife received a large payout from the disaster fund, she paid for the disabled section at Goodison to be built in his memory.

After the game, I joined the thousands piling out of the Street End and heading around the Park End to ambush the Leeds fans coming out. I was ten, and yet there were lads a lot younger than me in the mob. As we came down Bullens Road, we heard a massive roar; the fighting had started. Old blokes were coming out of the stands and most of them were encouraging us to "get the Yorkshire bastards". I couldn't understand why they were saying that; I knew what a bastard was but we were playing Leeds, not Yorkshire – lack of schooling was already taking its toll!

I was hooked. I saved every penny and rarely missed a home game after that. By now my dear mother knew what I was up to but was glad of the peace and quiet, and as long as I was in before my dad got back from his twelve-hour shift on a Saturday, it was happy days. Mid-week games were more difficult and it was a couple of years before I sampled one of them. I loved it even more; the atmosphere and smell of the place was wicked. Unfortunately Everton were now garbage on the pitch while Liverpool were Champions of Europe, but I didn't give a fuck. My sister's fella used to give me loads about how if I had been a Red I could go to watch the football every other week. I used to look at me mum and smirk; only she and I knew I'd had a season ticket for the Park End for three years.

By then I had seen quite a bit of trouble, the worst when Bolton came in the League Cup. They scored in the last minute to get a draw and after it was mental. We all went up Priory Road and Bolton were looking for it as much as Everton. They had young lads as well and our little mob caught a few. It was the first time I had punched an away fan. I took his scarf and he burst out crying; his mates all lost theirs too. I walked up Priory with my trophy thinking I was the dog's bollocks.

It did not last long. An older gang of Scousers came and saw the Bolton scarf. I was whacked in the mouth and lost it forever. It was a lesson learnt. I never put on another away scarf; instead they were stuffed down my trousers and then proudly hung on the bedroom wall. By the time I was fourteen I had quite a collection. I didn't realise it at the time but I had become a football hooligan – and there was no escape.

By 1977, the fighting was the main part of the day. I loved Everton and wanted them to win, we all did, but they were useless. If we could make a day better with a good result off the pitch, so be it. The number of hooligans at Goodison in those days was frightening. We would have four different mobs spread out around the ground, each consisting of about 500. Us younger lads would wait in Stanley Park, adjacent to the coaches on Priory Road, and when the away fans pulled up, we were behind then in minutes and would wait until the corner of Goodison Road before attacking. There was always another mob of Everton in the graveyard opposite us and by the time we kicked it off, they were parallel with us. Although it was not planned violence with cellular communications like today, it worked a treat. By the time the away fans had been run to the ground, they would meet another mob waiting by the Park End. Then they still had to queue to get in and would be welcomed by hordes of lads who had infiltrated the away terrace.

Goodison Park was no place for the faint-hearted.

BY THE START of the 1977/78 season, the Scousers were adopting the casual look that is still apparent at every club today. Many writers on football and fashion have covered this subject and to be honest it bores the arse off me. I really don't care if Stoke claim they had Stone Island underpants in 1990 or if Sheffield United started a 'tache trend in the mid-Eighties (they did). It matters not. Anybody who was around at the start of the 1977/78 season at Anfield and Goodison would have seen that the majority of lads had ditched the wool and had become football casuals. I have no intention of going through the complete boring history lesson as to who started it and where but it can very briefly be explained:

Fact A: Scousers were the best blaggers and robbers in the world.

Fact B: Although I hate to admit it, Liverpool Football Club were awesome in Europe in the late Seventies and took thousands of fans away.

Fact C: The Scousers started the casual era.

It does not take a mathematical genius to work out the equation above, A+B = C, and that a foreign city full of Scousers and designer shops equals the first football casual.

The start of the casual era saw a change in football violence at Everton. Our numbers dropped alarmingly because many fans who previously were in the thick of things were now no longer welcome, as they did not look the part. Initially it decimated our mob. Although 100 per cent Scallies, we were all aged twenty or younger. We had to go to places like Newcastle, Cardiff and Manchester and fight with mobs of loons wearing three-star jumpers and covered in scarves who nonetheless were in their thirties and could hit fucking hard.

On a few occasions in the late Seventies, we came off worst at such places, but we were a young firm and were growing in numbers. A few hidings when you are young do you no harm. That was our theory anyway. The worst beatings were suffered at Newcastle and Cardiff, although Cardiff to their credit let loads of young ones off the hook when we were had off there in the Cup in 1977. Later that season we were not so lucky at St James's Park. Hundreds of Geordies attacked our terrace and took no prisoners. Women, kids and the likes of yours truly, who thought we were the business but were wrong, were battered. No Everton fan was ignored in the carnage. It did put us in good stead for future years though. As the Seventies ended, we were all in our late teens to mid-twenties and had a huge, nasty mob that had served its apprenticeship. We now went everywhere and feared nobody. At home, the fact that we were all casuals made picking out away fans very easy.

The worst games were the FA Cup ties when Everton and Liverpool were drawn at home in the same round. Games were rarely changed on police advice in those days, and hence there would be large-scale disorder from twelve o'clock onwards as two sets of away fans parked on Priory Road. The worst I ever saw was in 1977, when we played Derby County in the FA Cup quarter-final and Liverpool had Middlesbrough in the same competition. Over 100,000 fans watched those two games just a mile apart and all the away fans used the same area to park their cars, vans and coaches. Both Merseyside clubs won and made it to the semis, but that meant nothing to the hooligans of both clubs. As we waited for Derby to come out and blocked Goodison Road, masses of Reds were doing the same outside Anfield. I have never seen chaos like it as we met with each other across the Park. Boro were getting legged toward Goodison and Derby were running in the other direction towards Anfield. Priory Road was like a battle-field. Everton were at it with both Derby and Boro, as were Liverpool, and there were even skirmishes between Derby and Boro. An hour after the match, there were away fans walking around covered in blood looking for their transport

2 THE COUNTY ROAD CUTTERS

MOST FOOTBALL HOOLIGAN firms have a name. Some mobs, like West Ham's Inter-City Firm, the Chelsea Headhunters and the Cardiff Soul Crew, have kept their monikers for years and still have the respect that their reputations demand. Others, like the Derby Lunatic Fringe, or the Lincoln Transit Elite, may have names but will never have that level of respect, as it needs to be earned. Very few firms have a tag that makes you think, *fucking hell, they're here*, as was the case with the likes of the Headhunters and the ICF in the Eighties. When they were about you had to have a full turnout or you were in big trouble.

We never had a name that other firms would know us by. Yet, if anything, our hooligans were among the first to have a distinctive label: even when I was a kid, Everton and Liverpool gangs were known as Scallies, with younger members being the Urchins – a tag still used by the younger lads who follow the Red Shite across the park. These were applied to all street gangs in the area, so I suppose that is why the names were not widespread in football circles.

Everton actually had a few mobs, run by different lads from various parts of the city, and at times it caused trouble, as they all wanted to do their own thing. On occasions we came unstuck because of these divisions. With our huge hooligan following of the Eighties, there were three mobs that few will know by name but rival hooligans would definitely and unluckily have met.

Tony C had a particularly nasty mob and caused a lot of damage home and away. They were the older lads and always followed their own path; they were anything between fifty and 200 strong, never had a name but didn't need one. They were a ruthless shower. I gave them a wide berth when I was younger and stuck with the main firm, as these lunatics seemed to be a bit of a suicide squad. Tony is a good friend of mine now and still crackers, he just channels his aggression in different circles and seems to do well out of it. Enough said.

Another mob that was insane was Kelly's Heroes. Like the commander in the film of the same name, Kelly would take his troops behind enemy lines and cause murder. They stayed with the main firm most of the time but at the odd game you would see them fighting in the home end or hear that a pub had been stormed and word would get back that Kelly's Heroes had done it. He still goes and is probably Everton's most heard-of name nationally. Unfortunately, every time it goes off he gets nicked, and I think he is the only lad at Everton with as many charge sheets as yours truly. Many Man United still have him on their hit list, as he got the blame for the slashing of Jobe Henry at Old Trafford in 1982 (see Chapter Three); he never did it though, end of chat, no back answers. He is a top lad and still as game as fuck. I class him as one of my best mates at the match and would want him with me if things were on top. Proper old school, his hair and looks have long gone but not his bottle.

The other mob that was about in the Eighties was the worst though, and we are talking by a long mile here. The County Road Cutters were a mob of younger lads who did more damage than all the others put together. Their deeds took up more space in the *Liverpool Echo* than the obituaries, and on occasions they nearly added a few to that page as well. They were, without doubt, evil. I do not condone what they got up to and was not part of their gang, but their story should be told, as Everton were, and some believe still are, regarded as the worst knifemen in the country, and I'm not going to sanitise that. It is the truth.

A lot has been made about the Scousers' reputation for using craft knives, and I won't dodge the issue. Many, even on the hooligan scene, think it is cowardly. I know where they are coming from – I don't like weapons myself – but I disagree. In all major cities there are gangs, and since day one weapons have been used in gang warfare. Blades, razors, various kung-fu weapons and even machetes had been seen in football fights since at least the late Sixties. In the days of long coats and six-inch flick knives, there was very little police presence and searching was rare. Once the casual era took over and body searches became more common, it was a lot easier to hide a craft knife. The introduction of "Stan" was another terrace innovation by the Scousers and, in its way, a cunning one: it was an easily concealed weapon that could inflict serious yet rarely life-threatening damage. If things were on top, one slice across a rival's chest or cheek was enough for many and off they went. It sounds bad but these were not public school boys playing hockey; they were evil football firms who wanted success and respect at any cost. If you didn't fancy the consequences, you could stay at home. I am talking about highly dangerous mass fights here involving people who willingly participate; the use of such weapons against innocent or "normal" fans was and is inexcusable.

This is the truth about the County Road Cutters, told to me in his own words by their leader. He was regarded by many as Everton's top lad. He still goes to the game now and again and makes the odd guest appearance on our tours. His story is probably the most harrowing account of football hooliganism you will ever read. I had no part in this tale. My psychiatrist says that I am crackers, not evil.

an eye for an eye

The chase was over and he was finished. The dimly lit cobbled streets had become his prison and were soon to become his graveyard. The cocky bastard was cocky no more.

As he stood penned in the cul-de-sac, his annoying Brummie drawl was making me madder: "Ere mate, give me a break, leave it out."

I don't know why I wasted my breath, but I did. "Shut the fuck up. You're not me mate and very soon you're going to get it, and no amount of cry-arsing is gonna get you off the hook, dickhead."

That was all he was worth. His fate had already been decided three days earlier when his little crew had attacked a group of Everton supporters, yes, supporters, not hooligans like me, just lads who went to watch the match, and that is out of order. They blinded one bloke; lost his eye, he did, when they smashed a brick in his face as he tried to fight back when his cheery FA Cup trip to West Brom turned sour. I read about it in the Echo *on the Monday and was made up we only got a draw at The Hawthorns, as I wouldn't have to wait long to get even.*

West fucking Brom. I stood there with a fresh new blade in my hand and still couldn't get me head round the fact that I was tooled up for West Brom. But I had to be, 'cos as the Good Lord says in the Bible, an eye for an eye.

He didn't look as hard now as he had in the ground, safe behind the fences and 100 bizzies. He was the one with the big mouth, singing:

> *He's only a poor little Scouser*
> *His face is all tattered and torn*
> *He made me feel sick*
> *So I hit him with a brick*
> *And now he won't see any more.*

Bum bum. Dead funny. That was his mistake, well his second one: his first was coming to Everton and marching around County Road, chest out in a bib-and-brace and silver baseball cap. His sort have no hiding place at Everton.

I loved the Upper Park End Stand, I did. Get in the front

row and clock the mouthy cunts below. After the game we would come out the same gate as them and were soon in with them, and then they were not so hard. The chase never lasted long.

Goodison was ace, it was, loads of little alleyways, no street lights, none that the kids hadn't smashed, anyway. And when the first punch was thrown and the roar went up, not many stood to fight.

This cunt was no different and he was gonna soon regret coming to Everton.

I ran at him in a frenzy and slashed him and just, well, carried on slashing him. Slash after slash after slash, through his clothing. But I couldn't get my target – I wanted his eye. He was on the deck now screaming, pleading for me to stop. Fuck off.

I tried to prise his fingers back from his face but he was a strong lad and he wasn't giving an eye up that easy. I cut his fingers to the bone but in the end his screams made me do one as the curtains began to twitch and the bizzies must have been on their way.

I had failed, but had given it a good shot. He was in a bad way but, unlike the Everton fan on Saturday, this mouthy West Brom bastard would be able to see his scars though both eyes. That pissed me off. Still, he would remember this night for the rest of his life.

So what? Welcome to Everton, you have just met the County Road Cutters.

the crc

The CRC were about forty-strong. We all knew each other, and knew each other well. Very fucking well.

It was how we operated so successfully. Loads of other mobs got raided because they let people in with them, people they never knew. That was not for us. If someone tried to get in with us and we never knew them, they got cut.

We had no strange faces in our mob; we had known each other for years. Take Andy, who has written this book: I saw him at the match for about five years before I spoke to him, and that was only when we were in court. I knew he was one of us then, as he got sent to jail, so after that we were mates, but before that, no way. No disrespect but that is how we were. There was no way anyone could have stood up in court against us, as we all knew where everyone lived and knew each other's families. That was our insurance policy. Family homes burn.

Those Cockney mobs must have been mad letting themselves get sucked in by strange faces wearing a new trackie. But they all did: West Ham, Chelsea, Millwall, they all got busted in the Eighties and it was down to them having too much trust.

Even recently they still hadn't learned their lesson. That Chelsea lad got filmed with the reporter MacIntyre for a season and ended up doing eight years. Well let's be honest, he must have been fucking stupid. If a bloke moved next door to me and had a new Everton tattoo and offered to take me to the match in a thirty grand Merc like that silly twat did, he would not last long, and that is fact. He would have been cut and his car repossessed, sort of.

Still, that's Cockneys for you.

In the twenty years I was at it, we came across every firm worth talking about in Britain and, to put the record straight, I can remember only coming off worst on four occasions. No doubt mobs of Everton have been battered at loads of grounds, but we are on about the main lads here, not the little firms from boozers in Kirkby or Breck Road that get ambushed at Stoke or Forest. Those sort of firms do normal fans in and think they've had a result, but anyone can do that. They are not worth a mention.

Four times in twenty years we got done, which isn't bad.

Twice by Boro, once at our place and for good measure once up there, which is no disgrace as they are good and game lads, a bit like us really.

We got done at Man United in the League Cup; that was our own fault because we all split up but I am no bullshitter and get done we did.

The other time, and I am being serious, was at Queens Park Rangers. Yes, at QPR, I know, but we did so it's no good lying about it. Lads still argue about it now and say it was Chelsea or a black firm off the estates in Shepherds Bush, but we were at QPR and we got fronted and ended up getting chased and those that were caught got slashed, so in my book we were done by QPR.

Apart from those hiccups, everyone else who crossed our paths did so at their peril. Some games stick in your head more than others. I was there for them all and still get them mixed up, not because I am lying, simply because there are too many to remember. If you think the following stories are a bit off the mark, think yourself lucky you are still around to tell your side of it, because believe me, lucky you are.

boro

We had a spate of games in the mid to late Eighties against Middlesbrough in the FA Cup. They always ended up as draws, leading to replays, so sometimes we had three major battles with them in about a week. It was boss.

Boro had never been mentioned as a fighting force in my time but they brought a massive mob on the train one Saturday. They stormed a couple of pubs around Lime Street and one lad got thrown through a shop window next door to the Yankee Bar. I wasn't there so don't know, but I heard Everton stood but took a bit of a beating.

We never went to town before the game unless the Mancs or Cockneys were coming, but word got around and we were all out and ready by the time their escort was brought up Scotty Road. We marched right into their escort as they came onto Great Homer Street and again on Walton Lane. The arrests

must have been into three figures and it was madness all the
way to the ground with both mobs even.

At the game, things passed without incident, apart from
about thirty Boro going in the Lower Bullens Stand and getting
battered. That wasn't our scene. We wanted their boys, not a
minibus full of clowns. We were not Stoke or Forest.

After the match, that ended in a draw, Boro came out of the
Park End up for it. But before they knew which way to turn,
two of their lads had been slashed for treading too far out of the
escort. The police moved in quick to avert any major trouble
and our mob of hundreds were scattered by vans and horses. It
was like the scenes at the Miners' Strike.

We holed up in The Brick and were all sorting out how we
needed to get it organised for the replay. Boro had impressed us
and we'd have to show them respect at theirs, no doubt. We had
been in the pub over half an hour when a house brick shattered
the window and a chant followed: "Boro! Boro!" They were the
first to ever do that and have my respect to this day for it.

We stormed out of both doors right into thirty Boro wanting to
know who had slashed their mates. We had, and we weren't
finished yet. The lad at the front was a Kevin Webster
(Coronation Street character) lookalike wearing a ski hat. I went
straight for him. I was onto the cunt like so many before him, and
once again County Road was to become his graveyard. He got two
quick stripes down his back and one on his hand. It could have
been worse: he was at my mercy, but did not deserve a face wound.

They fought and never budged. I had never had so much
respect for a mob before: how many lads would do what they
did for their two mates? We would at Everton, but not many
others would. The sirens went up and the fun was over – until
the Wednesday.

The phones never stopped for three days. We had to be ready
for this one and it needed sorting, fast. All the lads, not just our
firm but TC's and Kelly's Heroes, knew we had to stick together,
so we booked six of the eight Barnes coaches available. Apart

from a few seats, we filled them all, and it was a firm that would take some stopping.

On our coach, a box of Stanley knives was opened. There were plenty of takers. We had flare guns, coshes, machetes. This was real and it was no place for wankers. Boro were going to get it like never before.

What an anti-climax. For the first time ever, the police stopped us on the outskirts of the town and kept us there until the match kicked off. We were driven right up to the turnstiles and put straight into the ground, with lines of police dogs at both sides. It was the same after the game, no chance of anything. Loads of lads in cars got battered by Boro that night. Tough. There were seats on our bus that they could and should have filled.

The good news was that it ended in another draw and we won the toss of a coin and the second replay was back at Everton. Now it was their turn to get organised. They never, and paid for it big time.

The third game could not come quick enough and we had the bonus of a full week to get it sorted. We would be ready for them this time. One of the lads had a bird who lived near the ground, one of the little terraced houses on the doorstep of Goodison. It was the first of many times we were to use it as a safehouse and changing room.

We stashed all the weapons there and had loads of coats and jumpers ready to change into. It was boss: we would cut a mob up and while the bizzies were looking for, say, me in a blue ski coat, it would be changed. In minutes I would be right bang at it again, only this time in a green sweatshirt. Sometimes we would be in and out of the room getting changed like the bloke Mr Ben from the kiddies' programme. The bizzies' heads must have been chocker.

Boro came early but they were disorganised and all over the place. They split up into three pubs instead of filling one and it was a massacre. They were in The Abbey, the Blue House and The Netley, and only the latter escaped.

We steamed the Abbey first. Boro tried to block the doors but we were too many and too strong and they ended up crowded into one corner trying to avoid the onslaught. They got fucked good and proper. They were lads but not all the top faces we had seen at the last game and in the distance a massive roar went up from the rest of our mob that had moved up to the Blue House.

This was who we were looking for. We made the short journey to the Blue House and it was bedlam already. These were their main lads and we went straight into them. The pub was alarmed but you could hear the screams above the siren as the cutting began.

Boro were there for the violence but were not ready for this scale of attack and were soon clambering over the bar to get away. Some did, many never, and a few that did were pulled back into our mob and dealt with accordingly. The lucky ones got battered, the less fortunate shivved or slashed. We took no prisoners. They were fools to think they could take the piss two games running. It was a vicious fight and one of my all-time favourites.

We never made The Netley. The bizzies were all over the place by now, but for many they were too late. Soon the sirens were ambulances as the wounded were ferried to casualty. It was to be a busy night at Walton General. Fighting raged all night and, over an hour after the game, two Boro were slashed near Everton Valley.

The headlines the next day said it all: "Ten slashed in soccer madness." We were bad bastards and we loved it.

west ham

The ICF always brought a good mob up and were a bit like us. They seemed to be different from the other flash Cockney mobs and I rated them the best in London. We went there in numbers a few times but never really got the results we had at Chelsea, Tottenham and Arsenal.

They were in and out of the Second Division in the Eighties, a bit like Chelsea, and the first year they were back up they came in the Park End Stand, the first mob to do that. We only had about 100 in there before the bizzies shut the gates, and they were about 300-strong and took the piss a bit. After the game they had a small firm that tried to make a name for themselves and did okay, but only okay; I won't get into slanging matches about who ran who, let's just say I have seen their account of it and it was laughable. The rest of their mob disappeared and it is a mystery where they all went.

The next time they came there was no disappearing act and it was a horror story. It might have been a big game for both teams if results had gone the right way but they never, so it was a fuck-all game. But they had sold all their tickets and they came up in their thousands.

They were everywhere that night. We chased a big mob of them all up County Road to Goodison. It turned out it wasn't even their main lads but they were tasty and gave it a good go. We soon got word that they had come on coaches and had parked them up at Kirkby, and were getting the train to Kirkdale. That was typical of the ICF: they were organised. No other firm thought of that until ten years later.

We waited for them by The Oak on Spellow Lane and it was strange because it ended up like a big stand-off as both firms weighed each other up. Their mob was impressive; no kids, just pure lads. I clocked a few faces. It would do later.

In the ground it was charged, one of them games when the hair on your neck stands up. You just know it is going to go off. Golf balls, snooker balls, coins and darts rained from end to end and there were bodies dropping on both terraces. We were in the old Enclosure that is now the Family Stand. Today it is full of blokes sitting there with their kids who in 1985 were standing in there tooled up and ready to cut up the opposition. The McDonald's Family Stand? Don't make me laugh.

The game ended and we charged into the road at the back of

the Park End. We were met halfway as they bounced out towards us. We clashed in the forecourt until the police baton-charged both mobs and we were forced back down to our patch, County Road.

You could hear it going off up the road but we knew if we waited, they would have to pass us. There was no other way out. I could not believe my luck when I spotted him and his four mates, who five minutes earlier had been battling with us on the forecourt.

It was a giveaway – there were no black faces in our mob – and within seconds we were onto him. He ran at a lightning pace with the CRC hot on his heels. His mates were at first ignored; he was the one we wanted. He was too fast for us but looked back and ran into an oncoming car. As he landed, one of the lads hit him with a hammer on the back of his head and then the blades went into him. A young copper was only about ten feet away but turned his back and ran as the pack carried on. I will never forget the sight of that bizzie fleeing. He should have helped him but it would have taken a brave copper to front us, we were mental. (The West Ham fan concerned was named Peter Lawrence, and this incident, part of which I witnessed, is discussed further in Chapter Eleven – A.N.)

We all jumped a bus to town later and, when we drove past the spot where he had been caught, there was a chalk mark around where his body had been. We thought he was dead but were glad that he was okay in a few days. It was nothing personal. It was a bad incident for the majority of the football world but we never lost any sleep. It was in all the papers and the lad was on the television and radio asking for someone to grass us up. Nobody did – we were Everton. The police break-through came after the incident was on Crimewatch and a lad was nicked after bragging about doing it.

The silly twat got seven years. He was not even there.

chelsea

Everton and Chelsea enjoyed a rivalry in the late Seventies and early Eighties which started when they scored a major victory at High Street Kensington Tube station in 1979. I never went but everybody has their own favourite tale of the day and mine is that the Chelsea mob asked all the women and children in one carriage to leave the train before they attacked the Everton. It may well be bullshit but I like to think that it is true because Chelsea have always had style.

It was a few years later when I first met them. We had a big vicious mob by then and so did they, and every time we played there was fireworks. By now, they were the Headhunters and had some well-known faces. I met them at a mid-week game at our place before a Milk Cup tie. The CRC packed into the pubs along County Road, expecting them to march from Lime Street. But they were clever, Chelsea, and came on a couple of coaches. A kid spotter came running in telling us they were walking down Priory Road. They were smartly dressed with no police and were handing a few slaps out.

We made our way up Priory Road. The darkness cloaked our movements and soon, bang! They were right in front of us. The first one I saw, I hit with a wooden mallet that I had nicked from my dad's toolbox that afternoon. It was a mess and was slung, as it was covered in Cockney claret. They were all top lads and never budged, and it was fight after fight all over the road. It happened a bit too close to the ground though, as it was soon over when the police came. If we had met them further up the road, it would have been tasty, but it was still a very violent little battle and they knew we were out in force – nobody will ever forget Kenny High Street.

A few years later when they all got nicked in Operation Whatever, during the trial at the Old Bailey it came out that Terry Last had written in his diary that he got whacked in the face with a mallet at Goodison. I loved reading that!

Another run in with them was on a Sunday game that was shit and ended scoreless. We were all by the Blue House watching the Chelsea escort being ushered left toward some buses to take them to Lime Street when this mob broke out and turned right and marched down Goodison Road. I made eye contact with one of them and he shouted, "Come on then Mickey." I looked at him daft and it was only later that I was told it was slang for us lot: Mickey Mousers equals Scousers. Fucking knobheads.

I knew if we went for it here it would be like the last time and over too soon, so I pleaded with them to keep walking, 200 yards would do and the fun would begin. I saw his face drop as we led them away from safety and the fifty-odd of them were getting a bit windy, you could see it in them, they were starting to slow down and flap and I knew we would soon be able to open a few up. Two hundred yards was 100 too many and when they got to the Winslow pub they panicked and attacked us first. It was a get-out, as there were still bizzies about and they were only one street away from where we knew it was safe to have it.

One lad at the front threw a full roof slate at me but I ducked and was onto him, cutting at his chest and legs to get him down. His panic-stricken screams alerted his mates of the dangers and the shitbags left him. They were caught and punched, kicked and slashed at. One big, fat bastard at the back fell after he was hit with a piece of three-by-two. I then witnessed one of the strangest sights ever at a football match. As I bent down to cut him, the blade snapped completely on his back. My chance of a hat-trick for the day was gone, so a mate went to do him. Ping, same thing. He must have had crocodile skin. He screamed that he was not a hooligan, so we let him off and even helped him up. He was a lucky bastard.

Not so lucky were the couple we copped for by The Netley. They thought they had made it to the safety of their car and drove off shouting, "Scouse cunts," but they got blocked in traffic and one of ours opened the driver's door and cut his throat. He was gurgling and his mate foolishly got out and cried for help. None came and he got a stripe across his cheek for his troubles. I must admit I lost a bit of sleep over that, as the driver looked like he wasn't going to make it.

leicester city

We went there in two unmarked Luton vans in 1985. The year before, about forty of us had had it in their stand. It had been a close fight and now we wanted to finish it off. We arrived in the town about noon, were all tooled up, and the thirty of us marched around ready for anything. As we made the shops and a small market, it was as if we had arrived in Pakistan and, with the right-wing followers we had, it went off in seconds. They were mad and fought us all the way. One got punched through a fruit and veg stall and was out cold. They couldn't wake him up and soon the bizzies were everywhere. Straight away two were nicked and we were penned against a wall. It was not what we had come for: we wanted Leicester's lads.

We were escorted to the ground but got off by the main entrance and clashed with their lads, who were soon on their toes. A couple more got nicked and what was a tidy little mob was getting smaller by the minute, and the game hadn't even started. We won the match 2–1, Andy Gray scored them both and it was the start of a run that saw us win the League.

We left just before the end and were soon away from the ground and straight away bumped into their firm. We had them off again but were chasing them to the town centre and our vans were in the opposite direction. A few of them mingled in with us and told us to keep walking to the station. It was fair enough but then one of them uttered the worst words of his life: "We're gonna kill the cunts when they get there." He had mistaken us for Leicester and before you could blink he had been slashed across the face and his mates were set upon in a vicious attack. But what more did they expect?

We got to the station but the bizzies had us again and were

going mad, trying to find out who had done the slashing. We were just standing there shrugging our shoulders and it was making them madder. All the Leicester lads were as bad, trying to get at us, calling us Scouse bastards, but it was too late – we had done what we came for. They were a right gang of cry-arsing mugs and tried to get everyone nicked. Nobody got done for it, though a few got fines for the fighting, nothing major. We had to wait until nine at night for them to get bail and were still fighting with gangs of blacks on a housing estate even then. It was a great day.

There are so many stories to tell of the things the CRC got up to but they all seem the same to me: a mob came to Everton and we cut them up. It is not rocket science; dead simple, really.

There was the Geordies: both Newcastle and Sunderland got chopped the same season in the Blue House; Grimsby in '85 got cut in the same boozer; Villa got it bad before and after the Milk Cup semi-final in '84, but they had a good go; Spurs in '84, first game of the season, two got sliced by the betting shop on Goodison Road.

It wasn't always a Stanley knife. Two Leeds got shivved with a bread knife after we ran across the railway track in '85. Three Luton were stabbed with a lock knife during the same Cup run after an Everton lad was stabbed at their place when the first game ended in a draw. We always got even or better. Ask West Brom.

Both the Manc sides and us could write a book alone about the cuttings by both sides in the Eighties. I remember hitting one with a twenty-four-inch machete outside a pub at Old Trafford one season, and they cut a good few Scousers up over the years, believe me. It was a dangerous game but we thrived on it.

I rarely go now. All this on-first-name-terms with the bizzies frightens me, and all this Burberry cap shite is a joke; it is a fashion parade for some of them. My time has come and gone. I loved the buzz on a Saturday afternoon, but always preferred the mid-week night matches, and our favourite chant:

"Ten past nine is stabbing time."

3 MANCHESTER UNITED

jingle bells

MANCHESTER CITY BOY Mickey Francis was spot on in his book *Guvnors* when he said that the hatred in the Seventies and Eighties between Scousers and Mancs was rivalled only by those religious nuts that follow Celtic and Rangers. He was also spot on when he rated us as the gamest fighters that his mob came across. Thanks for the credit Mickey, but I can't repay the compliment. The Manc firm we rated was United.

Season after season, they would bring a huge firm to Goodison. It is no exaggeration when I say that I have seen a mob of over 1,000 boys marching towards our ground. These weren't your bad Man U woollybacks, they were a proper firm full of big hitters from Salford and the other rain-soaked hovels the nasty cunts used to drag themselves out of twice a year to try a bit of Scouse-bashing.

The first time I had the misfortune of meeting the so-called Red Army was on Boxing Day in 1977. They brought thousands and generally wandered around the place like they were at Southampton. To make matters worse, Everton were in second place in the League, chasing Notts Forest, and United were struggling, but they did us 6–2 and spent all game singing "Jingle Bells". After that game was the first time I had ever seen away fans kept in at the end, but to be honest I'm not sure who the bizzies were protecting, because that mob would have taken some stopping, jingle or no jingle bells.

Later that season was the first time I went to Old Trafford. Most clubs then took very few fans there, as it was a scary place and the Red Army were the most famous football hooligans in the world. That meant very little to Everton. Not only did we take a mob, but also one nutter took a home-made flag with "MUNICH 58" written across it. As soon as the game started it was unfolded and held aloft, and went down quicker than the airplane on that sad day in February 1958. The whole ground apart for our half of the Scoreboard End went ballistic, and we were attacked from all sides. The Manc bizzies kept coming onto the packed terrace to try to get the banner, but it was passed back and fore and hidden before appearing again somewhere else. To this day the lad who made it has it in his attic.

After that stunt it was a bit on top, but we had gone to United and, unlike all the other mobs, not given a toss for them or their reputation. It was the start of two decades of pure hatred between them and us, which resulted in more stabbings and slashings on both sides than surely any other football fixture has witnessed.

the birth of the scally

Later that season we went to their place in the League Cup quarter-final, won 3–0, and by all accounts got severely punished for it after the game. The twatting Everton took that night was a bit of a turning point though, as the next year was the beginning of the Casual Era, as it is now boringly called. We prefer to call it the Scally Era.

Regardless of what the younger Mancs will have you believe after a few shandies, the 1978–79 season saw Everton and Liverpool take firms to Old Trafford and scenes of 500 wedgeheads with skin tight Lois jeans and Stan Smith trainers steaming scarf-laden Mancs not only made great viewing but also laid to rest the myth that Manchester was the place where the football casual was born. It was at least a year later when the Mancs followed suit and ditched their wool for cotton. I can still remember having it with them in '82 when their gamest lad had on a long leather that he must have bought in the Seventies. That was the last time he wore it though, and it saved his arse when a blade turned it into a bomber jacket.

jobe

Things reached a peak in 1982 when, on a Wednesday night, about 400 of us went to Old Trafford in September for a League game. It was pretty calm beforehand with the bizzies collaring us in town and giving us a huge escort up to the ground. Just at the top of Warwick Road, we burst out of the escort and steamed United all over the forecourt. Everton were all chanting "Munich" and there was mayhem. They had never seen anyone taking such liberties on their patch.

We lost the game 2–1 and then tried something for the first time that was to be our ploy for the next ten years. We waited and came out last, then did a right behind the main body of fans and then a left, leaving all the fans and hangers-on to go their merry way to the station while we walked into battle with arguably one of the top firms in England.

If you want it, you get it, in Manchester. There will always be a moody firm hanging about. It may not be the top boys but when you're taking the piss on their patch even the fishwives want to see you get your arse slashed and are ready to pour vinegar in the wound. Soon we were at it with a good-sized mob of United's finest and we were right on top. They started to split up into smaller mobs and it was when we caught up with them near the Toll Gate that the slashing that shocked football took place. A tough, nineteen-year-old black lad named Jobe Henry was very badly cut across the back. He suffered six slash wounds that needed more than 200 stitches.

The story was all over the papers, with Jobe portrayed as a promising young boxer whose career was ruined that night by a Scouse coward with a Stanley knife. Everton, for their part, had him down as one of United's lads. Either way, he was a game fucker who came unstuck when his mates did one and he got whipped up as he tried to follow suit. Nobody deserves that many stitches but it wouldn't have happened if he hadn't been with their firm. There was a lot of racist bollocks about the cutting but it was nothing to do with colour. There was also the story that the lad who did it carved EFC in his back. That was a load of shite, as the lad concerned couldn't spell.

It began a tit-for-tat slashing regime which led, over the years, to scores of thugs – and yes, I won't lie, some inno- cent fans – from both sides ending up in casualty, getting stitched by some fat nurse who feels sorry for you until you leave, then goes back to the nurses' hostel for a seeing-to by a student doctor muttering that you got what you deserve and the NHS shouldn't waste money on such scum. Season after season it went off with United home and away. The worst was the 1984–85 campaign, when it went mental every time we met them. Unluckily for the faint-hearted, we played them four times that season.

pisstake

The first game was at Goodison in September and 200 Man U somehow got tickets for the Main Stand. They came on coaches, kept a low one before the game, then kicked it off for the whole of the first half. Everton went 3–0 up early on and there was murder in the seats; only a small number of Everton had got in there and it was well on top. Before we could get it together at half-time, they came bouncing down into the tea bar and we had to back off. They took the piss to be honest, but lost some respect when they steamed a load of old blokes queuing for the bogs.

It still makes me laugh though, when I remember the three black lads who came in a bit late behind the main mob and got sussed. They wouldn't come up the stairs and were then pissed on by a load of Everton on the stairs above them. I don't care how cool or hard they thought they were, when you're wet and smelly the rest of the day is a bit of a bummer. A copper sneaked up and managed to nick one of ours who'd had a load of ale and couldn't turn his tap off!

For the records, Everton were fourth and Man U second and we beat them 5–0. Their mob didn't do much after the game but in their eyes they didn't have to.

own goal

Four days was all it took to get a chance of revenge, as we drew them in the League Cup at their place. It turned out to be one of those nights when everything goes horribly wrong.

Start of the day, big-time firm, "Let's do the Munich," and a banner reading "Jobe, how's yer back?" dangling from the Scoreboard End. Sixteen thousand tickets we sold and, as is usually the case when you have numbers like that, the mob gets split up and a recipe for disaster is written.

We won the match 2–1 with a last-minute goal from John Gidman, who had forgotten we'd sold him and put one in his own net to send the Blue hordes barmy. There is nothing like a last-minute winner to make your day but it can have its drawbacks, depending on where you are when it happens. It would not be the only own goal that night.

We set a flare gun off at the final whistle and steamed out thinking nothing could stop a mob this size except its own stupidity, and this was the main fault with Everton's mob –

we were too clever for our own good at times. When the going was good we occasionally dropped our guard and a few times came unstuck because of it.

Hundreds bounced out of the ground but it was impossible to keep all the boys together as different mobs of Scousers and Mancs battled all the way back to Oxford Road and Piccadilly Station. Our firm was about 100-strong but was missing most of the top faces as we took the back streets down past the canals in the hope of avoiding PC Plod and finding their lads. Unfortunately we managed to do both but came right unstuck as the mob we met were all United's old boys and, after a couple of minutes, we back-pedalled up a hill. Luckily no-one was cut up, which was a result, as we knew that if anyone went down they would be made a scapegoat for the artwork Mr Henry had suffered previously.

The inquest had just begun when a huge mob appeared down a side street. We could see the plod keeping back the United firm that had just had us off, so went down towards the mob thinking that if we all got it together, the now-even numbers would result in a bit of a face-saving exercise. Wrong. We got about 100 yards from this mob and still didn't spot any familiar faces when the nightmare began. They realised we were Everton and blasted right into us. I had never, and still haven't, seen two different mobs from the same club as big as those two that night and for the second time in a matter of minutes it came on top.

The Mancs threw everything they could at us and we did lose ground but not face. We put up a better show than earlier, partly because we had to but mainly because one of the lads got the flare gun back out which, as well as scattering bodies, ensured that the bizzies were soon surrounding us, laughing as we licked our wounds and, worse still, our pride.

It's strange how the mind of the soccer hooligan works. Although we would fight and die for the club and wanted the team to do well on the pitch, after beating one of bitterest rivals twice in a week and going top of the League and a step nearer Wembley, the mood on the train going home was as if we'd been relegated. Many firms would have looked back on the night as a result but at the time we were one of, if not *the*, main mobs around and the fact that we hadn't killed Man U was regarded as a major embarrassment to most of the lads on the battered British Rail cattle coach the cheeky bastards called a train. Particularly the unlucky few who had been thrown or jumped into the canal trying to escape.

There were loads of lads missing on the train, and when we got back to Lime Street, we saw why. A couple of hundred were still milling about, telling tales of the boss time they'd had. Much to our dismay they had taken it to different mobs of United all the way back to town and been well on top. Our mob had not been as fortunate and the inquests went on for weeks about who was to blame. It taught us the lesson to stick together as one firm, a lesson we absorbed for about six months, when exactly the same thing happened at Chelsea.

the future's bright but not orange

Everybody deserves a little bit of luck in their life or even just a break. This was the day when I believed in God and used up every bit of luck I was entitled to in ten lifetimes. The return match at Old Trafford was always going to be violent, as United had shown that they were no longer a gang of three-star-jumper pricks and we needed to prove that, given equal numbers, we were still easily the nastiest and gamest firm about, if not the biggest.

When you know there is going to be serious disorder, it is wise to wear something that doesn't stand out in a crowd.

I wish someone had passed on that sound advice before I boarded the 10.50am train from Lime Street to Piccadilly, along with about 300 of Everton's finest. But no, instead of a cheeky little dark blue Lacoste sweater or even black or brown leather, soft lad here marched up to OT in a bright orange Hugo Boss hooded sweatshirt.

As was the norm in those days, we got picked up pretty quickly by the dibble, as the Mancs so fondly call what we term the bizzies, and they kept trouble before the game to a minimum. Everton were on course for the title by now and we filled the away end. Unlike today, very few football nuts would go and ninety per cent of our following was boys – if not all ones who would look for trouble, most who didn't mind if it came their way. The match finished 1-1 with both teams missing a penalty, and the atmosphere in the ground was hostile to say the least.

End of match, same old ploy, still not sussed, turn right, fans to the station, mob next left, bingo. Next minute, WHACK. "Where are you going, you Scouse bastard?" The grim drawl of his voice pissed me off more than the clack and before you could say "dibble" the Manc bizzie had me spreadeagled on the floor and took great delight telling me which hole he was going to stick his truncheon up if I wandered out of the escort again.

I blagged him that I was in a van and the hundred or so lads that were disappearing into the distance were also on the same form of transport. He gave me a glare and said, "Nice sweatshirt, poof." I should have taken the bastard thing off there and then and binned it but it had cost a ton and I had jackshit on under it, so I merrily jogged down the road to catch the firm up before the inevitable battle began. I didn't make it.

I got within fifty yards of the main mob when twenty lads came running out of a side street. We went into them thinking they were Mancs but this one soft lad pulled a half-Everton, half-Celtic bobble hat out of his jacket (they were a bit of a trend at the time to some of the plastic hoolies). He started wailing about hundreds of Man U chasing them everywhere. He was right; no sooner had he repositioned his sad hat than the Man U mob started whooping down the hill towards us.

The daft Zulu noise not only drew the attention of the Everton mob but also convinced me that this firm were not Man U's best, as at the game previous they made no noise, no fuss, just got on with the business – because they knew they could – without macho sound effects.

We made a line across the road as bricks and bottles smashed around us, then charged once the first wave of missiles subsided. They were off and I thought they were either very poor or were leading us into a trap, as not one stood or even threw a punch worthy of a mention. As we turned the corner it became quickly obvious that it was a trap. A good 200 were across the road ready to have it. Everton, with two previous poor shows, were outstanding, taking it right into them and forcing the Mancs back up the road.

To my left I saw a lad with an England rugby shirt rummaging in a skip – and they call Scousers rats. He spotted me and went to jump out but caught his arse on the skip and fell over about six feet away from me. Instead of running, he tried to jump back into the skip and, when I got level, I saw why: the shady twat had a machete in there. I quickly grabbed it and fronted him and his mob, expecting him to do one sharpish, as his blade – which was now mine – was a tasty number. He didn't budge an inch, he was as game as they come, but his mates weren't and did one, forcing him onto his toes when he realised that things were not looking clever. He didn't get very far but it wasn't one of our lot that did him; he ran straight into a lamppost and within seconds had been slashed. Most people there thought I had done it, and many still do, but I didn't, end of story. Still, I confess that seeing him with his neck wide open didn't bother me, as he hadn't stashed that machete with benign intentions. He would have used it, no doubt.

I have had scores of fights at the match and am not one of the Scallies who would chop you up as soon as look at you, but at times you do have to fight fire with fire. I don't recall having much trouble sleeping that night over being partially to blame for his injury. To his credit, the lad got back on his feet and made it to his mob before we charged again, this time scattering them. I got pushed to the front and led the charge, waving this machete above my head.

The joy was shortlived as the familiar sound of sirens filled the air and we turned from being a pack of blood-thirsty animals into an orderly group of fans who had lost their way to the station and required police protection from the nasty Mancs trying to knock the shit out of us. Well that's what we hoped the plod would think. How many things can you get wrong in a single day?

We split into small groups and I ditched the blade in a hedge just before a police van mounted the kerb and emptied its contents into the middle of us, those contents being a dozen of the angriest coppers I have had the misfortune of meeting, all armed with batons and a serious attitude problem.

The crowd that day was nearly 60,000 and there must have been hundreds of police on duty in and around the ground. So what were the odds of the same copper who had smacked me across the head earlier, and who I had bluffed about being in a van, being the first one on the scene a minute after we had nearly decapitated one of the locals? Very fuckin' slim, thousands to one. I wish I'd put a tenner on it because as soon as the first officer jumped out of the meat wagon, my skull hit the wall and a big brown leather glove slammed into the side of my head.

My already swelling ear just made out the familiar drawl bellowing, "Where's your fucking van now, you lying Scouse cunt?"

We were all searched and the bizzies started to march us back to town with the threat that the first one to step off the kerb would be nicked. We had got about half a mile when a couple more police vans pulled up alongside a cinema and we were told to wait. They lined us all up and then an ambulance stopped and out gets a rather bloodstained Manc with a huge pad taped to his neck, looking pissed off with the world and our mob in particular.

The wretched copper whose vocation was to make my life a misery directed him over to us with the instruction to "point the bastard out". As Rigsby always said to his cat, "Goodnight, Vienna." To make things worse, as we were lining up, I stood in a pile of dog shit. So here I am, my future in serious jeopardy, I'm trying to blend in with the crowd and I'm wearing a bobby dazzler sweatshirt with stinking dog shit all over my trainers. I might as well have put on a clown's outfit, complete with a spinning bow tie. Up he walks and a group of United start shouting, "It was him in the orange." Our Manc got level with me and whispered the immortal words, "It's your lucky day, Scouse, I'll never get any compo off you," and off he went back to the ambulance, which sped off to casualty where the fat nurse was waiting, needle and thread in hand.

A couple of years later, when hostilities were on hold and a truce was called between the ticket touts from both cities due to the continual trouble costing them money, one of Man U's boys pulled me and said that they thought it was me but if I had been charged it would have taken years for the lad to get a criminal injury claim. So he gave me a walkover and got £6,000 by the end of the year for the thirty-odd stitches that kept his head attached to his shoulders. So in the end everyone was happy. Sort of.

Monday morning, a fine Hugo Boss sweatshirt was dispatched to the local spastic shop, and I was glad to see the back of it. I decided to wear something a lot less conspicuous the next time we played them, and it was only a few weeks away: in the FA Cup final at Wembley.

the last laugh

We played United three days after we had won the Cup Winners Cup in Rotterdam, needing a victory to clinch the Treble. After the best part of a week in Holland, a trip to the decrepit Twin Towers was always going to be an anti-climax. The day lived down to our worst expectations.

We got to Euston at about seven in the morning still suffering from general over-indulgence, thanks to the fine hospitality that the Dutch pride themselves on. It was not a good start to the day when we saw one of the lads already waiting for the train home. He told us that they had been drinking near Arsenal when a mob of Cockneys burst in and slashed his back and arse into two. They then got legged everywhere and had bumped into a Man U firm and foolishly asked their help to front this Arsenal firm, a request which earned them another hiding. So he'd had enough and sold his ticket, swearing never to go again.

It's funny how a good kicking affects different people. Some dust themselves down and carry on regardless, others turn into revenge-seeking lunatics, and others jack in never to be seen again, which was the case with this lad. The way I see it – and I've taken a few hidings at the match – is that if you give it out now and again, you get a bit back. Sometimes more, sometimes less. Don't get me wrong, if I had my arse chopped in two it would piss me off big time, but I honestly would not bear a grudge, which is why I have so much respect for the Man U lad that had been cut a few weeks before.

We then met a good-sized mob of Everton that had done a main firm of United's faces in Paddington; they had walked into a pub not realising it was full of Mancs and got backed out until one lad pulled out a hammer and steamed into them. Before midday, Euston and the surrounding area was awash with football fans and thugs alike. The problem for us was that most of them weren't Everton, so we got off and went for a drink at Swiss Cottage. Same story. Off to Leicester Square. Same story. And so on; everywhere we went was chocker with Man U, not proper firms but lads who would have a go, and most of them were all pissed up and looking for it. So we fucked off to Wembley sharpish.

Of all the times I have been to Wembley with Everton, the 1985 Cup Final had the most one-sided support I have witnessed. United were everywhere, even mixed in with our seats. The game itself was shite, Everton looked bollocksed after their mid-week European success and it was no surprise when Norman Whiteside scored the goal that stopped us winning the Treble. A few minutes earlier, Kevin Moran had been sent off and a gang of United started playing up in our seats, calling us all sorts. When Whiteside scored the mood changed and they got wasted. A lesson to be learned: if in the wrong end, shut the fuck up in case you score.

Two things piss me off about that goal. If you ever watch it being replayed, look behind the goal as Norman scores. A bald-headed bloke in a suit does a toss over on the touch-line celebrating Big Norm's fine strike. The culprit? David Davies, who is now in charge of the fuckin' Football Association. Neutral MY ARSE. Secondly, Kevin Ratcliffe who was our captain, wrote in his book that after Moran was sent off the atmosphere in the ground was that bad he feared for the safety of his missus in the stands. If I'd have known that I'd have escorted her out myself, then run on the pitch and nutted the cunt Davies, as he has turned out to be a right annoying bastard.

As it was, I got slung out for fighting and sat on the steps under the Twin Towers as Everton let the fans down again. Still, I suppose the fans, or whoever dished the tickets out, had let Everton down because that support was pathetic. Fickle bastards really, because it was the most successful season in the club's history and still we were moaning.

The only good thing about losing a Cup final is that while the winners do a lap of honour, you can get all the boys together. We got about sixty-strong and, although the mob was small, everyone was up for it because we had lost. We headed off down Wembley way looking for a United firm.

In all the years I was a hooligan, I can swear that the number of people I fought who were not thugs or who didn't want to know could be counted on one hand. This day was an exception to that particular code of conflict. We had only got about 200 yards from the ground when we met a load of United who had been watching the match in the Wembley Hilton. At first we all said, "Leave them," but, as is usually the case, some gobby bastard made the mistake of calling us Scouse bastards and all hell broke loose. These pricks full of ale and Dutch courage didn't know what hit them as we steamed into them with traffic cones and the barrier railings that surrounded the walk from the ground to Wembley Central. The poor, sorry, silly bunch were in danger of being done for littering the pavement, such was the mess we left behind.

We then ended up in some road with big hedges lining the street when we came across a nice little firm of Cockney Reds. They had a go back but ended up getting chased down the street. We had one on the deck and I witnessed what blind fear can do to a human's adrenalin. This big lad was holding his own when he clocked one on the chin and, as he went down, someone shouted to slash him. The words "slash him" acted like a pure rock of crack as he rose from the floor and ran straight through a hedge. I mean straight through; there was a shape of him like in a *Tom and Jerry* cartoon.

We gave up the chase but seconds later he only comes running out of the next garden with a boulder weighing half a ton over his head. If it had landed on someone, they would not have been around to tell the tale. Fortunately he dropped it and ran off again. Once we realised the nutty fucker had done one, we tried to pick up this boulder and it was not possible. He must have been absolutely off his head or a serious steroid jabber. He was most probably in hospital the next day having his bollocks put back in place.

Before long we got picked up by the Met and slung on a train to Euston. We got off at Euston Square and walked to the main station, hoping to catch the Mancs by surprise. Surprise, surprise, as that phoney slag Cilla would say, we strutted onto Euston's concourse, all sixty of us, to be welcomed by 100 bizzies holding back a 400-strong United mob. We fronted it but would have been in serious danger but for the plod charging us down the platform and onto the waiting train.

At least we had caused a bit of damage but all in all it was a bad day, a bad result and a lesson that unless you are seriously mob-handed, Wembley and United are a combination that is just not worth bothering with. The end of a great season finished as it had started – at Wembley – but the look on everyone's faces gave the game away that we were not as clever or as well organised as we'd thought.

We had played United four times, two wins, a draw and a loss on the field, and to be honest off the pitch was about even. And after the best season in our history, they still had the last laugh.

wing and one

The next few seasons went a bit quiet as the Acid House and rave scene took off, but still every time we met Man United, something would happen.

There was the time when we ended up back at Piccadilly and ten of us went for a little scout around, got about fifty yards and bumped into their mob, who immediately slashed one of the lads, Kinney, so bad his kidneys were visible through the cut.

Another time, we went through the Arndale Centre like a plague of locusts and fucked off home by half past one, without a punch being thrown but well kitted out, free of charge. Then there was the infamous battle on the ferry when Man U and the West Ham ICF went for it; a mob of Everton was involved in that.

One of the best rows we had with them at Goodison was when they came into the Old Park End seats. At the end of the game, a tidy firm of us were at one end of the stand and they were at the other. We waited until all the fans left and went for it underneath by the tea bars: no police, no prawn sandwich fans, just two tasty mobs having a ball.

We went down the stairs and straight into all the Mancs leaving the terraces, thousands of them. We gave it a go and were doing okay until they saw how many of us there were. They chased us back up into the stand just as their other mob were coming down from the seats and it went off again. When the police got it under control they marched us out and, when the main mob of United saw how many of us had attacked their massed ranks, they started clapping us. A nice touch – then a dart hit one of our lads in the face.

Another time was when we had it with the Cockney Reds in a bar under the Adelphi Hotel in Liverpool. The Cockney Reds, now they are a funny bunch. As if there are not enough firms in London you can join up with for a barney. Well, we gave it to them that day. We piled into the bar, they threw a few bottles, we went out and they followed – right into a CS gas ambush. Sorted.

To be honest, I don't mind most of the Cockney mob. I went to the Liverpool–United FA Cup final in 1996 doing

the tickets and ended up in a pub a few stops from Wembley
when they all walked in. I gave it a low one but got recognised and should have taken a kicking, but a lad Messar and
another called Wayne smoothed things and they gave me a
walkover. I even have a beer with them now. They are a game
mob but I don't understand why they don't just go down
Millwall or West Ham for lumber. It's not as if they are
following United because they are now a boss team; these
lads have been going for years, even when they were shite.

I got to know the main Manchester boys after a mid-
week League Cup match at Goodison. The days of 200-
strong firms were a distant memory and, as we lost, we
pulled about fifty, which wasn't too bad for the time. We
waited by the Paddock and they came out but no Mancs
seemed up for it and they definitely weren't firmed up big.
In those days they didn't have Hibs, Oldham and the rest
that have latched onto them lately, so we walked around to
see if any were going back to Lime Street. Some kids said
they had seen a small mob come late in cars or by minibus,
so we waited by the park.

The shout went up, "They're here." We bounced over to
see a black lad getting ragged across the road by a little gang
of Urchins. It was always the same story at Everton: when it
went off, there was no hiding place for black people. Off he
went into the distance running for his life. Just as we
thought he was a lone unfortunate who had ended up in the
wrong place at the wrong time, BANG, I'm sitting on my
fat arse in the road. I had met the "Magnificent Seventeen"
as Massey, one of United's top lads, called them.

I got up and we had a nice toe-to-toe with their best. No-
one ran, no-one won or lost, just a top little battle with all
the main lads from both sides. I had total respect for them
after that because when I was on the deck they could have
booted me all the way home, but it wasn't their style. Wing
Commander (one of their elite) told me years later that the

black lad who had brought it on top for them wasn't a hooligan, just a lad Massey had got to drive them there. He got chased all over Liverpool, then when he got back to the car the windscreen was smashed. He never went to the match again.

He also told me that I should not be too dismayed by getting put on my arse by a single clout, as the administrator of the shot was known as "One Punch" and was famous for it. So I had met not only the Magnificent Seventeen but also Wing and One, who would have made a fortune had they opened a Chinese takeaway.

respect

After that night, I got to know most of United's top boys. They had great respect for Everton, particularly in the late Seventies and early Eighties, have always let it be known that Everton were one of the main mobs to bring it to Old Trafford, and pleasingly rate Everton much higher than Liverpool. As I said, Mickey Francis stated in his *Guvnors* book, "Liverpool always had the numbers, but Everton were the gamest fighters." That has also been said to me by Man U's top lads. Say no more.

Man U are still rated as one of the best mobs around; on their day they pull some amazing firms together and love the "super-firm" tag they get. I thought there would be murder at their visits to Cardiff for the numerous finals they play, as the Soul Crew are arguably the only mob which could pull the numbers to have a serious pop at them, but the police seem to have it boxed off down there and so far have managed to keep them apart. For the past couple of seasons United have brought over 200 lads to Everton. I didn't rate the firms as that impressive; if anything they were too big for this day and age and were half full of bluffers, but they still had eighty-odd in their mid-thirties who should know better and grow up!

I know most of their main lads and quite happily have a beer with them now. They have given me a walkover a few times when I could have had a good hiding, so you have to respect them for that. The one thing I will say is that they have become a bit of a rent-a-mob, with lads from all over latching onto them, not just the Cockney Reds, who have a tidy little firm of their own, but the Jocks and even one or two Leeds faces at the England game at Anfield, which has caused a rift amongst the ranks. Whatever next, Liverpool teaming up with them to fight a combined Everton and Man City mob? Somehow I doubt it.

Whereas I think Everton and United respect each other, there is a real hatred between the Mancs and Liverpool. A couple of years back, a small firm of Liverpool turned up at Salford Quays, attacked a boozer and slashed the throat of one of their boys. A couple of Scousers got nicked and, when they went to court, Man U ambushed them as they were leaving. A lad lost a couple of fingers when he got hit with a machete protecting his head. Now I've had some bad results in court, but give me community service over a machete-chopping anytime. The lad that did the original slashing is the most hated person in Manchester and if the Manc on the receiving end wasn't now doing an eight-stretch for drugs, I'm sure the slasher would have been done in, because he wound everyone up by bragging about it.

I get a bit of stick off our lot for being matey with United but the majority of them are grafters and can always put a few pennies your way, particularly with the tickets and swag at concerts. With Champions League matches you can easily pull two or three ton every game, so to me it seems daft to give up the easy dough for two minor scuffles a year. I've had my fun over twenty years.

The 2001/02 season was a perfect example of how things

have changed. At the game at Goodison, one of their top lads came with me and we watched the game from the Executive Lounge. We took another five or six United "heads" on the ale after the game. Years ago, that would have been unheard of. At Old Trafford, I watched the game with Wing Commander and they took me for a good drink after. It very nearly went horribly wrong though, as I got a call from the Everton mob leader for the day, Larry, who told me they were on their way to steam a bar full of United. It was the very bar I was in, so I made my excuses and left before they got there. Luckily they never made it, as the Manc bizzies copped for them, but it was a close call and shows that for some the hatred and need to battle with them will never go away.

No matter what happens in the future, you will never, EVER, replace the days when we played them: 400-strong mobs, running battles from dawn to darkness, stabbings, slashings and looting, the full shooting match. English football will not see anything like it again.

4 SOUTH OF WATFORD

WHILE I LOVED away games at Manchester the most, I rarely missed a match in London. Whereas Manchester was a bit compact and on top, once you got south of Watford it was a big adventure and always a great day out. It was never a school trip, though, but a dangerous place. Maybe that's why I liked it so much.

I think the whole set-up of the place gives football thugs the buzz they crave. There is never a dull moment in London; you need to be on your guard and have your wits about you from the minute you pull into Euston. If you didn't, there was, certainly in the Eighties, only one likely outcome. I have seen many people nursing bad wounds on the way home from our capital city and London was and is in my book not just the capital of England but of football violence.

If ever there was an invention created to assist football hooligans in their quest for total mayhem, the person who designed the Underground train system was sent from heaven to oblige. The Tube was an Aladdin's cave of mischief and bedlam, and how there were so few football-related deaths in the Eighties is a miracle on par with feeding the 5,000 with a loaf and a couple of kippers. The place was evil. Whereas we had the little dark alleys and tower blocks of Walton and Scotty Road to prowl in and attack from, I was always envious that we never had the Tube system. The Cockneys were masters of it and used it to full advantage every match day.

Of all the London clubs I visited, I have to go with the majority and rate West Ham as the worst place in town. Everton's mob had results at all the other grounds where there was a firm, including Millwall in 1989, but I have to be honest and admit that we never had a result at Upton Park – not in all the times I went there, anyway. We did Chelsea in '84 at a Friday night game, we did Spurs two years running in '85 and '86, and I lost count of the times we chased Arsenal back down Highbury Hill. West Ham was different. We never seemed to take the same firm there as we did to the others and it is no good anybody arguing; it was the same fucking price to Euston no matter who you were playing, so in my eyes people must have jibbed it because they were wary of the bastards. In my experience, you had every right to be wary but that should never stop you going.

I don't agree with all these hooligan league tables that you see but if I had to rate the Cockney mobs in any order, it would be West Ham, then Tottenham, Chelsea and Arsenal. We never played Millwall much and the others are not worth a mention (saying that, the worst spanking we ever had in London was at QPR, so I suppose they should get a little bit of glory).

Tottenham being above Chelsea may surprise some people but Spurs always brought a firm back to Euston and we had battles with them long into the night, literally hours after the game had ended. Chelsea, on the other hand, only worked their own patch. The one time they did stray further than Edgware Road, they got pummelled and cut up at Kings Cross. Arsenal got better with age and it was a pretty nasty place by the time I got nicked and jailed there in 1988. They had a massive mob about in '86 and, of all the London clubs, arguably had the best results at Goodison. They always seemed to look for it, and found it, at our place, whereas the others would look for it when it suited, usually when the place was swarming with bizzies.

West Ham never had the numbers that the others had away, although they were like us in the fact that the majority of their away following were pure "lads". Spurs, Arsenal and Chelsea brought the numbers, but had loads of taggers-on. The ICF didn't, and for their numbers they always did well, although Cass Pennant must be snorting too much of the Devil's dandruff if he expects anybody to believe that forty of them ran 700 at Everton in the Eighties (in Cass's book *Congratulations: You Have Just Met The ICF*). I suppose it sells books but it needs to be kept real.

The following are my personal accounts of how we fared home and away against London's finest. I was there at all these battles and don't bullshit. If I did, I would leave out the story of how QPR battered and ran us in '85 when we thought we were hard!

the hammers

I have been to Upton Park, or the Boylen Ground as I prefer to call it, eight times. Of those times, I have been chased twice and had the bus smashed up once, and it is the only football ground I have ever visited where I have stopped and asked for police help. It is a rough ground in a rough area full of rough bastards. In a nutshell, it is fucking evil.

The first time I went there was 1984/85 when we won the League. We took a tidy firm on the train and it was reasonably quiet. We had a massive escort to and from the ground and, apart from the odd skirmish, no trouble. I got home and wondered what all the hype was about. I had been to worse places – that season it was more violent at Chelsea, Spurs, Arsenal and QPR. We won with a late goal and as we boarded the Tube we were all chanting, "Easy, easy." There were a few old geezers growling but it was, as the chant said, easy. The following year was not, and "easy, easy" came back to haunt us.

At the home game the ICF came into the old Park End Stand. It was a mismatch. Although we tried to get in there in numbers, they'd got in early and, as a few skirmishes broke out, the bizzies forced us all out. We only got back in in a very small mob of about fifty. I shit it when, in the second half, they came piling over, all chanting, "ICF!" But to their credit they saw we were not mobbed up and that the place was full of lads and dads, so they retreated and told us to wait till after the game. This must be the match Cass blags about.

As we came out, I saw the black lad that had led them into the Park Stand; he was wearing a blue diamond Pringle jumper and outside struggled to blend in with the crowd, for obvious reasons. West Ham did get out of the escort and they did make it down Everton Valley and it is true forty of them stood against maybe 700 of us and had a proper go. But to say they ran 700 is just bollocks. Forty could not run that many Scouse schoolkids; in the mayhem people would get split up and don't forget it was a nasty place with all the blade business. If you got split up, you were cut up.

They were penned in by the all-weather pitches and it was a great battle. They had all the faces at the front and they were big blokes. We were mainly in our early twenties and were wary of them but they took some flak and the bizzies saved them and eventually got them back to the station. That is my version. Read Pennant's and make your own mind up. But remember these are factual books, not fiction!

The following season we went there and had a crap mob on the train. We were about sixty-strong and were missing all the older lads. I thought they must have been on another train but it turned out they had hired a coach, for some daft reason. We went to the Rising Sun near Kings Cross and before we had ordered a drink, a small mob of Man City fronted us by the main doors. We went out to them but the first few of ours then came running back in. I thought this was a joke, as the City lads were the Young Guvnors and, although we were not firmed up, I had seen this mob earlier at Euston and was not impressed. As it was, the first lad out to front them had been slashed to ribbons. They had pulled him down, striped his head and slashed his thigh down to his knee. Once they'd done the damage, they were off, with Everton giving fruitless chase. It was a bad start to the day, and not even twelve o'clock.

Everton were going mad about it but I thought they were hypocrites, as many were guilty of similar wrongdoings. Kettle, pot and black sprang to mind. The lad was rushed to hospital and we were one less out of not many. City were at Arsenal and a lad came down in a car and told us all the main Everton lads were drinking near Liverpool Street Station. As more City were due in at Euston, we got the Tube but were not a confident firm, and it was a quiet journey to meet the lads.

There was a top mob when we got there. All the old lads were out, but it pissed me off, as it was typical of the lack of organisation that so often was our undoing. We ended up rowing about how we should get to West Ham and were divided, so they made their way on the coach and our meagre mob got back on the Tube. One wanker got on the bus but another lad told the rest to fuck off and came with us. I have to admit that, had I been him, I would have stayed on it. They got to the ground, fronted the Cockneys and were put in the away end while we were on our way to face the music.

I had been on the ale and was bursting for a piss as we pulled into Upton Park station. I waited for the lads to go up the stairs and had a quick piss on the empty platform. It was about quarter past three so I thought it would be quiet outside, but as I shook the last drops from below I could hear it going off outside.

I ran up the stairs hoping to see Everton starting on a few West Ham late-comers who had been a bit lippy on the Tube, but it was the other way around. As soon as

Everton had got up the stairs, the Cockneys had kicked it off, alerting all the Under-Fives who hang around outside the Queens Market. I could see Everton forcing them back down the ramp, with Carlos yards in front and straight into them. But me and my mate Pat Halkyn, who went to every game with me in those days, were 200 yards away and were spotted by a mob of about a dozen West Ham. One pulled a blade and it was either run through them or back into the station. I opted for Plan B and we scurried back into the Tube, knocking over the ticket collector who thought we were jibbing the train, not trying our best to avoid being stabbed.

A train pulled out as we got on the platform and we could hear the feet piling down the stairs and their cries of excitement and shouts of "Kill the Mickeys". There was nowhere to go, so we hopped across the lines. Thinking of it now, it was a crazy thing to do, as a slashed arse is better than being run over by a train or frazzled on the lines, but at the time it was a gamble worth taking. They didn't fancy it and we escaped up the embankment and got out into the streets at the very back of the market. There were lads on every street corner and this was no longer "easy, easy". We split up and walked on different sides of the road but still got sussed out and chased to the ground. This was the West Ham I had heard and read so much about and I was not keen on the place.

I made it to the turnstile but it was shut, and immediately I was set upon by a load of kids. They were only in their teens but were lawless and a copper had to start whacking them with his truncheon before they got off my back. He then proceeded to piss off into the West Ham end to watch the game. The second he went, they were back and I was chased again. I spotted a bizzie on horseback and asked him for help. I had never done it before and have never done it since, but that day, had I not, I would have been slashed, make no mistake. The little fuckers were like ants and the bizzie told me to go in the West Ham section or fuck off home. The ants were loving it and as I went into their bit, they joined me by the turnstile and were booting me up the arse, saying I was going to die. I had no reason not to believe them, and as soon as I got in the ground I asked for a move to our own section. If I'd had one wish it would have been for Scottie to beam me up, pronto.

By now it was half-time and Everton were a sorry, divided mob at the tea bar. Loads had been whacked outside as I was getting chased, and the ones on the coach agreed to come back with us. It was too late, and although after the game we got a bit of respect back, it still rankles with me that they were the cause of much pain that day. It was a bad, bad day and a scary one, proving that if you went to West Ham unprepared, the stories were true and you would come seriously unstuck.

Back at Euston, the coach picked them up just before Man City came in and we had another little go with the Young Guvnors. It was the same lot we had met before the game and we were ready for them. When I was wandering lost around West Ham, I had found a blade on the floor and put it in my pocket, and when it went off at Euston I pulled it on the Mancs. I was never a blade man but I'd had enough and it was a case of fighting fire with fire. City backed off and were cry-arsing to the bizzies that I had a blade. I was nicked but had ditched it and, in fairness, one of the Mancs came to the police room in Euston and said it wasn't me and I was released. I saw the lad that had done the earlier cutting at the Rising Sun and I am ninety-nine per cent sure that he was in the later "Guvnors" trial at Liverpool Crown Court, when much of that gang was jailed.

Later that night, the coachload of Everton met all City's top lads in Hilton Park service station. These were the Cool Cats, the predecessors to the Guvnors. Everton murdered them. The newspapers reported that six City were slashed and one woman fainted when the lift opened and there were two lads in there unconscious and cut up. As Everton drove up the motorway there were City lads two miles away sitting on the hard shoulder. The next week some lads were still buzzing off the revenge they had gained for the slashing at the Rising Sun, but to me it was fuck all; we had been playing West Ham, and to this day I believe they let the lads down by getting that coach to the game.

West Ham came to Everton again that year, the game when the Lawrence lad was badly cut up (see Chapters Two and Eleven). The next time I went there was a Sunday game and we were all on coaches. We were in no mob as such and we melted as we got near the ground. I even bought a BNP paper to blend in with the crowd. It pissed me off again. Had we been at another ground, we would have been bang at it, but West Ham's reputation did put loads off and, as I say, we never seemed as up for it there as at the other so-called tough grounds. That game we did have a bit of a result though, as right on full-time we opened a gate and a few of us got into their section, with one of theirs being stabbed. It was nothing much but better than usual.

The next battle I had with them was on a Monday night after an FA Cup quarter-final. We booked a coach but did not fill it. Still, forty of us went looking for it. We were older now and I personally didn't give two fucks for their reputation any more. We had been a few times since the bad day and drank in the Blind Beggar (where Ronnie Kray shot George Cornell for calling him a fat poof) every season with no hassle. The ICF seemed to have died a death, so our forty seemed a good bet to do some damage. Wrong again!

This was the game when we got off on seeing the flood-lights, only to find we had about three fucking miles to walk to the ground. We did a lap of the stadium and saw no opposition and were then fronted by a few of their old boys who told us to go to some wine bar after the game if we wanted it. Everton lost, so we did, and got spanked again!

We made it back to our coach and should have gone home with damage limitation, but we were just getting it together as a mob and thought, *bollocks*. As the fleet of coaches turned left, we went right and within seconds were off and having it with them. We pulled up outside a boozer and could not believe we had found it so quickly, so only a couple got off to have a nose inside. I was at the front telling the driver not to leave anybody when a lad walks up to the coach and cracks the windscreen with a hammer. Next minute, we were under attack and the windows were going in. A traffic cone flew over my head and hit the driver; it was indeed the pub we were looking for.

We piled off but they had the upper hand. They were already all around the coach, they were tooled up and the bar was chocker with them. We gave it a go but in the end were backed off and done in, really. One lad, Kevin, got a bad slash to his arm and was in hospital down there for a week or two. The bus was wrecked and it was a cold journey home as yet another four-hour inquest was held as to what went wrong. During the fighting, Franny had pulled a lad over and battered him. As he went down, we tugged his jacket over his head before he ran off. We still had the jacket, and on the coach we found his address book. When we got to Watford Gap for a piss and a warm, we were going to phone his bird and say we'd kidnapped him, but thought better of it, in case he answered and told us we had been done again by the ICF.

They came to ours mob-handed one final time and I had a lucky escape. It was just after the Hillsborough Disaster and they were a couple of games away from being relegated. As I walked out of the subway near the library, I bumped into about 300 of them. They gave me a walkover but it was a tasty mob. They also brought the same mob to Anfield for a mid-weeker, when they indeed got relegated. I was glad to see the back of them, and it is a painful reminder writing this chapter of how poorly we did down there. But as I said earlier, it is fact, not fiction: Everton have never really done the main ICF mob but bullshit is bullshit and 40 running 700 is the biggest load of it I have ever read.

chelsea

The first time I set eyes on Chelsea was on the last day of the season in 1978. It was like a cup final for us, as our star striker – and my schoolboy hero – Bob Latchford needed to score twice to reach thirty goals for the season and win ten grand from one of the national newspapers. At thirteen you still had heroes, and Bob was mine. I did not think Chelsea would bring a mob, as very few teams did in those days and anyway they had little to play for. So when I saw a firm legging it over to Lime Street, I just had to take a sneaky look, despite my wariness.

What I saw caused me sleepless nights for weeks after. A little mob of Everton were chased out of the station's main entrance, and I was following them, when I clocked a one-armed black man leading the Cockneys out of Lime Street. Apart from watching Pele on the telly, this was the closest I had ever come to seeing a real black person, as there were none where I lived, and the sight of one with a stump like a tree trunk freaked me out. Before the game, all the talk was of this bloke, and as the Chelsea mob were taken into the Park End it was like a circus freak show as hundreds of little Urchins stared – from a safe distance, by the way – open-mouthed as the legendary Babs marched his firm into the ground.

We hammered them on the pitch and were 5–0 up when we were awarded a last-minute penalty. Latchford had scored one already and, as he smashed the ball past Bonetti, hundreds invaded the pitch. After a few minutes there was a shout to attack the Park End, and I had reached the halfway line before a flashback of that tree trunk stump brought me to my senses and I climbed back into the Gwladys Street a happy lad. Chelsea later got done by all accounts; don't know, wasn't there, but it was the first time they had brought a mob to Goodison and it was a tidy one. In school on Monday, all the talk was about this one-armed black fella and even the teachers were made up with the tale of Babs.

If Chelsea did get done after that match, they did not have to wait long for revenge. The fixture list came out for the new season and there it was, first game: Chelsea away. I never went. The furthest I got in those days was the Midlands, as I worked bit jobs when Everton played away to pay for the home games. London at the age of thirteen was only a place you saw on the telly. Everton took a load down there on the train but got the worst hiding they have ever had, and to this day people still tell stories of Kenny High Street. Although I never went, I have listened to many tales of it and what follows is the most common one told.

Everton had a good turnout and over 500 were on the special to Euston. It was not 500 lads but there were plenty on, not the barmy day-out brigade by any means but plenty of fighters among the normal fans. From Euston, Everton were escorted to Fulham Broadway, and were in the ground safe and sound to see Andy King score and secure us a 1–0 victory. It was a dream start to the season; the nightmare to follow was less than an hour away.

Everton were escorted back to Fulham Broadway and the odd fight broke out, but generally those on the train were well protected by the bizzies. Those not on the train had a torrid time and I know one lad who has never been back since, claiming to have had enough kickings that day to last him a lifetime. But a full contingent of over 500 was on the

Tube and it seemed Chelsea had decided against taking them on. Everton were a bit cocksure until they realised the train was stopping at every Tube station; it was not a special direct to Euston.

At Earls Court, a good mob of Chelsea was waiting on the platform and piled onto the very last carriage. As the train pulled off, they went for it and began battering all the Everton before making their way forward to the next compartment to repeat the process. The Everton further down the train could hear the commotion and some went to help when suddenly the train stopped again. It had reached Kensington High Street, and for Everton it was the end of the line.

The platform was full of them, all of Chelsea's mob: skins, punks, scarfers, the full complement – and they were tooled up. The first lot bricked the train just as the doors opened. It was mass panic on board and very few fancied getting off to have a go, by all accounts. The Chelsea already on the train stormed through the carriages and Everton were fucked good and proper. Anybody who slightly resembled a lad was battered and loads were dragged off the train and booted all over the platform.

The Cockneys were not letting it go and had fire extinguishers jammed against the doors to stop them closing, which would allow the train to leave. There were only a few British Rail police and they left it and ran up the stairs for help. Everton by then were in a sorry state and Chelsea should have left it but then the power in the station was turned off and it kicked off again. The papers later reported how Chelsea had planned to stop the train by cutting the electricity. I don't know if that was true but the train did not leave Kenny High Street for over ten minutes and that is a long time to be under siege.

Eventually Everton fought back. I spoke to a top Chelsea lad at an England game years later who said that, had they retaliated quicker, the damage would have been a lot less. Loads of the Cockneys that joined in were not even Chelsea, just lads who fancied a bit of Scouse-bashing. The Everton fightback saved a bit of face and a few legends were born. I know one bloke, JC, who put a fire bucket over his head and went straight into them. He was deaf for weeks after, as they were bouncing all sorts off his makeshift helmet, but he had a right go and saved a few lads. Others eventually got off and Chelsea ended up running up the stairs, though nobody claims Everton ran them. The police were arriving.

When the dust settled, it resembled a battlezone. A few Everton had been stabbed and loads needed hospital treatment. Chelsea were gone and the police were left shocked at the severity of such a vicious and well-planned ambush. Not as shocked as the lads on the train though; by all accounts the only words spoken on the long trip home were "bastards" and "revenge".

Leaflets were printed before the subsequent home game but a massive police operation prevented a riot. The wounds had healed but the mental scars of the slaughter were not forgotten and the amount of weapons found at Goodison that day proved that no matter how long it took, Chelsea would be repaid for that ambush. Their showing at our place was not brilliant and they made no attempt to get out of the escort to or from the ground. Everton had thousands out and we were doing our kiddie spotter job, but Chelsea didn't want it bad enough. Had it been West Ham, I think that day would have seen deaths on Merseyside, as they would have come for it and, with the nastiness of our mob, they would have got it. Chelsea got home safely and later that season, were relegated. Payback could wait.

If a week is a long time in politics, five years is a lifetime in football violence, but that is how long it took us to get even. When we did, we laid the memory of Kensington

High Street to rest. We played them in a Friday night match in August 1984. They had been promoted amid mad scenes at Maine Road, when they were in all the ends of the ground and took the piss out of City. All summer the papers were full of Chelsea this and Chelsea that, and they even had one of their lads rating who would be their main terrace rivals. He said Stoke and Everton. Don't know about Stoke but I knew we would be going there.

We had just won our first trophy for fifteen years, beating Watford in the FA Cup final. Then we beat Liverpool in the Charity Shield. Things were looking good. Everton were in demand and the game was picked as the first-ever Friday night live game on BBC. I was glad about this, as we were getting a bit of a bandwagon following and we knew they would not fancy Chelsea on a Friday night. Early optimism was pissed on as we lost our first two League games, and we took the usual suspects only on the half past two out of Lime Street. We had about 300 on, which I thought was a little bit short to take it to the so-called hooligan kings of England.

At Euston, there was a mob waiting on the concourse and I thought, *here we go*. We bounced up the ramps but it was about 100 Everton who were working down there or in Bournemouth, as was the trend then. We marched out of the station together and I stood on a wall to get a view. This mob looked the business; there was nobody who was not ready for a battle. One of the lads, Colin, stood in the middle of the road and said, "This will do Chelsea." It was a simple, matter-of-fact statement but was all that needing saying.

There was no point in pissing about. We got the Tube straight to the ground and walked down to The Shed. The bizzies had not clocked we were Everton and we went into a boozer directly opposite the famous Chelsea end. It went right off but you could not get near the doors and Chelsea could not believe we were taking the piss at their place. All everybody was saying all day was, "Remember Kenny High Street, remember Kenny High Street," and it was as if it was spurring everyone on.

We were given the entire end opposite The Shed and must have looked a poor following as just 450 stood in a section that holds ten times that amount. All game they were singing, "Is that all you take away?" Yes, it was, and soon they would regret that we never filled the end with the usual knobs that stood there. This mob sitting spread out on the barriers did not give a fuck for the singing and chanting. It was there for one thing, and that was not the football.

We won with a Kevin Richardson goal. With a couple of minutes to go, John Bailey had a bit of a set-to with Chelsea's Paul Canoville. All the Chelsea in the stand to our left were going mad, so to get it going a lad fired a flare straight into them. It was off. They went crackers trying to get on the pitch and a mob in the stand on the other side started to give it the big one, so we fired another into them. Apart from the blokes in the pub before the match, the Cockneys must have thought we had no mob, but now they'd had their wake-up call and a few got over the barriers into the no man's land in our end. There was only a couple of flares left so they were kept for later while we tried to smash the gates down to get out. The bizzies forced us back, so we opened a gate in the fencing and nearly got on the pitch before more bizzies intervened.

We were kept in for about thirty minutes and escorted back to Euston trouble-free. We never saw a single lad on the Underground, a real anti-climax. At every stop lads were saying, "They will be at the next one," but they weren't. Apparently loads of Chelsea watched the game on telly and, due to our poor numbers, thought we had not shown. One told me years later in Sweden following England that when we scored it showed us just standing there not giving a fuck, and you could see it was pure lads. Then at the end, when Jimmy Hill was doing his talk, you saw a flare go into their stand. They knew we were there and he reckoned it took them some time to group up and get ready for us, and that is why it never went off when we came out of the ground. That's Chelsea's view and may explain why they never met us on the Tube. There is no argument about the next hour's events that night, though.

At Euston all was quiet; the bizzies took us in and we went down to the platform without so much as a whimper, leaving the local "OB" to congratulate themselves on a job well done. They happily went back to their stations to clock off. They had totally misjudged our mood, though, as the night was still young and the job not even half done. We knew that Chelsea would be somewhere in the area and if it took all night to find them, we would. "Remember Kenny High Street, remember Kenny High Street," was still being mumbled in our massed ranks as we walked out of Euston with not a police officer in sight.

We headed for Kings Cross, having a peep in all the boozers on the way. One of them had a few lads in but no real numbers and it was not a time to start banging a few and bringing the bizzies back on top, so we left it. I looked back up the road and saw them leave and reckoned that they had thought it better to piss off. As it was, they were Chelsea boys looking for us; they had gone to collect the rest of their firm from another couple of pubs set off the main road while we went towards the main station to check the bar out. Unbeknown to us, they were looking for us while we were looking for them.

At Kings Cross there was no sign of them, so foolishly but predictably we split up and went on the rob. There was a Wimpy burger bar next to a small amusement arcade and two separate mobs went in while another mob walked back to the pub on the corner, the one that Man City would cut us up outside the following year. It went off in the Wimpy when a lad snatched the till before so much as a chicken nugget was ordered, while next door we were smashing open the machines. A huge one that you slot a 50p in and hope it pushes a load out for you was tipped over, while the tramps trying to win a couple of quid for a bottle of meths stared at us in amazement and prayed that a few coins spilling from the wreckage would land at their stinking feet. For a few minutes we were like Leeds fans; going on the rampage was not usually our scene but money was money and there were no Chelsea to fight. Yet.

A few lads ran in and shouted, "They're here," and we thought they meant the bizzies, as staff from both the till-less burger bar and the wrecked arcade must have called them. We were slow to react and a mob ran past us, turned about-face and panned across the road. Another lad came in and bellowed, "They're fucking here, Chelsea are fucking here." We piled out to join the ranks and indeed they were; there was a good-sized mob of Cockneys running towards us and a load pulling scaffold pipes off a nearby building. There was not even all the usual "stand" bollocks. Everyone knew that what we had come for was about to happen.

Chelsea slowed and I knew from that moment they were finished. They did, too. We were not the kids and fans that they had battered five years before; we were all mid-twenties and older, as well as having a score to settle. For those who were at Kenny High Street, this was payback, while those who were not there can rest assured we paid back with style.

A Cockney at the front of their mob pulled a big blade and there was a stand-off until a lad ran from behind him and hit him over the head with a metal bin. The lad was with the mob of Everton that had gone to the boozer, so now we were in front and behind them and they crumbled. I thought they would have been better but you cannot even say we were toe-to-toe, it was more toe-to-heel as they were chased all up Euston Road. The lad with the blade got his comeuppance; playing with fire got him burned as he was slashed four or five times while scrambling on the floor for his own blade that had long gone.

In the fight to cut him, one of my oldest mates at the match, Karl, fell over him and, as he got up, had his throat cut by a fellow Scouser. Karl went into shock and we flagged a cab down to rush him to hospital (luckily he survived). As the lad that slashed him was apologising, I saw the most ruthless act I have ever witnessed. Another lad shouted for the blade, walked over to the cab Karl was bleeding in, collected the knife from the apologetic slasher, pushed everybody out of the way and then slashed the Cockney (who was called Denny) again. He held his head up and laughed as he gave him a six-inch stripe that I am sure he can still see every morning when he combs his hair.

One Chelsea book has claimed that the mob tried to slash EFC into his back. That is not true: it was apparently meant to be KHS, the initials of the 1979 massacre site. The lad doing the cutting told a few Urchins to finish him off and every time the victim tried to get up he was kicked back down. A mob appeared out of a side street and attention turned to them, allowing Denny to get up. I was glad to see he was alive as he ran past me before falling over in the road, shouting for help.

By now we were chasing Chelsea everywhere but were getting split up and lured down dark little streets. I shouted at one small mob to get back, as the ploy was working and Chelsea were splitting us up. We regrouped minutes before the bizzies – who earlier had been reflecting on a job well done – arrived and realised it was a job fucked up. A mob of Chelsea were chased into a pub and it was smashed up, so the bizzies nicked a few of our lot, but we got the van doors open and everybody got back to Euston free men.

Basically we battered Chelsea and ran amok. The Cockneys I have spoken to who were there admit it, and that will do for me. Payback was complete.

At Euston the bizzies were going off their heads and forced us down the platform to a waiting "special" that had been quickly ordered to get us the fuck out of there. The best part was that as we were being battered onto it, Holly Johnson, the minging pop superstar from Frankie Goes to Hollywood, was forced on it as well. He was nearly crying when he showed the bizzie his first-class ticket and was told that there was no such thing as a first-class Scouser. In the eyes of the London constabulary, we were all scum, and he, like us, got a boot up the arse and no cheerio as we waved our goodbyes to the capital.

The trip home was legendary. We terrorised that horrible bastard Johnson. His band had just been number one with the song "Two Tribes" and all journey you could hear people doing the start of the song that went something like, "Awww awwww, let's goooooo." Some Urchins soaked his compartment with a fire hose. One of his records had a lyric about the disgrace we brought to our city with all the slashings. There was talk of him getting a bit of a cut himself, but no-one would take the risk.

We did our Leeds act again and trashed the buffet bar but it was empty, and I got home at four in the morning without one drop of alcohol having passed my lips all day. That put to rest the myth that football hooligans were fuelled by drink or drugs, as ninety percent of that day were clean. It was the violence we got high on, not lager or charlie. How did I reflect on the brutal events of that day? At the time, I thought it was the best day of my life.

The following season saw another good turnout for Chelsea away but it was never going to be the same as the Friday night payback sketch. We probably had more on the train but it was not a nasty mob like the year before and many had turned out only on the strength of the previous showing. Some were making their first trip to Stamford Bridge. In my eyes, everybody's first trip should have been the season before.

A small mob of us got there early and were drinking in the George outside Euston before the main mob's train arrived. We were shackling the bandit – we used to make a good day's money with little home-made devices that would trigger off credits on the fruit machines. As we were huddled around it, a couple of lads walked in and flashed a telescopic truncheon at us. It was meant to scare us but seconds later the train was due in with hundreds on, so we left and directed our arriving firm straight to the boozer now occupied by the truncheon-carrying Chelsea spotters. It was a picture as the Cockneys who minutes earlier were calling us wankers bolted the doors and then bolted out of the fire exit at the back of the boozer.

We were a big mob but split into two, as one lot wanted to go up to the ground and another lot wanted to stay on the ale. It was typical Everton again, divided with no leaders. The load who stayed in the boozer would come to regret it. We got to the ground unopposed. We saw a firm at Earls Court but they were not bothered with us; such was their lack of interest that I did not even think they were Chelsea. About twenty minutes into the game, in came a sorry-looking bunch of about sixty Everton who had been done at Earls Court. The mob I had seen had indeed been Chelsea's finest and although our lads were not in a bad way, they had taken a bit of a ragging. None was slashed but a few had stripes down the backs of their leather jackets. It was quite a bad fight by all accounts, and one of the Headhunters, a lad called Jeremy Bodkin, did jail when he was nicked and they found his diary bragging of his involvement. They put the Tube train windows in and fired a flare, and he said an Everton fan was on fire. That was crap, as I saw no-one resembling Guy Fawkes that day, but the judge believed it and the silly twat got six years.

After the game, we stayed as one and Chelsea ambushed us again at Earls Court. I was fast asleep on the Tube when a massive crash hit the window and I looked out to see the platform full of lads trying to smash the train up. We thought it was going to be a top battle and lads on the inside were swinging on the hand straps trying to kick the windows out. Eventually the doors opened but Chelsea ran and in the end the bizzies battered us back onto the train. One lad took a right hiding from them, and an off-duty policeman on another platform later put an appeal in the club programme for him to come forward. When he realised it was not a trap, he did, and a couple of bizzies got sacked for it, while he got a bit of compo for his beating.

That was it with Chelsea; there was never another major off with them. There is no doubt they could be a massive, dangerous mob on their day, but to me they were the Manchester United of London, and never really a tight-knit unit like West Ham. I seriously think they were overrated.

Of all the grounds that have been redeveloped, Stamford Bridge is the most unrecognisable. Since the Russian bloke with money to burn took over, the club has left Joe Public behind. I'm no mingebag but it's £45 to get in, which is taking the piss and pricing the true fans out of the market. It has killed their hooligan following at home, believe me; Abramovich has fucked their mob up big-time!

I had one more good great day there in the 2000/01 season and was in the boozer opposite The Shed talking to a few of their old school about past battles. They had good respect for us. One mouthy cunt was giving it all the Scouse-thieving bollocks though, so to teach him a lesson I dipped his season tickets from his pocket. They all got a bit lippy and started singing, "You're not welcome in this pub," so my mate Hopper and I showed the tickets and threw them back to him. The place erupted and a Cockney then opened the emergency exit and told us, "Out. Not negotiable." He was being kind and we just made it before we got killed. It was a lucky escape, but typical Chelsea, giving it the big one with numbers but not following it up. Had I been stupid enough to pull that stunt at West Ham I would not be alive to tell the tale.

queens park rangers

Easily the worst result we had in the capital, and we are talking about off the pitch here, was at QPR just a few weeks after we had destroyed their West London rivals Chelsea at Kings Cross. We always took a big following to Loftus Road and it was regarded by many as one of the easiest grounds in London to visit. It was the sort of fixture where you would take your younger brother as a little taster for harder games in the capital. We had some great results there too. We won 4–0 the year after they finished runners-up to the Red Shite, and the year after that won 5–1, with Bob Latchford getting four of the goals. It was always trouble-free and we wandered around the place in numbers as if we were Cockneys ourselves. That all changed in 1984.

Like I said, it was only a few weeks after we had been at it with Chelsea and there was talk of them paying the ground a visit for revenge. But before the game there was no sign of them or Rangers, and we had a few beers unopposed in several of the pubs near the ground. It seemed the gossip was exactly that, and during the game, which was a dull goalless draw, there were very few Cockney boys on show. The highlight of the afternoon was when our psycho full-back Pat Van Den Hauwe was put on his arse in a fight with one of their players, which saw them both sent off.

After the match we had a tidy firm going back to the

Tube and whichever was first – White City or Shepherd's Bush – saw the main body of fans and a few of the lads disappear into the Underground. Twenty minutes later I wished I had been with them. As we were milling around the stairway, a few Cockneys fronted us and were chased off. They were only about twenty-strong and I thought they had a death wish, as we still had eighty-odd hanging about in the hope that Chelsea might show. They kept coming back for more and must have been sent packing three or four times before we ended up leaving the Tube station entrance and following them.

There were no bizzies with us whatsoever and we should have realised we were being set up, but we were Everton and had just done Chelsea, so who the fuck were QPR? We got near a park and this small mob, being led by a proper mouthy cunt, turned on us. Some say it was McGregor, their main mouthpiece. I had seen him around Euston a few times and don't think it was. It did not really matter; whoever he was, he set us up big-time.

Within seconds of us bouncing into them, a lad ran into the middle of us and smashed a huge bottle onto the road. It was full of ammonia or something like it and everybody was coughing and spluttering when a huge mob of mainly blacks came piling out of the park tooled up like the Zulu army in the film. They were all chanting, "War! War! War!" It was a scary sight. Loads of them had scaffold poles and one fired a flare into the middle of us. Then they charged. It was well on top, with people still blinded by the initial ammonia attack. After a brief toe-to-toe, which was very brief if I'm honest, we were put on the back foot, despite screams of, "Stand, it's only QPR." No matter who they were, they had planned it to perfection and we were getting had off.

As I was running, there were blacks with bats overtaking me and pulling back Everton lads. They were legging us but we ended up whipping a few of them up as they were a bit eager and mistook us for Cockneys. We were on our toes for a few hundred yards and sought refuge in a large garage forecourt. It saved us a bit but a load of cars were smashed up as we massed behind them and the Cockneys threw everything they could lay their hands on.

It was one of the worst attacks I have seen at the match and was relentless. As soon as we got it together they would come back with more and extra. They must have been collecting missiles and weapons for weeks. One lad was thrown through a bus shelter window and another had his arse badly slashed. That was a bit of a turning point, and we regrouped and bounced them back down the road a bit.

One bizzie came on a horse and eventually we were escorted to the Tube. They must have thought there was more of us than there was when we backed them off a bit, as when they saw us being escorted they were trying to get past the bizzies and do us again. They were deranged and were walking along one side of the road still tooled up in full view of the police. It is one of the few times at a football match that I actually thought I could get killed, such was the ferocity of their attack.

We eventually made it to the station but were in disarray. A few were beaten badly but there was none of the usual inquest bollocks, as everybody accepted we had been done and had come unstuck. I looked down the platform and there were lads with their heads in their hands looking like they had suffered a family bereavement. It was indeed a sad day for our firm, and many of the lads took it personally. But it was a waste of time pointing fingers at the first lot that had gone on the earlier Tube or the other lot that ran into them when we should have stuck closer together. The point was, at no stage that day did we think that we were in any danger. We were taking liberties and paid the price for it.

People still say that it was a mob of Chelsea or a mob of blacks from an estate near the ground that did us. That doesn't wash with me. It was at Queens Park Rangers so we were had off by QPR. Plain and simple. It taught us all a lesson though about how dangerous a place London was, regardless of who you were playing. Had we been at one of the so-called "harder" grounds, that incident would never have happened, but we weren't and it did. So you have to take your hats off to QPR, because like it or not we took a proper spanking there that day, and no amount of covering up or bullshit that it was somebody else will make me change my mind.

Later that season we clinched the League title against them and they had a few hundred fans up. No lads came at all and it didn't matter, it was our first Championship for fifteen years and a day of drink and drugs, not football thugs. It was a hot, sunny Bank Holiday Monday but the memory of that dark night at Shepherd's Bush was still at the back of my mind – until the players did a lap of honour and the beer began to flow.

The following season we took a huge mob there hoping to save face but it was a waste of time; there were no lads about and it was a bit on top with the bizzies. They too had learned from the previous year. We have played them once since, in 1995. A few of us bunked into the main stand at their place and, with a minute to go, made our way to the front, just as Hinchcliffe hit in a free-kick to put us 3–2 up. He ran towards us and I jumped onto the pitch, as it was a top win with both sides fighting relegation. A steward nicked me and, as I was getting frogmarched to the police room, a big fat Cockney booted me up the hole. I was only cautioned and was out in minutes, but a few QPR were waiting to do me in. Luckily Steve had seen me getting nicked and had a little firm waiting outside, and they put the Cockneys on their toes in seconds.

It was a funny one, that, as I had borrowed my mate's

Railcard to get there and simply glued my picture over his. When the bizzies searched me, they found the Railcard, processed his details, and "Phil Spencer" was banned from Loftus Road, which was no great loss, as he's never been to an away match in his life.

As they are a mob that never travels, I doubt if Everton will ever get the chance to pay them back for that embarrassing day. We thought we were the dog's bollocks after Chelsea, but that day at QPR the only thing we had in common with dogs' bollocks was that we got licked.

arsenal

I have tried not to get involved in the soccer casual debate but can lay to rest the myth that the Cockneys were at the forefront of this terrace trend. I went there in 1979, a time when, if you are to believe them, they were all dressed in Pringle and Fila. Well I can say hand on heart that the only lads fighting for them that day were a load of punks dressed in Sham 69 donkey jackets, while the faithful London green flying jacket was also seen during the odd scuffle. They had indeed stopped wearing scarves by then, unlike the vast majority of the Mancs, but apart from the odd sheepskin coat on their better dressers, they were still a couple of years behind the Scousers.

I never rated the Gooners on their own patch but they did have a few results of sorts at our place over the years. They came in the Park End Stand a few times and at one Friday night game they fronted it on Scotland Road before and after with a small firm. They will always have respect for that, as at the time it was unheard of. Their main lad, Denton, was a name we all had heard of, and I can vouch that he was a game bastard and kept them together loads of times when we had it with them.

It was a pity they were nothing at home, as the away end at Highbury must have been designed by Denton himself. You were situated in the middle of the Clock End, and had to enter via their section. It was madness, and half-time was a free-for-all downstairs. Only the brave, dehydrated, those with weak bladders or lads looking for a fight would venture down on the pretence of needing a piss or cup of Bovril.

As the Seventies were forgotten, we took some top mobs to Arsenal, and in the early and mid Eighties I can never remember coming off second best there. We were not a mob that turned up early at grounds but always seemed to do so at Arsenal. We got in a few of their boozers early and had some tidy battles keeping them out.

One year we had been there all morning and had chased them time and time again back down the hill to the Tube, but they were a proud mob and always seemed to come back for more. After the game, we were on the Tube and pulled into a station a couple of stops from Highbury. The platform was full of them, and it was one of the best firms I have ever seen in London. The Transport Police were on the ball or that would have gone off big time. It seemed like every one of them was Pringled up and it was a very impressive sight.

Another time we went there nearly saw an incident that would have been up there with the very worst. It was the season we won the League for the second time in three years, with a goal from Wayne Clark, who lobbed the keeper from about forty yards. We were neck and neck at the top with Liverpool, and when news came through that they had lost at home to Wimbledon, the place erupted. By now, the bizzies at Arsenal had sussed that the away end was a bit dodgy, so we were in the section to the left of the goal. A few Arsenal in the stand down the side were chucking coins at us, so my mate Grant slung a thunderflash into them. It exploded and knocked a bizzie out sparko for a few minutes. When the St John's fellas brought him around, he was in shock and started lashing them with his truncheon. We were pissing ourselves and the poor ambulancemen had to leg it until the nutty bizzie was restrained by his mates.

We thought it would be murder outside, but the following week Arsenal were playing Liverpool in the Littlewoods Cup final and tickets were on sale, so apparently they were all in the queue. A few weeks earlier, Liverpool had been down there and seven Cockneys and a police horse had been slashed. Our rivalry with the lovable Reds from across the park was as intense off the pitch as it was on it, so one of our lot decided to better the Liverpool score of seven and a horse. There was a load of people waiting at a bus stop and he wandered over ready to carve up the lot of them. It was pointless and he was bang out of order, so we stopped him. He laughed and made the sign of the crucifix with his blade in front of them all as they cowered in fright.

They'd had a lucky escape. Had we lost the League that day, I don't think he would have been so accommodating.

tottenham hotspur

The first time I went to White Hart Lane was about 1979 and there was murder. Having been done at Chelsea, the Battle of Seven Sisters was a great victory. We had poor numbers but it was an evil little mob and as Spurs ambushed the Tube they were beaten off by Everton who had dismantled the fluorescent light strips and used them to cut "the Yids" to ribbons.

The following year was the infamous jeweller's sketch at Kings Cross, on the last game of the season. Everton had a few hundred on the train and rampaged out of Euston all the way to Kings Cross before looting a jewellery store. I was in a van and was amazed in the ground at the low turnout we had there. Soon we got word that loads had gone home with swag and loads had been nicked. All match the bizzies were searching lads and anybody with so much as a gold watch on was taken away for questioning.

For the real mob versus mob battles you need look no further in your *Rothmans Football Yearbook* than seasons 1983–86. Those were the years when we clashed every game with the Yids. They brought it to us and we took it to them. Both teams were up at the top of the League and both mobs always had a full turnout home and away, and for those three seasons, you needed it. White Hart Lane had one of the longest walks from the Tube station; it was twenty minutes to the ground from Seven Sisters. That was if you knew the way and had no lumber. It was never like that, and on occasions it took us nearly double that to cover the distance.

In 1983/84 they came in the Park End Stand, the first lot to do it when we had a mob in there. We had it with them just as the game kicked off. I was at the top of the stairs when I saw a mob of unfamiliar faces gathering. They were joined by a mob of black faces and the game was up; Everton they were not. I waited at the entrance and shouted to the lads that they were on their way up and, as they tried to surprise us, I lashed a cup of scalding tea in the leader's face. We battered them all over the seats. They had a young black lad with them and he was crying his eyes out as all our Urchins were threatening to cut him up.

We went there just after Christmas for the return and had them following us all the way to the ground. We knew it would go off any minute and, when we reached the away end, a load of them made a line across the road to block us. One of our lot pulled out a massive blade and it was like the parting of the sea as we marched through the gap, giving it the big one. Not a punch was thrown even though it was like a time-bomb waiting to go off. How it never erupted I don't know, as it looked on top until the steel was flashed. I saw the young black lad from the home game, standing with his mates and giving us loads, but once he was reminded about his Kleenex antics in the Park End he shut it and went on his way.

Ten minutes before full-time, we got out and went into the old stand above the away end and had it with them. I was punched by a big lad at the front of their mob and slipped on the stairs. As I went to get up, I was booted all over the place and was half expecting to get slashed at any minute. I was screaming for the lads to help but none came, and when I eventually got to my feet after spewing up, I saw why. There was not a Yid in sight; the London bizzies had been the ones attacking me. I had concussion for days and was black and blue for weeks; it is still one of the worst hidings I have ever had. It could have been worse though; they could have nicked me!

Later that year, we had them in the FA Cup fifth round back at our place and they brought thousands. They even had a big mob in the Upper Bullens, which nobody had ever done, and at half-time there was a full-scale battle down in the tea bar. It was started by one of the lads, Kiddy, who had been sitting next to them all game and was covered from head to toe in their spit. We won 2–0 and it was mayhem after. The mobs from both sides were big and it went on all the way to the station. At the time, that was the best firm of pure lads that I had seen at Everton apart from Man United.

The next time they were up was for the first game of the '84/85 season. We had won the Cup and thought we had a chance of the League but they thrashed us 4–1. The mob they had was quiet. They seemed to be that way, Spurs; if they lost, they always had a load of nutters to swell their numbers, but if they won they were quite happy and left it to the real thugs.

We also lost the next game at West Brom but then lost only a couple more times until we went to Spurs on a Wednesday night in April as top of the League. They were second and it was billed as the Championship decider. Over 48,000 were there, including the biggest following Everton have ever taken to a League game in London. We had a great mob on the train and burst out of Seven Sisters. They attacked us when we got near the shops and a load came piling out of Boots the Chemists. We had too many for them and you could here them all shouting in there annoying accents, "Facking hell, there's handreds of the cants." They were not wrong and it was one of the most enjoyable walks I ever took in London. It was going off all the way down to the ground and we took ages to complete the journey, so we missed the kick-off.

It was one of the great nights in Everton's illustrious history as we won 2–1, virtually clinching the title. After the game we were buoyant, and the support was unbelievable, but it was football support and, with that, we lost the togetherness of the mob. The bizzies blocked the road to Seven Sisters and all the supporters were told to turn left and get on special trains laid on at Northumberland Park station. Most took the easy option and there were only about fifty of us left trying to turn right and go to the Tube. The bizzie in charge told us that there were hundreds of Yids waiting on Seven Sisters Road and we could go there if we wanted but with no protection.

We started to go left with the other Everton hordes when one of the young lads, called Spike, stood on a wall and, as loads melted towards the police escort, he began making chicken-clucking noises. In my eyes that saved Everton from copping out, and we earned the respect of London that night. His mockery worked and, as the bizzies went left, we said "fuck it" and went right and started walking, albeit very slowly, towards the hundreds of Tottenham that a flimsy line of police was trying to disperse.

We got level with a boozer called the Black Bull, I think, and they were crammed in there. Spike was off again and started shouting, "Champions! Champions!" Spurs tried to force their way out. A huge roar came from behind us and I thought I was about to die a happy man but the mob behind were Everton and the road filled with a few hundred more who had followed our example. The easy option was well and truly sacked; if we were going to get done we would get done together and the chant got louder and louder: "Champions! Champions! Champions!" It was one of those times when your hairs stand up on the back of your neck, and they still do now as I think about it.

We went across the road and straight into Tottenham, who were gutted; they were mobbed up and hoping for easy pickings. Thanks to one young lad taking the piss, we were saved, and were indestructible all the way back up the Seven Sisters Road. The bizzies then decided we were round the twist and told us to wait for an escort, but we did not need one: we were champions-elect on the pitch and champions off it, and we boarded the Tube as one, with the Yids not able to get near us. It was great, and the buzz of times like that would addict the Pope to football violence.

Spurs showed at Euston – they always did – but got had off. The same thing happened the year later after a mid-week FA Cup tie. They were one of the few mobs that always came back to Euston and I respect them for that. If you played them there was a chance of a fight until you were on the train and it had pulled out of the station.

We had some top results against the Yids and the 1985 Championship night I will take to my grave. We did have one iffy trip there, though. It was an August Bank Holiday Monday and we got off at the wrong Tube station looking for them. We spotted a load of moody-looking blacks and luckily, before it kicked off, realised we had somehow walked into the middle of the Notting Hill Carnival. There were hundreds of them. We never ran but it was a quick walk back to the train!

London was always a great day out and I loved it, but it is a dodgy place to go and needs to be shown respect at all times. Whether you are there for a shopping trip or for the football, it does not matter; if you drop your guard or take liberties you will be sorry, particularly when on the hooligans' paradise called the Tube system.

5 ACROSS THE PARK

THERE ARE MANY myths in this world, some feasible and some totally ridiculous. Some people still believe, for instance, that all black blokes are well endowed and can dance like John Travolta. Nonsense. I know a black lad with a knob like an acorn and who bops along like he has his shoes on the wrong feet. The most outrageous, however is the one that Everton and Liverpool fans are all best mates, stand shoulder to shoulder in the Kop or Park End on derby day and, regardless of the result, spend the night drinking together, cracking each other up with their Scouse wit. If Everton or Liverpool have no game, goes the legend, we watch the other and help cheer the Reds or Blues to victory, as it is a good advert for the city.

What a load of bollocks.

Agreed, Everton v Liverpool is not like Celtic v Rangers, what game is? It is not even close to Man Utd v Man City, or Newcastle v Sunderland. But to say it's a family day out and there is never a punch thrown because we all love and respect each other is about as accurate as the time a smackhead from Kirkby claimed he saw Elvis buying a fish supper at the local chippy.

Years ago – late Seventies, early Eighties – the lads from both firms did sometimes go together and fight, mainly against the Mancs and some of the Cockney mobs. Still, derby day was iffy and, although we put up with each other, there was the odd scuffle in the ground. The scarfers did go in each other's ends, but why kick off on them? They don't want to fight. But believe me, the city centre at night was a nasty place to be. The violence between us was not organised in those days, it was just inevitable that, after a day on the ale and what was usually a defeat for us, by nightfall it would go off.

To prove this point, I have been arrested about twenty times for football-related offences and six of those have been against the Liverpool, or the Red Shite, as we affectionately call them. I have been glassed, thrown through a shop window, kicked up and down Church Street and held down while a Kopite twat searched his coat for a blade to open up my face. I am not moaning about it, as for all those beatings I have paid back in bags-full. But I hope people reading this will wake up to the fact that we are not all like Jimmy Tarbuck and Billy Butler. I, along with hundreds more, would love nothing more than to see the Red bastards relegated and would prefer it if their gobshite followers never set foot in our beloved, although crumbling, Goodison again. Their fans, if they are honest – and some are – feel the same about us and pray that one day our annual flirtation with relegation will result in us going down. In fact it has become an obsession with many of them, and they have become as sad as us!

The fact is that the vast majority of fans from both clubs hate each other with a passion, and I am no different. However, the lads from both clubs did once team up and fight for the city, and friendships that were made and respect that was gained then will not go away. That is where the confusion arises. Loads of the old lads from both clubs work legally and illegally with each other, and most of the doors in town are a mixture of old Park End and Anfield Road End Scallies. That does not mean that Everton and Liverpool games are trouble-free, and only a fool would suggest such a thing.

bitter and blue

Like I say, derby games in the Seventies and early Eighties were a bit of an uneasy truce, and when other firms came to

the city they invariably ended up taking on lads from
Everton and Liverpool. I have seen top lads from Liverpool
on the train with us to Manchester and vice versa. The turning point for many Evertonians came after the tragedy in
Heysel. The rules changed. The hatred shown to the Reds
was getting worse every year, though most of the lads from
both firms still got on.

Today even that has changed.

I cannot really slag them off for the trouble before the
1985 European Cup final against Juventus because, as
you will read later, I was there. It resulted in all English
clubs being banned from Europe. We were the League
champions and a week earlier had won the Cup Winners
Cup, so fancied our chances in the top European competition the following year. The ban fucked all that up and
the rest, as they say, is history. Our best players and
manager left, we missed out on millions of pounds and
the club once known as the Mersey Millionaires now live
in the shadow of the club many believe are to blame for
it. Nobody will ever know what would have happened
had that ban not been imposed. I and all Evertonians are
sure, though, that we would not be £40 million in debt
and bringing in players on free transfers, with the TSB or
whoever phoning up and asking our board of knobheads
to flog Wayne Rooney and clear the overdraft, while
Liverpool attract world stars at the click of a finger. It is
very hard to swallow.

The past two or three years have been especially bad and
the number of fans from both clubs watching from the
other's ends has dropped by the hundreds, as it is not safe
any more. I have never seen so few away fans at both
matches as in the past couple of seasons. The bastards signing
Nick Barmby also stirred it up and the signing of Xavier on
the cheap, when he had obviously been tapped, added to
the bad feeling. The fact that both signings flopped soft-

ened the blow but the fact that players left us for them still stirred hatred.

The game in 2001/02 at Goodison was a prime example of how things have changed. The season before, we had played them on Easter Monday with a 7pm kick-off. Everyone had been on the ale all day and there were loads of scuffles. We got bad press for ruining the minute's silence before the game but, to be honest, how many of these do we have to go through? The general consensus amongst many, Red and Blue alike, is that the Hillsborough victims should be allowed to rest in peace once and for all. No Kopite will deny that, at the time of the terrible tragedy, there was not a club more supportive than Everton, but years on they criticise us for showing no respect. They should think of the respect some of them show about the Munich air crash before throwing stones in glass houses.

So the next season, on police advice, we had a morning kick-off. It worked a treat and the trouble in the ground was non-existent. You ask the Scouse football intelligence how happy they were at midnight though, trying to keep Everton out of the Red boozers. The problem was sorted to keep the TV and football authorities happy but it didn't go away, it was just postponed for a few hours.

I'll be honest and admit I hate the Red Shite more than I hate anything else on the earth. They call us the Bitter Blues and they have a point. It doesn't stop me hating the team, the ground and the slimy bastards that reside in it though, or Doctor Fun and "You'll Never Walk Alone". Most of all I hate Phil Thompson, their assistant manager, as he stands for everything bad about them. Even most of his own players hate him and I have that on good authority, by the way!

But those few (!) examples apart, I cannot hate my many mates who support them, and that is where the confusion regarding Everton and Liverpool being best buddies is born.

How can you hate lads you were brought up with, or your relatives, or your best mate in work, who would do anything for you, just because you hate the team they support? In my eyes it's not possible, but that doesn't mean there is no trouble on a derby day.

church street

For years, Liverpool have drunk in town and we have kept to Walton, mainly down County Road. Liverpool are like Manchester United and have thousands of foreign supporters, mainly the Paddies, so town is a stop-off on their way home. That is the main reason they have bigger mobs there. Over the years, the extra numbers have come in handy for them when we have entered their areas after a derby defeat.

The worst kicking I ever had from them wasn't after a derby match though; it came when we were nearly relegated in 1994. We arrived back in town from Leeds after a 3–0 defeat, leaving us in big danger of going down. As we got off at Lime Street, we heard the bastards on the platform singing about our plight, and so we soon scattered the Devon and Dublin-bound woollybacks. We then headed into town but were stopped from entering The Crown, a big pub near the train station, as the bouncers were Everton lads and would have lost their jobs had we totalled the place. True Blues though, they told us Yates's Wine Lodge was full of Liverpool. I jogged to the front of our mob and we headed straight for them. It was a sunny evening and there they were, all around the doorway, singing, "Going down."

I told the lads to join in with the chant and, as we walked towards them, they thought we were Reds. I stepped up the pace and drop-kicked the one at the front with the biggest mouth. He flew back into the crowded doorway. I managed to stay upright and waded into them before they knew what had hit them. They caved in at first but, on seeing the size of our mob, they got a bit braver and came back out throwing bottles and glasses at us and brought it on top with the bizzies.

We went to The Hanover and a few came in asking who had started it. I didn't give a fuck for them but, as our numbers left, it came right on top and only a handful were left when the place filled with Reds. We had no option but to get off and it was typical of us not sticking together, causing ourselves a major headache. It very nearly caused me a lot more. I didn't realise that they had followed us out and, as we went up Church Street to the Crocodile, they attacked us, as usual from behind!

Larry and Vic, two very good lads who did not give a fuck about numbers, were caught straggling at the back but never budged an inch as the twenty-strong mob swarmed them. We heard them shout us back down the road. It never entered my head not to go down – a few more with the same attitude would have been handy, by the way – and so I failed to notice it was a trap. I grabbed one of the Liverpool and ran him into a phone box, smashing his head through the glass. They were onto me like a pack of wolves. I got hammered over the head with a pool cue and went down on my knees as they fought each other to boot my head back up the hill. I was losing consciousness and went onto all fours, then into a ball trying to cover my head and kidneys. The kicking stopped and I thought that was it but, as I went to get up, I was hit over the head again. One of them was shouting to his mate, "Pass me the blade." That was it – I got up onto my knees, bit the cunt's thigh and managed to get away. The other lads were still at it but it was even numbers and they hadn't seen the pasting I had taken.

We made it to the Croc but I was spewing blood, so went to the Royal and was kept in for a few hours. I had a couple of broken ribs and two fingers bust, but I was lucky not to have a five-inch slice across my cheek. I still hear the horrible cunt asking for the blade when I'm sleeping after eating too much cheese before bedtime, and often wish I could meet him on a dark night when the shithouse was on his own without tools.

the blob shop

Another time I got done was actually in Yates's, although it was nothing compared to what happened to a very good mate of mine. That night they cut him up. Very badly, too.

Again it started in The Hanover. We had a tidy little mob in there, most of them full of ale, but not a mob we could trust. After another defeat, they got it into their heads to have a pop at the Red Shite in their main boozer, Yates's Wine Lodge, commonly known as the Blob Shop. I was never keen on going in there, as not only their lads drank inside but also every Kopite from Aberdeen to Dover while waiting for their trains home. Anyway, an ale-fuelled plan was hatched and, against my better judgement, we decided to go in, have a little nose and hold the door area if we had enough bodies. We never intended to go on a suicide mission, but that is what happened. It was madness really – there was no way they would ever try a similar attack on our boozers – but year in, year out, we had little kamikaze squads on a mission, and I was always up for it.

By the time we got there, our fifty was twenty, as some preferred a Big Mac to a good hiding and disappeared into several establishments we were not heading for. As we entered, we could see the place was full of them. We assessed their numbers – easily 200 – and decided to fuck off. At last some of the lads were seeing sense, and if you have ever been in there after a Liverpool home game, you will know what

I mean, as the place is rocking with the horrible bastards.

Before we got back out, two birds started fighting. A glass smashed and the whole boozer looked at us. To a thick Kopite, two plus two made five. A massive roar went up and they slaughtered us. Only their sheer weight of numbers and a CS gas canister I had saved us from being killed. They had that many, they couldn't get at us but one of my mates was forced to the floor and, as I went to help him, a Redneck smashed a bottle and dug it deep into his cheek. It was horrible but I managed to gas the lad with the bottle and get my mate to his feet.

There were glasses and bottles flying everywhere and the place was wrecked. They must have thought we had a bigger mob, as loads of them just stood huddled in the corner slinging anything they could pick up at us. Women were screaming and a few were joining in the target practice, as they all thought we were to blame for the carnage. I suppose in theory we were, but we were being paid back for our foolishness, big time.

I am not sure how, but we got out alive. It was a bad night and many lads should hold their heads in shame when they think about it, especially those watching the drama unfold from the safety of McDonald's. My mate whose cheek was opened was a good lad and had a top sales job, which he duly lost when his wanker of a boss saw his scar and feared it would scare off potential clients. He came good in the end; with his pay-off he opened his own business and has done very well for himself. That was the only good thing to come out of that night though.

My lasting memory of it sums up the whole day. As I walked across the road, a pool ball hit me on the back of the head. It was thrown by an Everton lad at the Reds piling out of the Blob Shop, but missed them, hit the wall, bounced back and hit me, nearly knocking me out. That was it for me. Time for bed and goodnight.

the cunard

One of my better nights with them came in the Cunard near the Royal Court. Only a few of us were in there when a mob of thirty Urchins came in. I was a bit older than them and was waiting for a lad called Mark Duvall. He was a main Liverpool face who had been in jail with me a few months before, and also did three years for the slashing of Jocks at Carlisle services.

My best mate Billy made the mistake of calling these Urchins "Red Noses" as they were singing by the bar, and a lad called Dellar nutted him. I went mad and asked him if he fancied a go at doing the same to me. He fucking did and my nose splattered across my face, but before I could have a go back his mates pushed him outside. I walked out and asked him for a one-on-one and he agreed but, as I took off my jacket, he did me again, and I took a bit of a slap if I'm honest. Undeterred I went and got cleaned up and kicked it off with them inside. I didn't give a shit for them or their numbers and went crackers. The few Everton lads were pleading with me to leave it but there was no chance. I was going to have this cunt if it took me all night.

Duvall turned up, went mad with them and, to his credit, took my side. He made Dellar go outside with me again and this time I was aware of his moves. As he tried to get inside me, I roundhouse-kicked him under the chin and wasted him across the street. The Reds, with Duvall reffing, let it go, as it was a fair fight. As he tried to pull me down, I was too strong for him and I ran him into a pet shop window. All the parrots and birds in the cages were going crazy. In the end the bizzies came and, to his credit, Dellar told them we were fighting over a bird – not the ones in the shop but the female variety. We shook hands and the only time I have seen him since was at Mark Duvall's funeral.

Mark was killed in a stupid fight with his brother, who

allegedly hit him with a piece of wood. Mark had been with me fighting with a Leeds mob weeks before and had taken a brick on the head. It left a soft spot where his brother caught him and he tragically died, leaving his family wrecked, as his brother was sent down on a manslaughter charge. It was one of the saddest funerals I have ever attended. His brother was allowed to go but had to watch the cremation whilst handcuffed to a bizzie. It was a disgrace and I will never have an ounce of respect for the police after that.

The day after the Cunard fight I was in agony but still turned out for the British Legion in our Sunday football league. After the match I went on the ale and forgot about the pain but by the Monday my head was that swollen I thought it was going to pop. I went to the doctor and told him I had clashed heads playing football. I'm not sure he believed me, as a clash of heads with Herman Munster would not have caused such damage, but he could see I was in a bad way and sent me straight to the x-ray department. I had a treble fracture of my nose and cheekbone and had to have an operation that day. I was in hospital for a week and looked a right mess. I believe my looks have never returned, and quite a few girls have binned me off since the operation as I snore like a twat in bed.

One of the lads who I had been out with earlier on the night of the match phoned me and, having heard of my heroics, admitted that he had spiked me with an Ecstasy tablet. This explained my energy for all those hours fighting but I was gutted, as I thought I was super-hard and fit. Still he kept it to himself, so all the Red twats thought I was a nutcase.

scousers united

Those were the bad times off the pitch with the Reds, but we did have a few good ones, prior to Heysel. Another quote from Mr Francis in the *Guvnors* book was that we always teamed up with Liverpool to fight the Mancs. The truth is that it did happen but now only on the odd occasion. If we had a nothing away game and the Mancs were in town, why not turn out and have it with them? But it certainly didn't happen all the time and, apart from the odd European game, I for one was not a fan of spending the day at the match with the lovable Reds. I think more of them used to come away with us and, because we had a shit team, we took mainly lads away whereas their success saw them followed by hordes of pricks. There was more chance of trouble at our away games as we were always together and looking for it. Hence quite a few of their lads came for the violence, and good lads they were too. People like Mark Duvall were game as fuck and I never had a problem with them being Reds.

Games when a few Everton went with them were for the Milk Cup finals against Spurs in '82 and against Man United in '83. It was a day out and, as there was no chance of us getting to Wembley, we looked at it as a bit of a beano. Those two days were well on top though. The Spurs one was mad. There was not a punch thrown before the game but Liverpool won 3–1 in the end and all hell broke loose. I was waiting on the steps outside, as I had no interest in seeing them show another cup off. As I looked to my right, what appeared to be an army of ants was marching around the ground. It seemed every Yid had a black and white "beanie" type hat on and, from a raised position, it looked impressive. I went back in and it was a case of the devil and the deep blue sea: watch the twats parade a trophy for ten minutes or get chased around Wembley. It was not a hard choice, by the way.

As Liverpool came out, they got battered. Spurs were mental. It went off all the way back to the Tube and the London bizzies lost it in my eyes. They let a lot go that day and Liverpool kids and families were caught up in it. I'm sure the Bill let a few have it as they were sick of all the hassle the Scousers caused on every trip to the capital. I got back unscathed but wished I had been with my own mob as, with all due respect to Liverpool, they did not seem up for it that day and it was one scary journey back to Euston.

The following year a few of us went to the Man United final and, if anything, it was worse than the year before. We got the "ordinary" train to Euston but most of Liverpool's lads were on the specials, which got you in later but were half the price. They always were a mingebag firm. We were there for about ten and the station was fifty-fifty with Scousers and Mancs. There was the odd skirmish but nothing major. I wish I'd known the Mancs as I do now, as they all went to Swiss Cottage before the game and had a tom shop off for a big-time earner.

After the game, which the Kopite bastards won again, all the Scousers got together on the grass verge outside one of the blocks and marched into the coach park. At first they steamed United and things were looking good but then United regrouped and came back and managed to split us into two groups. One lot ended up at Wembley Central but we ended up at Wembley Park. It was Sod's Law that their main firm would turn up at the Park, and they did. At first Liverpool had them on their toes twice before, once again, United forced us back and in the end we got chased for what seemed like a good two miles, with battle after battle being broken up by the bizzies. They kept United back and put us on the Tube to Euston, and when we got there it was full of Liverpool. There were no United in sight and gradually more and more Liverpool got on the specials. After half an hour, United showed, led by Cockney Sam. They took over the station and ran amok. Had Liverpool stayed together it may have been a close one. They never and it wasn't.

mersey cup finals

The first time we played them at Wembley was in the 1984 Milk Cup final, and on the Saturday night we had a combined mob of thousands all over London. No Cockney mobs came near, despite all the threats that we were going to get done if we showed. Before the game, thousands were locked out and millions worldwide watched as lads jumped off the towers and were pulled into the stadium through the window-like openings by Red and Blue supporters. A few didn't make it and were lucky to be alive to tell the tale, as it was a forty-foot drop. We drew the game 0-0, but as usual against them were robbed by the referee. We lost the replay at Maine Road when at least Man City turned out and had a go, unlike the Cockneys days earlier.

The tide on the pitch was turning and we were the first side to win a Merseyside derby at Wembley when, after winning the Cup later that season against Watford, we beat the Red Shite in the Charity Shield. Again we took London and for two nights nobody would entertain taking us on, apart from a big, nasty bouncer. Before the match we went into a club in the West End and we were playing up a bit, nothing serious, just being a bit silly. This bloke came over and warned us that if we didn't pack it in he would fight us one by one or all at once and that "there would only be one facking winner." He seemed a nice bloke so we stopped playing up and he was sound with us. I'm glad we took his advice as later we found out he was Lenny "the Guv'nor" McLean. This was before he had cropped hair, as in *Lock, Stock and Two Smoking Barrels* – he had horrible long sideburns, no neck and shoulders like a bull gorilla, and he looked an absolute monster. Nice bloke, hard bastard, no takers!

The following season we won the League and the Cup Winners Cup and were runners-up in the FA Cup, but all that made the sports news was the Heysel Disaster, and that was the straw that broke the camel's back for many. The next season we lost the Double to the bastards and there was trouble after the game at Wembley, which we somehow managed to lose 3–1 after being one up at half time. We had still been together before the game as word was around that Millwall were at Leicester Square. It was a false alarm so we looted the place instead.

After that came Hillsborough and I don't really want to go into the actual event, as in my eyes a lot of bad things happened that day that will never come out. One thing is for sure though: the Cup final, never mind the re-played semi, should have been postponed or abandoned, as there was only going to be one winner and it wasn't going to be Everton or Nottingham Forest. As it was, for the good of the game and in remembrance of those who died – or was it the financial implications and potential loss of revenue? – the FA decided to play it. They took down the fences and gave both clubs extra tickets.

It was no surprise that we lost the match, as the world rightly wanted Liverpool to win that Cup for the ninety-six that lost their lives on that tragic day in Sheffield. But it was a crap match and off the pitch was like a testimonial, with people who knew nothing about football joining in the remembrance service that was in reality still the FA Cup final. They made a mistake taking the fences down though, as when we scored in the last minute to force extra time, thousands invaded the pitch and it took ages to restart it. It had a happy ending, as the Red Shite won. Their fans invaded at the end and, fair play to them, fucked up the lap of honour for their team! It was a fitting result, I suppose, particularly for the bereaved families, though I couldn't feel much warmth for the thousands who jumped on the "Hillsborough Cup Final" band-wagon.

Before that game, a joint mob arranged to do a jeweller's full of Rolexes but the lad with the sledgehammer had cut too much off the handle and it got stuck in the window after the first hit. The alarm went off and we legged it, leaving him with both feet against the glass like Spiderman, trying to pull the hammer out. He escaped but was an Evertonian, so it was a really bad weekend for him: no silverware in more ways than one.

A week later, Arsenal came to town and the rest of the football world waited while they rolled over and gave the Red Shite the second half of the Double. They didn't read the script and a last-minute goal won it for the Gunners. As the Arsenal coaches went down Priory Road, gleeful Evertonians were stopping them and giving them ale for the victorious trip home. It was a great end to a shite season, and the sight of Steve McMahon in tears made me piss myself, it really was that funny

three of the best

We didn't always lose to the bastards. For a few years we could do no wrong against them and were their bogey side. Of all the games people watch against their bitterest rivals, they always have favourites. These are my top three.

The best derby game I ever saw was the 4–4 draw in the FA Cup. We went one down and a gobshite in front of me started jumping about, so I smacked him. He turned around and, although he looked a mean bastard, just sat down. Within minutes of the second half we scored and I went mad. As I went to sit down, he belted me plum in the mouth. I was shocked but thought, *fair play to him*. They scored again, so I gave him another, which he repaid when we got our second equaliser minutes before the end. Then they went three up, and I told him that if he wanted to jump up when they scored, to fuck off into the Park End. Before we made it three each, he had skulked off. He missed the end and another three goals. There was no sign of him at the replay, when we won 1–0. Had I been in his shoes I'd have been in the hozzy or nicked, as I'd have gone ape, but he couldn't half take a dig.

Another great day was our first win at Anfield for fourteen years when Graham Sharp scored *Match Of The Day*'s Goal of the Season in 1984. We had about a third of the Kop and loads got on the pitch when Sharpie scored. We all got into the Kemlyn Road Stand when the game restarted. The Reds were well pissed off with us and started leaving twenty minutes before the end. At full-time, the ground was nearly empty of them. We sang, "Going down," as they were in the bottom five in the League and we were top.

My best ever, though, was Joe Royle's first game in charge. We were bottom, they were top and we beat the bastards 2–0. Duncan Ferguson scored the first and Paul Rideout got the second in the last minute. We were all at the front ready to get on the pitch when the second went in and I ran on thinking there was hundreds behind me. It was live on Sky TV and I was the only fucker on there. I looked a right soft bastard running around with the police and stewards chasing me and the Liverpool fans in the Bullens Road booing me, so thought *fuck it* and jumped into the Red Shites' end. They went bananas. I was covered from head to toe in spit and took a few digs but the stewards got me out and the Park End gave me a standing ovation as I was led to the police room. It was one of the proudest nights of my life.

life and death

Those days of "friendly rivalry" in the ground are over and I don't think they will ever come back. It is hard for me, as many of my mates are Reds and I can earn top money from a couple of them. I hate everything about the club but won't fall out with people who I respect, and they feel the same way too.

I was in a pub recently and saw a bit of a meeting going on between about a dozen top lads. When it was over I went and had a chat to the ones I knew well and it turned out it was the weekly meeting of the main lads who work all the doors in town. Each firm had the main bloke and his number two and they sorted out all the narks that had been triggered after the weekend activities. Mr X would agree one of his lads was out of order belting somebody and they would pay for his new teeth. Mr Z would let a door go for one nearer a club he ran. It was all sorted out in about an hour. Nearly all these lads were old football hooligans and were Red and Blue alike. Is a bit of palaver about who's got the best mob going to undo all that trust and potential earnings? No.

I also know gangs of Everton and Liverpool lads who are the best robbers in the country. One time it took a firm weeks to plan and rob a major designer shop in town, but when they did they cleared thousands. Would a couple of lads turn that down because the bloke who hijacked the dustbin lorry to carry the fifty sacks of swag away was a Red? Would they fuck.

It isn't always as successful as that raid, though. Another job was planned and, after ten hours of chiselling a hole in the roof and breaking into a massive warehouse supposedly full of cigarettes, it turned out that the place was packed with sacks of salt. The lad who sorted that job, who we will call Peter, also turned up at my mate's shop with a blanket and opened it to reveal a huge chandelier. Peter thought it might be worth a few quid as scrap and my mate kept it in his shed for a night. The next day it was in the *Liverpool Echo* that it had been stolen from St George's Hall while the hall was being painted and that it was worth a million quid. They dumped it in the road and the taxi driver that found it was a hero on Merseyside for weeks.

The tickets are another top earner but if the lads from both clubs could not work together then it would fuck it up for everybody, as at the first sniff of a kick-off, the chance of money would be gone. That also applies in Manchester, where half the touts at Old Trafford are ex-Man City lads. We all need money, and I am glad that when I fancy a few soft quid I can earn it from the Reds. There is a lot more money to be earned outside Anfield when they play Barcelona in the Champions League than when we are at home to Crystal Palace the day before in the Worthington Cup!

This renewed success Liverpool are having has hindered their hooligan firm, as the club is like a business. Unlike at Everton, the man in the street is now being forced out of Anfield to be replaced by whoppers from Devon with a pocket full of cash to waste in the club shop. It is virtually impossible to get a ticket for a game on a Saturday at Anfield; midweek is easier as it's a bit far to travel from Devon and Dublin on a Tuesday or Wednesday and the flights from Karachi don't land at John Lennon Airport till gone half-time!

As a mob, they struggle to get thirty good lads nowadays, although they seem to have a decent firm on their hooligan website, especially during half-term and when the libraries are open. Their old football intelligence officer, who we called "Will Carling", was often at Everton away games, as it was far more likely to go off than at Anfield. I also know the bizzies were dreading us getting into Europe through the back door, as it would not be like the Liverpool games when all is well. The tragedy at Hillsborough finished it for many of them, but that does not mean they were never there. On their day Liverpool were as good as anybody and caused more damage than most. They can still pull a nasty mob if they need to, and always show at Old Trafford, but most of the lads of my age are into making money, and won't risk it all for a scuffle at Ipswich. Bill Shankly once said, "Football is not a matter of life or death, it is far more important than that." What a load of bollocks. Your family, friends and money are far more important than two games a season against the Red bastards and only a silly old Scottish fool would say otherwise.

In conclusion, Everton v Liverpool is not Rangers v Celtic but it has never been as hostile as it is today. The hatred shown by Everton towards them after Heysel is now going full circle. They now hate us whereas a few years ago, I really believe quite a few of them wanted us to win the Cup final against Man United. Those days are gone and I am honest enough to admit I do hate the club and the majority of their supporters with a passion. In the words of our ex-captain Brian Labone, "One Blue is worth twenty Reds." I don't hate my mates though, and through no fault of their own loads of them support the Red Shite.

6 BORO

OF ALL THE rivalries we have had at Everton, none has been as bad or violent as the one with Middlesbrough. It dates back to 1977, when we went up there in the FA Cup. I was only fourteen and kept out of the way, but it was a nasty place and easily the worst ground for hassle I had been to in my short career as a football hooligan.

It always seems cold up there and the match in January 1977 was no different. We lost 3–2 and there was a bit of trouble before the game, but after, Everton went mad and it was going off all the way back to the coaches. Boro had a good mob and youngsters like myself were out of our league and just bystanders as the older lads from both sides fought for what seemed ages. It ended with Boro getting chased and, as one lad, Kevin Sawdon, climbed over a wall to get away, he was stabbed straight up the arsehole – as in, right up it. There is a picture in this book from the press showing the blade that was used; the lad on the receiving end was close to death. I remember the police holding all the coaches back and looking for the stabber, but he was never found. The lad responsible had a lot to answer for; from that day, Everton v Middlesbrough games have on numerous occasions resulted in bloodbaths, with many more stabbings and slashings on a par with that initial incident twenty-five years ago.

It was quiet for a few years after that, mainly because we were in different divisions, but on the odd times Boro did play at Goodison, their fans were poor travellers and never showed, and when we went there they didn't seem to have a mob any more. It all changed in about 1985 though, when we drew them in the FA Cup at our place.

I was in the city centre early, and a few of us were having a drink in The Crown, which in those days was a bit of a meeting place when we ventured into town. It is a big, spacious pub a minute's walk from the station, and before CCTV was installed was the perfect lookout for strays. It had one entrance but two exits and used to be ideal for an ambush. It was a short walk from the Yankee Bar too, which although popular with Liverpool, was also used by us when The Crown was full or the bizzies were onto us in there

I had just ordered a bottle when the doors opened and a huge mob walked in. A big cunt wearing a baseball cap walked to the bar and jokingly ordered 200 pints of bitter. I think he was joking anyway, but I'm not sure, as I didn't hang around to see if he paid for them. We shot to the Yankee Bar to see if there were any lads about, and only about thirty were in there. One of Liverpool's lads, Ged, said to me when I told him about the 200 Boro, "I'll get them out of there."

He kept his word, as the minute he walked in there, the pub emptied and he was chased back to the Yankee. They filled the road outside and we had no chance of getting out, as the door was only wide enough for one at a time to go through. Boro didn't give a fuck and started to force their way in and we had a battle to keep them out. They were dead game and, although the first few were getting battered, the lads behind them kept forcing their way in. It was bedlam until one of our lads threw a stool through the window and a few of us got out behind them. For a few seconds they backed off but they weren't on the run. They seemed to take a look at our smaller numbers and then started to walk away.

Had we left it there and let them have a bit of a victory, I am sure they would have given us a walkover. We were a bit humiliated, however, as it had been years since any firm had shown like that so early in the day, apart from the Mancs. We got it together and ran into the back of them and another massive fight broke out. By now word had got around and we had been joined by loads of lads from the other pubs around the station and even blokes who were shopping and queuing for the pictures across the road. The Boro lads were shocked as well as surprised, as I am sure they thought we would leave it, but once we were on top we were not letting go and for a few minutes they got battered. I was fighting with one lad when a bloke I have never seen before ran over and shouted, "Who's Everton?" I just nodded, as I was not winning this battle, and the bloke grabbed the Boro lad around the neck and threw him through a clothes shop window. My saviour grunted something like, "Cheeky bastards," and then went back to his daily business.

We ended up getting backed off when all the Boro regrouped and saw we were well outnumbered, and we were chased back into the Yankee. It ended up a stand-off, as we were not going out and they could still get through the door only in ones and twos. They left at the first sound of the police sirens. As they were walking away, a lad threw a big piece of plate glass at us but missed and Mark Duvall picked it up and was a better shot, nearly taking a Boro lad's head off with his return of serve.

The bizzies were well on their case now. Meanwhile, we all got taxis up to the ground and there got a massive mob together. Loads were shocked that Boro had turned up with big numbers, as very few had heard they had a top mob. It wasn't long before they got to the ground but they had a huge escort and were boxed off. We were hanging around when the bloke that had first walked into the pub and ordered the ale came over and asked who wanted a go. He was a fucking monster but Carlos fronted him. The lad just turned his cap back-to-front and booted Carlos in the shin. He was a nutcase, and walked off laughing.

After the game, a draw, there was no real trouble, as they were kept in and most of them were put on buses back to the station. I was glad to see the back of the cunts, and hoped we could take the same numbers up there for the replay, as I was sure we would need them. The thing I remember from that day, apart from the nutcase in the cap, was that they didn't have many fans at the game, but those they did have were nearly all boys. That reminded me of Everton as, until our team was successful, our away numbers were poor at some games, but when the turnout was low it was all lads. That helped us in the Eighties, as most followings had a large majority of normal fans, whereas we were ninety per cent hooligans. If we took 500 to London – and that is all we took to many grounds before it was fashionable to go – 400 were lads. Many fans that travel away now would have crapped themselves during the free-for-alls of the "unfashionable" Seventies and Eighties.

The replay was on top. We took a huge mob on coaches but the bizzies had them sussed (see Chapter Two). Loads who went in cars and vans had a rough ride and many took a slap. We got another draw and won the toss to have the second replay at our place. I got there late and never saw if they had the same firm, but afterwards it went mental and seven Boro got stabbed or slashed. These were the horrific events related by the leader of the County Road Cutters in Chapter Two. The cuttings were out of order, but it is true that Boro did come looking for it, and the harsh reality of those days was that if you came down County Road for hassle, you got it, and the rule book was out of the window. The papers understandably made a big thing about the knifings. All I can add is that Boro did not learn their lesson.

The first time we went there by train as a firm was in about 1989. It was towards the end of the season and was a nothing game, we were doing crap but still took 100-odd on the ordinary. I was with Kelly, who all the way there was saying he was going to give it a low one, as he was already on a football charge. We got off the train and walked out of the station and a few lads fronted us. Kelly kept his word for about a second before putting the first one on his arse, and was nicked within a minute of arriving.

We bounced into the street and there were no great numbers of them, just small mobs, but they don't care up there, and we fought all the way to the ground. They were waiting in shops in groups of five or six, letting us go past and then charging into us. They were fucking crackers, and battle after battle took place as they ambushed us. It was a fair way to Ayresome Park and the walk must have taken over an hour. It was toe-to-toe all the way. One lad walked into a bin when we were in the town centre and a bizzie told him to pick all the litter up. He made us carry on and then followed us, leaving the litterbug to get battered by them. Even the coppers were bonkers. There is a big ICI chemical factory up there and I'm sure there has been a leak that sent the place haywire, because I have been all over the world and can say hand on heart that Middlesbrough is the nastiest place I have visited.

By the ground, they mobbed up and came down alleys towards us. In those confined spaces they had it sussed, as no more than a few could get at them, and some of the most ferocious fighting I have ever seen took place. You could not run or get off if you didn't fancy it, as there was no room to move, so you had to have it, and a few made names for themselves that day on both sides.

At the end of the match, we got out early, but were forced back in by the sheer weight of numbers on their side. All the small mobs before were now as one, and they had an awesome firm. We were kept in for ages. Later, about fifty of us got away from the escort but didn't find their mob. One Boro lad did meet us at the station and instead of all the usual abuse that is thrown around, he said we were a boss firm and had given them their best go before a game for years. I wish there were more like him; nowadays all you seem to get is bullshit and posting crap on the Internet. It's one big yawn.

They had a few bad seasons after that game and were relegated, and by the time we played there again our mob was a shadow if its former glory. We tried to fill a couple of coaches but ended up with three minibuses. It looked like we were headed for embarrassment but it turned out to be the day a new mob was formed: the Snorty Forty. That trip became legendary,

We parked up at Darlington Station and were not picked up by the bizzies, so had a few drinks and took the train into Middlesbrough. We piled out of the station and straight into their boozer. They must have thought we had big numbers, as they kicked the fire door open and ran out to escape. We stayed put in the bar and when the bizzies turned up, they could not believe forty-odd had taken this Boro stronghold. Outside the street was filled with disgruntled "Smog Monsters", as the Geordies call them, and we were herded out and marched through them to the ground. When they saw how few we had, there was a furious inquest in their ranks and we could see them kicking off with each other.

The venue and its name had changed, but it was still the same old walk to the ground – you had to battle all the way. Whether it was Ayresome or the Riverside, there was no easy route, they made sure of that. They were in front of us, behind and all over the other side of the road. It went off at every junction and crossing, and they had the mentality that the police did not exist. They just kept fronting us. The local bizzies would say, "Pack it in, Billy," or, "Stop it, Joe." They knew every fucking one of them, but rather than nick them they'd dish out the odd slap or a baton thwack across the legs. We sussed this out, and once we realised we were not going to get nicked, we started taking it to them. We had three or four major offs and only two lads got nicked:

Jeff for spraying them with CS gas and Kevin for not heeding his fourth warning to stop punching people.

We made the ground, which was a lot less hostile than Ayresome. There were no alleys and the big forecourt outside was easier to police. It was also easier to see how many they had, and the sight of the Snorty Forty marching towards their masses chanting, "We are evil," was one I will take to my grave. They were distraught, and even a few local bizzies said to me that we had done well getting there in one piece after our attack on their boozer and backing them off all the way to the ground. They also added that we had done the easy bit, and that after the game they would have four times as many. The bizzies up there were round the twist.

After the game we were again kept in the ground for our own safety, and you couldn't really argue with that, as they had hundreds waiting for us. Once out, as always, we went looking for it, and got away from the escort, briefly fronting it with some splinter groups of Boro as the police chased them all over the place. We got level with a pub at the railway crossing and it came badly on top, with the police really struggling to keep them back. All sorts was flying over our heads and mobs from all four sides were breaking through. They had lads mixed in with us saying that any minute we were going to die. We were only forty-strong and they had ten times as many but, as frightening as it was – and we are talking scary here – it was still brilliant. I loved it when it was like that. As has often been said, there is not a rush to match it: Class A's, a Swedish page-three model, fine claret and fifty-year-old blended Scotch, I've had the lot, but give me that buzz at Boro any day. It's different class and only people who have been there could begin to understand that.

I don't know how, but we made it to the station, and even there we were still fighting them on the platform. One knobhead was giving us shit, claiming we had been battered even though we were virtually unscathed and were still as one, forty-strong, so nobody had been put on their toes. This guy was one of their lads, as I have often seen him; he has either the worst inherited curly mane or a bad home perm and always stands out. I told him that, with the same numbers at Goodison, they could not do what we'd just done. He lied that thirty of them had chased Everton off Lime Street on Boxing Day. I laughed and informed him no trains run on that day. He went red and fucked off with his bad perm between his legs.

We got back to Darlington and the fighting should have been over. Perhaps with any other firm it would have been, but we were Everton, so we got in our minibuses and drove straight back to Boro. We collected the two lads from the nick and then parked by their pub, but a police van pulled up and we had to do one. By now even the Cleveland Police had seen enough of us. One lad nipped in and told the Boro that we were back and a few came out as we were being escorted away. Years later, a Boro lad told me he thought we were mad that day, and said when we turned up at eight o'clock in the evening they were flapping, as most of their firm had got off. They were even glad the bizzies had turned up, as they knew how game our small firm was. We never did Boro that day and they never did us either, but it was a day we earned respect, not just from them but from ourselves. As a mob we would never fear going anywhere with the Snorty Forty.

The next season, Boro played at our place in one of the first games in the new campaign. I was expecting a big turnout from them but intended staying away, as it had been only a few weeks since my arrest at Aberdeen (see Chapter Eight). A couple of Hibs lads, James and Richie, came down for the weekend to sort us out with a decent brief and give us the ins and outs of Scottish law. It was a load of crap to us. All this Sheriff bollocks and High Court stuff was very confusing and worrying, as we were on a riot charge and had been told to expect seven years. Both the Hibs lads had been on similar charges and knew the score, putting us right on a few points, which was a help.

Though we weren't going to the game, we drank in The Oak until about ten minutes before kick-off, then had a wander up to see if any of them had showed. At the top of the road by the Winslow boozer, we met up with a decent little mob of Everton. Seconds later, Boro came around the corner – led by Bad Perm! They had more than us and there was a bit of a stand-off while everyone sussed out who was who. Their undercover bizzie was with them; we recognised him from the Berghaus fleece he always wore. That may have been their reason not to kick off, but if so, it was a poor one. Bad Perm was giving it loads and how it never went off I don't know. We were all mixed in with each other and the bizzies were flapping about. James noticed a lad from Hibs he knew who was with Boro and pulled him over. The lad was in shock and asked what he was doing with "the Scouse cunts". James took his number before Boro were put in the ground, while we went back to The Oak. We phoned them and told them to leave it after the game and fuck off up to The Arkles by Anfield, saying we would be in touch.

About six o'clock, we phoned them and they said the bizzies were still outside, so quite a few of our lads got off. Half an hour later, we got a call from them and they said they were on the move, the bizzies had done one and they would meet us at Everton Valley, at the junction of Scotty Road. I had heard all this bullshit before and did not believe they would get anywhere near Scotty, whether they meant it or not, so stayed in the pub. It must have been nearly seven by now and a load of young lads came in saying Boro were past Anfield. A lad went up in his car and came back with a positive. They had meant it and were nearly at Scotty.

We piled out. I did not fancy our chances, as the away mob, if a proper mob, is usually the stronger in my book, and loads of our lot had got off. I walked past The Netley and The Queens feeling a bit wary. We gathered pace, the two lads from Hibs at the front with big Shaun and me. There was a roar and Larry and Stewy came from nowhere and were into them with a load of the Urchins. Boro panned out across the road. I looked behind and the numbers were dead even. Shaun shouted for everyone to move it and we went straight into them. They stood firm, as I had expected, and from the back of their mob came a load of lads with big rocks. One had a fence pole. Had they kept hold of them, we would have been in lumber, but they threw them at us and backed off. A huge rock knocked James over but he just rolled back onto his feet and charged into them with it. His mate copped one in the face and looked fucked but never moved an inch. Say what you like about the Jocks but these two were the very best, and with them at your side it was easy to get the upper hand.

I picked up the fence pole, as we were getting pushed back. As their next wave attacked with anything they could get their hands on, I ran forward and hit the biggest fucker they had clean over the head with the pole. It snapped in two. I rammed the broken stake into his chest and waited for him to crumble. And waited. He shook his head, picked up the other half and came into us with it. Shaun got one around the chest, I'm not sure if it was from Boro or my back swing, and weeks later he was still badly bruised. How the Boro lad stayed up I will never know, but he did. He was the hardest bastard I have ever fought.

They battled like mad but in the end they went. We chased them before they stopped and fronted it again, but this time they had casualties and got done in. One lad was stabbed in the arm and a couple more were unconscious on the pavement. Shaun stopped the two lads getting slashed, as a couple of Urchins were ready to stripe them. Soon the police came, but they were powerless and we charged once more. One lad was still having a go. He picked up a piece of concrete and got ready to throw it at Shaun, who in fairness had just saved their lads a trip to the stitch department in Fazakerley Casualty. I drop-kicked him and that was that; Boro were finished and we disappeared up Everton Valley.

From the top of the valley I looked down and it was carnage. There were cars stopped on the dual carriageway, a body on the pavement, another on the road, debris and makeshift weapons lying everywhere. More police arrived and I ran through the alleys up to the ground and got a cab into town. We drove past the Boro mob being escorted to Lime Street. They looked a sorry lot, with their clothes ripped and loads limping and bearing cuts. As I was on bail, I didn't even go into town for a beer, just went home, had a fine bottle of Châteauneuf-du-Pape and celebrated my favourite victory against our biggest rivals off the pitch. The next time I saw the Hibs lads was a few seasons later. They were with a big mob of Man United who chased a few of us outside Wetherspoons. They go with United quite often now and I'm sure they are well appreciated by the Mancs, as they would improve any firm.

It wasn't that long before I saw the Boro boys again too. We had to play them away on Boxing Day and, although I gloated that night in bed, deep down I knew we would be in for a rough ride. There was no way they would take the humiliation they suffered that day lying down. That was another call I should have had a big wager on.

I am not a great fan of Christmas football. It gets you out of the house away from the visiting in-laws, and I suppose if the game's at home it's okay, but whoever sorts the fixtures out must be a Jehovah's Witness, as time and time again you seem to play teams miles away. Still, I suppose you could say that "Boxing" Day was the right occasion to face Boro. If you need an excuse to bottle out of a game that could be a bit tasty, Christmas is the ideal one. If you have kids, you don't get stick for not going, and I have heard the "I was pissed and slept in" blag used many times. Quite a few used it that day, and expectations of 150 going up there were well off the mark. We had a coach and a fleet of minibuses ordered but in the end the minibuses were a dream and there were even a few seats left on the coach. Although most of the main lads were on board, many who for weeks had been harping on about the "Battle of Boro" were spotted playing Kerplunk with their little brothers or Twister with their sex-starved mother-in-law.

We got there nice and early at about twelve and made it to the town centre without a bizzie in sight. We pulled the coach over outside a pub and had a quick nose in but it was nearly empty, so we got everyone off, with the usual "stick together and no running" sketch. We were wasting our breath. We had a few young lads on the coach who had been with us on Scotty when we did them. They had been expecting more of the same and, as the last few got off from the back of the bus, they were already disappearing around the corner. A lad came out of the pub, one of their boys I had seen loads of times. He was sound and asked, "How many?" I told him fifty-odd, but a good fifty-odd, and he laughed; not a sly, piss-taking laugh, but a "don't fucking bother" laugh. He even told me to leave it and go for a drink with him, but that was not an option. I asked him what Boro had out and he said, "Hundreds." I nodded and walked away shaking my head.

He shouted me back. I will never forget him saying, "Nicholls, six hundred an hour ago, get your lads back on the bus and fuck off home. You're gonna get killed, the whole town is out for this one." Seconds earlier I had thought he was blagging but this time his tone was different. Although I didn't want to believe him, I knew I had to.

We were indeed in big trouble. I never considered getting off but did wish I had kids, which might have prevented me attending the impending slaughter!

I caught up with the mob, still believing they were Cock of the North, and we got level with a pub near a bridge, which is like a small tunnel. Inside, the boozer was full of them. We fronted the main door – we had been there less than a minute and it was ready to go. A few came out and there was a massive roar, but they turned and pushed their way back in. The lad at the front of our mob I had never seen before, but he seemed a game fucker and pushed into the doorway, punching the first two lads trying to get out into us. One went down and the other held his chest. Boro ran back in and it looked like a poor show from them. The lad at the front turned and I saw him put a blade into his coat; it was obvious he had stabbed at least the lad on the floor and possibly both of them. That explained the so-called poor show. As he moved away from the door, Boro steamed out, and we were forced back under the bridge as wave after wave of glasses and bottles landed around us. I was screaming for our mob to hold our ground, as if Boro got out tooled up, we were finished. Briefly we got them back into the pub when they ran out of missiles. Still there was not a bizzie in sight, and we regrouped and moved up the road towards the next boozer.

As we looked up the hill, it was a sight to forget, but one I never will. There was a light blue or grey car driving slowly towards us with a mob of hundreds behind it. I thought it was a police car, albeit a clapped out one, but it revved up and drove straight into us. There were lads jumping out of the way and we soon sussed that it was being driven by one of their lads. I tried to put his window in with a bottle that had seconds earlier hit me in the chest, but I missed and within seconds our mob was scattered. They were behind us, at both sides of us and the road in front was still full of

them. You could not see an inch of tarmac, just masses of
lads piling down the road. Loads had coshes, and we were
still being bombarded by the pub mob. I thought I was
going to die. We were getting forced back but Franny went
the opposite way, straight into them. He got pulled down
and a few of us went back for him but he managed to get
up without being killed. They were around him and you
could hear them shouting, "Bite him, kill him." He took
the brunt of it but still got to his feet and fronted them
again. A few of us went to his aid, a few never, for the size
of the Boro mob was too much, and I will not condemn
anyone who didn't fancy it; it was a scary fucking sketch,
believe me.

At last the police arrived. I'm sure they had let it go on as
long as they did to teach us a lesson. They surrounded us but
Boro went through them and we were chased back to our
coach. We were lucky. I think they had so many that they got
in the way of each other, as only Franny had taken a kicking,
although loads had minor injuries. Even back by the bus,
they came at us, but left it in the end. We looked a sorry lot
getting escorted to the ground. One lad, a big-muscles character who was one of their main faces, stood there in our
faces screaming, "You're shit, it only took us three minutes to
go straight through you." *It would have taken a lot less if they'd
had 400, not 800,* I thought. A police van stopped the escort
and they nicked Kelly. In the van were two lads who had
indeed been stabbed. They told the police they had the
wrong lad and Kelly was let out. The lad responsible did one
and I have never seen him since. He was lucky though, as
Boro wanted him dead and the bizzies were desperate to nick
him. The Boro lads were top drawer for that, as they easily
could have blown up the wrong lad, and with Kelly's record
a judge would have thrown away the key.

We were silent all the way to the ground and Boro left
us alone. I was embarrassed that our stupidity had cost us

and the myth that our forty could go anywhere and do it was blown out of the water. In the ground, I never saw any Boro lads. At half-time, their bizzie came over with Everton police spotter Pat Cook and said we were in for a rough ride after the game. He strongly advised us to stay in the escort back to the coaches. He said they were going berserk in town after we had attacked the pub and that the two lads who had been stabbed were well-known faces. I asked him about the Boro mob and he admitted the whole town was out for us and all the pub and club bouncers were with them. It was their biggest mob for years and he still reckoned we had done all right. They had the more severe casualties, so I suppose he had a point.

After the game, we came out behind all the normal fans and stuck together like glue. Pat Cook and the Boro bizzie were with us but there was no real escort. Cook got out his telescopic truncheon. I swear he didn't look too happy and I don't blame him. Up ahead you could hear it going off, and loads of Boro were on the opposite side of the road pointing us out, but after a load of scarfers up front got banged, we made it back to our coach with relative ease. We even had the cheek to filter off and try to get across the railway crossing to their pub but it was a half-hearted effort and we didn't get very far.

Once on the coach we were surrounded by the bizzies and were all searched for weapons and traces of blood. We were kept for ages before they let us go. It was a long, silent journey home and we never even bothered with an inquest. Regardless that two of their lads had been stabbed, we had been done fair and square by sheer weight of numbers, and no amount of arguing was going to change that. A few lads came out of it with credit and a few never, but the letdowns were those who were playing games or happy families at home when we were getting roasted.

A couple of months later, we got them in the League Cup or whatever it was called that year, but again the turnout was poor. Our bus was nowhere near full but still we went; after the Boxing Day annihilation, we just had to. The difference was that there was no way they would have that firm out in mid-week. Our plan was to go straight to the ground and just go for it outside. We were not playing heroes this time with forty, but at least would show and let them know we were still about. It was a nasty firm on board and a well tooled-up one, but on arrival near the ground we got stopped and simply turned back. No arguments, we didn't have a chance. A local bizzie got on the bus and read out a letter saying we were all known hooligans and were being refused entry into the area in the interest of public safety. They had a point. I was just glad they didn't search the bus, as we would have been still inside now such was the seriousness of the armoury on board.

We were escorted out of Middlesbrough and all the way to Leeds, and when we turned off to go into the city centre for a mooch, we were picked up by the Yorkshire bizzies and escorted to Lancashire: road blocks, motorway lanes closed, it must have cost thousands. We got home and went on a bender, as Everton had won 3–2. I don't remember the results of our other games against Boro, as we weren't there for that and it wasn't important, but we listened to this game on the bus radio as we had fuck all else to do, and it was sound. Cup fever!

The following season, the game at our place was on a Wednesday night. We mobbed up in the Red Brick and had a tidy firm around the ground looking for them. They never showed, which I think was the beginning of the end for our tit-for-tat clashes. We always went there, even when we knew we would be hopelessly outnumbered, but the first time they came without all their boys, they bottled it. Those are not my words, but those of one of the seven Boro lads who did turn up and were given a walkover before the game outside the Paddock. They had just managed to fill a minibus which, given the history between us, was pathetic. We won 5–0 and their team was as bad as their mob. Their boys left early and we couldn't even be arsed going after them. It was no surprise when they were relegated that season. It was a bit harsh, as they had points deducted for not turning up for a game at Blackburn, but it helped us as we were near the bottom again.

Middlesbrough came straight back up the next season but many of the lads had lost interest in them by then after their no-show at Goodison. A new generation was breaking through in our firm and the younger lads had no axe to grind, as they had not been involved in the violent history between the two clubs. It was a bit low key when we went there that season. I went up for the game but neither firm was out in force and nothing was planned or happened.

They were due to play at Goodison in the last week of the season. That time is a bit like the third round of the FA Cup and usually guarantees a good turnout, so it was no shock when, a few days before, I got a message from a Man United hooligan to phone a Boro lad he knew. They were going to Blackpool on the Saturday night and wanted to sort out our problems on the Sunday once and for all. They obviously still had the axe and wanted to grind it. I phoned him and he was serious, saying they had a full complement out for the weekend and gave me the assurance that we would need our top mob out or we would be in for another embarrassment. I told him that bringing eight in a minibus on their last visit to Goodison was an embarrassment, not fifty of us getting steamed by 1,000 after fronting their main boozer and shivving a couple. It would be sorted, I added.

I let everyone know but wasn't that hopeful, as Boro were no more at the top of everybody's hitlist. I got a few calls in the morning from them and they reckoned they had three coachloads. We went up early and had all of six in the Red Brick at opening. I was ready to call it a day and go home. Soon, however, the place began to fill up and within an hour it was bouncing, so I cancelled my retirement plans and phoned them up. They had pulled up in Widnes to get the train in, but got collared. I don't know why they did that, as they had never had trouble getting to us before. It was the first sign of a bluff to me and I was right; the three coaches turned out to be one and a bit.

They were escorted to Anfield and put in a bar called Sam Dodd's, so a few of us went up. They did have a good mob but nothing like they had claimed. They phoned to say they were walking down, albeit with a massive police escort, and we got together. We had a top firm and blocked the junction by Priory Road, but we were a bit early and the bizzies were going mad, charging us with horses. We struggled to keep it together and they got Boro into the ground. I kept in touch with the Boro throughout and it was agreed that they would stay in at the end and then walk to Anfield, where we would meet. I don't know why but instead they came out early, chased a few kids and fans, and got put on their bus before the game ended. They even turned their phone off. I honestly think they blew it on purpose. I got a call at about eight o'clock saying this had happened and that had happened but it was a load of bollocks and I lost respect for them that day. We were there when it was arranged and when it mattered and they weren't.

The following season I was nicked at the Riverside, not for anything to do with violence or their mob; it was a set-up, covered in Chapter Seven, when the police tried to get me banned, which they still managed to fuck up. Anyway, Boro again didn't show at Everton and it really looked like it was all over for both sides.

In the season 2001/02, I got a call from a Sunderland lad

warning me to watch out because Boro had arranged buses and were expecting a big turnout. As it was the second game in and their first Saturday away game, I thought he might be right, so I got the Boro lad's number and on the Friday night I spoke to him. It looked like they were indeed up for it again. I phoned him again on the Saturday morning asking him for a meet but now he was shady about numbers. He said he would call me when they got there and to be fair he did, but he was still a bit cagey and wouldn't say how many handed they were. He told me to come to The Arkles pub, but in the end we agreed to meet alone a few streets away. I didn't really fancy going in there on my own, as it only takes a few narks with a scar or grudge against you and you can get filled in before the others can stop it, but I trusted these lads and was prepared to do it. A few of our lot said they would come but I would not take any more with me, as you lose all trust and that can make things worse. If you are prepared to meet them on your own it earns respect and that is what I have done with loads of different mobs over the years. I have walked into – and surprisingly out of – many pubs full of the enemy unscathed. The police have told me they cannot believe either my balls or lack of sense. I prefer to call it a code of conflict.

We met and he was honest that their turnout was piss-poor. Two minibuses and a few cars on the way were all they had. I had a drink with him and then their mob turned up. I could have bolted but could not see the point in this lot battering me so thought, *fuck it*, and I stayed put. There were a few big lads with them but they were well down on numbers and many of the old faces had gone. Like us, they had been replaced by young lads who had no real nark, as when it had mattered they were still in junior school. One lad came over and showed me a big scar across his eye. It was nasty and he explained he had actually lost his eye in an attack. I thought, *fucking hell, I hope he didn't get it here*, but of course he had, in the FA Cup replay years earlier. He asked me did I know who had done it. I joked that it could have been any one out of 100, but he was still bitter, and rightly so, and didn't muster a smile at my inappropriate wit. Soon the bizzies turned up but didn't clock me for about half an hour. By then the Boro lad had arranged with me where to go but had asked me to tell the lads, "No steel." I could not guarantee that blades would not be in abundance. I was a thug, not a bizzie, and in no position to tell lads what is right and wrong as, like it or not, in any organised violence there are no rules for some people and victory is all that matters.

I went to the ground and told the lads that Boro were on their way with an escort that they could get away from. I had drunk with and talked to them and seen their numbers and, more importantly, their attitude, and I decided to fuck it off. Apart from a few of them, they did not want to know, and were on edge. The police had seen me with them and I would be the first nicked, so I just skipped it knowing I would miss nothing. Boro went home without so much as a bad word exchanged.

That was the end of it with Boro. It went on for over three decades and was as good or bad, depending on how you look at it, as it gets. There were casualties, some very bad. I think they hate us because of the blades, but also respect us, as we always showed. I would say our two mobs were about even. We certainly respect them: apart from Man United, I rate them as the best. They are game but fair and I have to be honest that, unlike ourselves, they never used blades. The mutual hatred will never die, though.

7 OCCUPATIONAL HAZARDS

a case for the defence

With anything dodgy, there is always the chance that you will come unstuck and get nicked. I suppose it is an occupational hazard. Being a football hooligan is no different, but in recent years the punishments handed out for what is often no more than a bit of a street brawl have been like Jordan's tits – way out of proportion.

In the Seventies, when I first got into violence at the match, you quite simply didn't give a fuck if the police were about. They were there to keep rival fans apart and the vast majority, I'm sure, used to enjoy the mass punch-ups as much as the hooligans they were out to keep an eye on. The early Eighties went a bit daft, and some courts, Birmingham for one, started to make a big thing of the culprits contaminated with the so-called "English disease". Then things started to go really silly. Maggie Thatcher got fed up with the continual problems we were causing at home and abroad and, overnight, offences which would cost you a couple of hundred quid in fines suddenly started costing you four- to eight-year stretches.

Now I'm all for maximum sentences for the sly twats that mug old ladies to feed a pathetic smack habit. I even know a couple of Everton lads that got big-time jail for slashing. Fair enough. If you can't do the time, don't do the crime. But some of the jail those Cockneys got for little more than keeping a scrapbook about their days out at the match was well out of order. We are talking of TEN years here for a bit of a fight. Child molesters don't get that, and I know who is more danger to society. I bet some of those Chelsea and West Ham boys hadn't even hurt anyone. They got banged up in their prime for having a hobby that had the potential to be a bit nasty and for being stupid enough to keep a scrapbook of it all.

I have been lucky, of that I have no doubt. I have been nicked about twenty times for football-related offences, and the worst sentence I got hit with was a month in Brixton in 1989. I have had a few close calls though, the worst being at Aberdeen, when at one stage we were looking at a seven-stretch. You take the rough with the smooth; sometimes I've been unlucky to get nicked, other times I've been lucky not to have had the key thrown away. All points considered, British justice has been pretty kind to me.

coventry city

The first time I got nicked was at Coventry in about 1981. We played them in the League Cup and before the game I went around the box office to try to blag some tickets. The casual era had now arrived but only the Scousers, Mancs and Cockneys had latched onto it. It was freezing and I had these sheepskin mittens on, which for some daft reason were a bit trendy at the time. Some lad in a blue bubble coat asked me if I had a ticket. As he was quite well dressed, I thought he was an Evertonian, so was off guard when he launched a head-butt into my face. He shot off but bumped into some of the lads who could see me holding my nose in place, so he back-pedalled and I caught him with a top-of-the-range left hook, putting him straight on his arse.

A bloke came over and said, "Good shot that, mate." Just as I was sticking my chest out thinking I was hard, he followed up with, "You're fuckin' nicked." The shady bastard was an off-duty copper that couldn't keep his nose out, although at least he had a nose; mine was spread over my face like a tomato.

A van pulled up and they cuffed one of my hands to the seat and the other to the floor rail. If they wanted they could have kicked the shit out of me. Luckily they were not Scouse coppers, or I would have had more than a bloody nose. They kept me for about an hour, then brought the lad to identify me. He was a top kid, looked at me, had a chuckle about my nose and said he'd never seen me before. Fuck all they could do, so they slung me out and I walked up to the ground with what must have been the first Coventry City casual.

cops and robbers

It wasn't long before I was locked up again because of football, but this time it had nothing to do with hooliganism. I was arrested for looting a sports shop; we got caught when one of the lads booted a football out of the shop and it set off the alarm.

The police came and chased us for about an hour through gardens and across roofs. It was half two in the morning, and like a Benny Hill sketch. I got away but the other two lads were nabbed. I was made up at having escaped, but after all the running about, the iffy curry and twelve pints started to surface and I ended up spewing in a garden. Before I finished getting the starter up, this big, horrible fucker comes bouncing out of his house in his vest and underpants and we start swapping punches because he's taken offence to me decorating his prize roses with a chicken madras and lager splash.

His missus calls the cops and we end up in the next cell to my mates, who have been charged with burglary. Just as I'm getting a caution for the spew-and-fight offence, they bring out one of the lads and he blurts out, "Fuckin' hell, Nicks, I thought you'd well escaped." Caution complete, back in the cell on the burglary charge. Nice one.

We went not guilty on the grounds of pure cheek really, because they'd caught us red-handed with the swag. The only thing they never saw was the window going in and we didn't do that, just the looting. Anyway, this clever plod gives it the big one and tells the judge he saw us do it. The top forensic bloke says we never, as they did tests on our clothes and there was no glass on us. They have a big barney in court and we get a case dismissed. Top result. We even asked could we have all the sports gear back, but the judge gave us a look that had "fuck off while the going's good" written all over it.

the red shite

I received my first fine after what was to be the first of many times I got nicked against Liverpool. They beat us 5–0 at Goodison in the real bad old days when they were good and we were bad; no, they were very good and we were shite. They had Rush, Dalglish, Hansen and Lawrenson. We had Ainscow, O'Keefe and Glen Keeley. Keeley was sent off on his debut and Rush got four in our worst derby defeat for about fifty years.

I was nicked at 1–0 for fighting in the Park End Stand with a few Irish who believed in all the standing side by side crap that was in the papers. I know a load of the Liverpool lads and they are sound but how some IRA-lovers can expect to get away without a slap when they start singing, "Blue and white shite," is beyond me.

The norm then was that you were locked up for an hour, cautioned and then set free to have another go, if you wished. The thing to do was to fuck off to the pub or, safer still, home, but as soon as I got out and heard the score, it wasn't long before I was at it again and got nicked before John Motson had finished his match report. The look on the copper's face was a picture when he asked me had I ever been arrested before.

"Three times, officer."

"When was the last time?"

"Half an hour ago!"

No hope of a caution, and my first-ever fine. Twenty-five quid, at £2 a week. Five pounds for every Red goal or for every Irish Kopite I'd hit. It was worth every penny, depending on which team you supported.

aston villa

Over the next few years I had the misfortune of another two court cases, both after cup games, one at Villa, the other at Bradford. The Villa one was quite straightforward. We played them in the second leg of the old League Cup, and although we lost 1–0 on the night, we won 2–1 on aggregate and made it to our first final for seven years. Everton took thousands to Villa that night, and at the end we all got on the pitch to celebrate. Some chance. I'd been on the grass all of a minute when a fight broke out with the Villa stewards, who were pissed off that we had won and were making their lives a misery.

Before the first chant of "We're on our way to Wembley, we shall not be moved" had begun, I was on my way to the cells, never mind the Twin Towers. By the end of the night, there were seventy-eight of us nicked and the Birmingham police had to put a coach on to get us all out of the city, such was the hatred towards us following the hassle we'd caused. We all got bailed and had to go back a couple of weeks later.

A mob of Villa were waiting at New Street Station, so the cops kept us all together and we had a proper escort to the court, with horses, dogs and vans. It was mad. Shoppers were asking who was playing, and looked on in disbelief as a bigger mob than most clubs took to the match was herded into the courts. The judge was a terror and from the off started to throw some silly fines about. The duty solicitor advised everyone to plead guilty and most of us took notice. I got a £150 fine and asked to pay a fiver a week. Judge Dread looked at me like I had two heads and said, "This is a punishment, not a hire purchase repayment. You will pay it in fourteen days or go to jail."

Fourteen days, I thought he was winding me up. I was on only £60 a week in those days and we were going to Wembley in a month. He was having a laugh. But I said nothing and was glad because the next lad up asked to pay £1 a week and the judge said the same as he said to me about HP. So the lad gives it, "That's all I've got, I'm on the dole." The judge finds him in no financial position to pay and sends him down for seven days. The next lot all went not guilty, hoping the same judge would not be on the bench for their trial. He only goes and requests that he follows all the cases to completion. The twat must have been a Villa season ticket holder. He had a big grin on his face as he told all those who went not guilty that they would have to sign in at the local police station every Saturday, clearly thinking, *that's fucked your day out at Wembley, you Scouse bastards*. The very same big grin that would have been wiped off when he found out that the final was on a Sunday!

In the end, most of the lads were fined £400 and banned from the match, which was quite rare in the early Eighties. It was one of the only times I was glad that I pleaded guilty, as four ton was a lot of coin and a year's ban from the match was a nightmare. It would have been sound in most seasons, as we were crap, but that year Everton went on to win the FA Cup, then followed it up with the most successful twelve months in the club's history.

Loads didn't take any notice of the bans but those that did missed out on the lot: Wembley, Europe and our first League Championship for fifteen years. Me? Well, I got a bank loan for a grand, paid the £150 fine and had the best year of my life watching Everton conquer Europe, on and off the pitch.

bradford city

The next time I was in court was for fighting at Bradford City in the FA Cup. What a carry-on that turned out to be. I'd got a bit of work in Germany and flew home for the match, as we were going pretty well at the time and we all love a cup run, although in those days they lasted longer than the round or two which has been the norm with Everton lately.

We got to Bradford and it was a bit iffy, with little mobs everywhere and the odd skirmish breaking out. I wasn't expecting any hassle so took my nephew Pud, but I didn't have tickets and it was well on top with the plod, being only a year since the fire that had destroyed much of the ground. I got one ticket off a tout and did a "double click" with my nephew: you know the sketch, put him in the front, hand over the ticket, give a big push and, bingo, two for the price of one. Only this time some steward was on the ball, caught us and slung us both out. None for the price of one.

I managed to get Pud in with one of the lads, just before it went off by their main stand with a load of Bradford backed up by a tidy firm of Leeds. I don't know if Leeds were there to join up with Bradford but together they were a tasty firm. It was on top for a few minutes, as no-one knew who was who, and I saw a few of our lads getting done in, so I waded into the main mob. We backed them up the hill that brings you down to the ground. It is a dodgy place for a fight and they took some stopping with the numbers they had and the slope of hill, which is an advantage if you are at the top. It was the first time I ever saw an Asian casual: quite seriously, this lad was swapping punches with us dressed in Lacoste and Armani and wearing a turban. He was a bit of a kickboxer as well, so I didn't get close enough to see what make his turban was.

Next minute, my feet were off the floor. A copper on a horse had gripped me by the hair. I'd like to see him do it now, as the worry of such incidents has had a dramatic effect on my hairline. Off he rode with me in tow, but lost his grip and I was able to do a quick one back around the Everton end, leaving the rest of the lads to finish off the battle with Leeds, Bradford and the turban casual. Still with no ticket, I went for bust and hurdled over the turnstile, and got in just as the game kicked off. Within five minutes I was in a police van, cuffed, on a charge of threatening behaviour. How the fuck can you get charged with that for jumping a turnstile? You may well ask. Simple: another steward collared me and I threatened to knock his head off, so it was a fair cop.

In the van, which was one of those box cell numbers where you are locked in a little cabin with no room to manoeuvre, the copper who'd had me by the hair earlier recognised the multi-coloured jumper I was wearing. It was like Man United two years before all over again. He gave me a bit of verbal but I thought that was it with him.

In the nick we were all in a big holding cell, with most just getting cautions. This Asian kid was going on about what he was going to do to us all when we got out, and I was made up when just the two of us were left waiting to get booked. The bizzies had started to use the plastic ties, like you put on pipes or use in the garden, instead of handcuffs, and mine was loose, so I took my hand out, gave the Asian lad a dig and was back in the tie before the door opened to see what he was yelping about. Just for luck, the copper gave him a dig as well for being too noisy.

I was last out. When I gave my address in Germany, they started to wind me up, saying I wasn't getting bail, so I had to do a swift one and give them my old dear's address. That's always a pain in the arse, as they go around to check you live there and bullshit that you are in big trouble. The problem was that I *was* in big trouble, as the eagle-eyed horseman had identified me from the earlier fight and, instead of a caution or a breach of the peace, I was on an affray and assault charge.

I flew back for the case, which I'd managed to get adjourned a few times, as I was hoping if I had a bit of coin behind me they might want to hit me in the pocket rather than give me jail. This was becoming all too common, with Maggie Thatcher promising the nation that she and her little pipsqueak Colin Moynihan would rid the game of all the nasty hooligans who were spoiling it for everyone.

I was wrong again, as my solicitor was honest enough to tell me that if I got a guilty for affray, there was only one place I was going, and it wasn't back to Germany. The prosecution were that confident that they dropped the charge of threatening a steward and went full steam ahead on the affray, but I had a bit of luck early on when that was dropped to Section Five due to lack of numbers. While I had been in Germany getting it adjourned, loads had been dealt with, and you can't have an affray with yourself, so it was reduced to a Section Five.

The only evidence they had was this copper and his description of my multi-coloured jumper. It was a corker; all along they kept harping on about this loud, colourful jumper and how it stood out in the crowd amongst all the other casuals fighting. So the judge asks for the picture they took when I was arrested. It was only in black and white. Bingo, reasonable doubt, case dismissed, costs to yours truly, flights home, loss of earnings, the lot.

British justice at its best or worst, depending on whose side you were on: Maggie Thatcher's or mine!

a face in the crowd

I kept a low one after that for a few months, as I knew I'd been lucky and the police at the match had started to give me a bit of grief. They seemed pissed off that the Bradford case, which was quite high-profile, had fucked up.

During the next season, I got nicked twice at the Merseyside derby, home and away. Depending on who arrested you, it was usually a caution at that game, due to the numbers that were in the cells and the lazy Scouse coppers not being arsed with all the paperwork. It did make me realise, though, that my face was getting noticed. The second time they nicked me was in the Yankee Bar, a big Liverpool boozer near the train station, and I was just dropping off tickets for some Reds. The bizzies locked me up but didn't charge me. They were making my life a bit of a misery as well as costing me money, because they had a funny habit of letting you out when the game had just finished. A pocketful of tickets was not a lot of use at quarter to five when it was a three o'clock kick-off, and the bastards knew it.

I then went a whole season without getting nicked at home, but that was mainly because I was working abroad and rarely got back for the match. Then I decided to come home for Christmas, and it was a bad call. On Saturday, December 19, 1988, Everton played Arsenal at Highbury, and twenty-nine of us got nicked for fighting outside a boozer called The Woodbine.

the everton twenty-nine

I hadn't been to Arsenal for a couple of years, so went down with a few of the lads, not really in a firm but more for a Christmas drink. We got to Euston and were met by a good-sized mob of Everton who had come down by coach.

They had a different agenda to our little mob: they wanted Arsenal, and it didn't take much persuasion for us to join up with them on the short Tube journey to Highbury.

We came out of the station and took a walk up Highbury Hill, heading for The Gunners pub, where we were told their boys were waiting. We had only got near another boozer called The Woodbine before it went off. Although it was December and quite cold, it was a sunny day and there was a mob of lads drinking outside. As we got level, they noticed us and one threw a glass before they tried to make it back into the pub. A few did, a few didn't, and the unlucky ones got a pasting. We started to put the windows in and were surprised that no-one put up much of a fight, as they had a bit of a reputation.

Within seconds, police surrounded the place, and one copper with a loudhailer was taking great delight in telling the whole of North London that we were nicked. We thought it was a set-up until a lad pointed to the building next to The Woodbine. We all stared in disbelief as it became apparent that we had launched an attack on a pub that was next door to a police station … a station that was full of officers being briefed on the crowd control requirements for the day's big match.

We might as well have brought our own handcuffs. Some made a run for it and about half got away, but after a couple of minutes the rest of us were herded all of ten yards into the yard at the back of the station. It was like Christmas come early and the plod were pissing themselves laughing. The Government was spending millions of pounds on undercover police operations and we go and kick it off in full view of them while they're having tea and biscuits.

We were still in the yard when another ten Everton were brought in. They weren't hooligans and I thought they were being kept for their own safety, as it would be a bit tasty outside by now. They told us they had walked up to the police station and asked for an escort, as the Gooners were having a go back. They were told to wait in an alleyway, then got marched over to be with us, all under arrest! One by one we were taken into the station and searched, before being charged and then locked up. There was twenty-nine of us, and about ten were known faces, so it wasn't looking too clever. A few were right pricks who shouldn't have been there; it was obvious they were not thugs.

Just as I thought things couldn't get any worse, a copper came in the station carrying a bucket from the police yard. He tipped it on the desk and there were fourteen blades, ranging from Stanleys to a big dagger. "Now we are in the shit," I remember saying to myself as the cell door slammed. We were lucky to get bail, as I thought there was a fair chance they might put us before a special court and remand us, so getting home that night was a bit of a bonus.

highbury corner magistrates

The court date was set for the Monday, so back to London we went to appear before the stipendiary magistrate at Highbury Corner. It was then that some of the lads got the worst legal advice ever given out. The stipe, we were told, was a bit of a savage and if we pleaded guilty he was sure to send us down. Now that was already a certainty for some of us: I had three previous for football, Macker had a page-full, including a wounding conviction, Regan had a full house, Karl Titch, Foulksey, Richie, Kenny and Jock all had football previous, so it didn't need Mastermind to see where we were going. But it would be adjourned until after Christmas, and the longer it goes on, well, you never know your luck.

The rest of the twenty-nine, which included one Cockney who supported Chelsea – and to this day I don't know why he was with us – had very little previous, so I'm sure if they had gone not guilty on the day, most would have walked eventually. The turning point of the pleas was when the case before us started. It was a Japanese tourist who had been nicked for drink-driving. Now the Japs are small and this bloke, the court was told, had drunk eight pints and a few whiskeys and driven off down the wrong side of the road. To him it was the right side but not in England, so he was nicked.

Anyway, up he goes, acting the dumb tourist, "No speekee Engleesh, velly solly," and all that bollocks, and the stipe, being a festive soul, sends him to prison for two weeks. The Jap hit the roof – well, he would if he'd been taller than four foot one. Amazingly he got the hang of the language too, swear words, the lot. We were pissing ourselves until the old magistrate warned us we would be going with him in ten minutes if we didn't shut up. That, we decided, was a good hint for a bit of silence in court, only interrupted by a young duty solicitor, who had taken it upon himself to throw a bit of advice our way and tell everyone to go not guilty in a group. Now to the few of us who were deep in the mire, that was a top idea. But why most of the group decided to do it, I will never understand.

The thing with a group trial is that you are all in it together, guilty or not guilty. You can't have sixteen who are guilty and thirteen who aren't. To put it simply, it's shit or bust. When you've acted as one in a group, it means that if there is reasonable doubt any of the group was not involved, you all get off. The prosecution has to prove you are ALL guilty. That's the theory, anyway. In practice it was a load of crap. But it sounded good, so we all went up together, pleaded not guilty and a date was set for the trial. While the drunken driver Jap was on his way to Wormwood Scrubs, we were on our way home for the Christmas festivities. British justice at its best. For now.

the trial

Christmas came and went in a haze of egg flip and plum pudding but, try as I did to enjoy myself, in the back of my mind I had a bad feeling. The trial was a joke. The evidence was weak, the police stories were all different and we had a few good witnesses that were spot on. We also had in the dock about ten lads who hadn't thrown a punch in their lives, all with good jobs and most whose mums and dads were in court to see that the big bad beak didn't harm their little soldiers. That was the case for the defence.

The prosecution had very little, except for a few officers who were laying it on with a trowel and a couple of pissed-off Cockneys that had been slapped. They did, however, have one thing that really gave them a chance of a result: a magistrate who seemed to have grown up with a hatred for two things in life – football hooligans and Scousers.

As we sat in the dock and watched things unfold, I cracked, "Like the midwife said when Mrs Beardsley gave birth to her baby son Peter, this is not looking good." The trial lasted nearly three weeks and we had a good laugh for the best part of it. We all had to sit in the same seats every day so the stipe could familiarise himself with our names. I had the misfortune of being sat next to a lad called Regan. He was sound, only eighteen but a top heavyweight boxing prospect who by all accounts was in with a chance of turning pro in the ring. He had one thing stopping him though: he was crackers. How he lasted as long as he did in the court before he got jailed, which was after about ten days, Carol Vorderman would have struggled to work out.

From the first minute, he treated it as a joke, pissing about, farting, swearing, sleeping, eating, drinking, wearing a hat. If ever there was a case for contempt of court he was sent from hell to cause it.

The stipe would say to him, "Are you eating?"

"No."

"What's in your mouth then?"

"Chewing gum."

"Well, you're eating."

"If I was fuckin' eating, it would be called eating gum."

The rows they had were endless and all the time a not guilty was looking more and more unlikely, as the stipe would have happily sent twenty-eight innocent people to jail if it meant his worst nightmare Regan went with them. Another day, he nudged me and said, "If that cunt (the magistrate) looks at me funny again, he's getting this." And he pulled out a blade in court. He was mental.

There was some confusion about who had actually nicked him. He said it was a mounted officer, yet a copper on foot was his arresting officer, so according to the prosecution Mr Regan was lying. So the stipe asks him how he knew it was a mounted officer. Regan looked at him like he was a Muppet and said, "Cos I know what a fuckin' horse looks like." We were in bits and the whole court was in chaos for ten minutes while the stipe sat there pondering how long to give us.

Then we had a bit of luck. During a lunch break, Regan went on his usual shoplifting trip and got collared by a store detective, who he duly tried to stab. Straight to jail, do not pass go, and things looking up for the now Everton 28. We didn't see him again during the trial. He got remanded and then, when he got out, did an armed robbery in a Liverpool nightclub called Quadrant Park. He got a year for every grand he had in his bag when they caught him, which was bad news as he robbed eighteen big ones.

Regan's absence made no difference. Against all the evidence and all the reasonable doubt, Magistrate Bruce decided we were guilty. I knew we were going down when a load of security came in. One of our briefs told us that he had never seen so many in court. Also there were no Probation Service present, who you normally have if you're in with a chance of a pre-sentence report. There was uproar in court as he didn't even bother with the reports, he just sat back, made some speech about us being undisciplined rabble, smiled and sent us all to jail for twenty-eight days.

While the ten or so innocents held their heads in their hands and their mums and dads cried and had nightmares about what the neighbours would say, the rest of us shook hands, waved goodbye to Mr Bruce and burst out laughing. Twenty-eight days? A right result, out in two to three weeks and all the hassle over with. He brought us back into court to tell us we were also banned from watching our beloved Everton for two years, which was a bit of a bummer, but who cared, we knew we'd still go anyway, ban or no ban.

prison

We were put in the cells for an hour, then got a meeting with our brief, who said he had lodged an immediate appeal for our release, on bail, as the magistrate should have asked for pre-sentence reports. It was a Friday and he said that we might have to spend the weekend in jail, as Bruce was not prepared even to review his decision. That turned out to be the case and an appeal date was set for the Monday. The prison officers were on industrial action and were not accepting any new inmates, so we had to be held in police custody in stations all over the place.

We got split up and me, Jock and Mick were put on a minibus with some police guards and were told that we were going to Melton Mowbray, a small market town near Leicester famous for its pork pies. Personally I'd never heard of it but it was bound to be better than The Scrubs, the only prison which had agreed to take a few of the lads. A lot of the young ones got sent to a detention centre, which was not a kind option – six young Scousers and half of London's urchins wasn't my idea of a four-star weekend break in the capital.

We stopped at another police station on the way to Leicestershire and the copper handcuffed me to a bloke that they brought out. It was dark by now and this bloke was suited up but he had long hair and a mad beard, so I thought he was a bit of an odd one. After about ten minutes this foul smell was making me retch and for the next hour of the journey I did well not to spew my guts up. I couldn't really make out who it was and, with this bloke next to me having a suit on, I thought that it must be a bloke behind us, who was a bit of a scruffy bastard. We pulled into Melton Mowbray police station and they called out the names of me, Jock and Mick, which I was glad of, as it meant we'd be in there together. When we got inside the station they took the cuffs off and I looked at the bloke in the suit. He had a pair of football boots on his feet, Gola mouldies! He was a stinking tramp. The screws were pissing themselves but I was in a right one, started itching all over, and they did let me have a shower when they stopped laughing.

The nick was sound. We were looked after by traffic cops on overtime. It was a doddle and we were given remand privileges, which meant we could send out for food, books and other little luxuries we would not get in a proper nick. As it stood, a month in Melton was nothing short of a holiday. One night a lad was caught burgling a local house and he got locked up with us. The occupants of the house were away on holiday and he was caught red-handed with their television and video recorder. The bizzies set it up in the recreation room, took 50p out of all our wages and we watched films on Exhibits A and B every night. One night they got us *One Flew Over the Cuckoo's Nest,* which was fitting considering some of the crackpots locked up with us.

It all went wrong when the solicitors representing us put in an appeal against the sentence after losing the first one regarding the judge not giving us pre-sentence reports. We could not believe that some of the lads were not happy with a month, but we all had to go with the flow and after a week the second appeal was granted and we were released. We were gutted: the three of us were guilty and were happy where we were. The police were after an easy time, gave us no shit and were a credit to their profession. I'm not sure if the authorities would see it that way, but to us they were sound and I was honestly sorry to be released. We had only two weeks to do and a retrial would last another three weeks, which was all money out of my pocket, as this time is was to be at Southwark Crown Court. Another thing playing on my mind was that at the end of it, if things went bad there was nothing stopping a new judge giving us a longer sentence. It was a gamble and one I would not have gone for, but some of those sentenced had done nothing, so I suppose it was important to them to clear their names. I just wish they could have left us where we were.

The retrial did indeed last three weeks and, after a promising start, turned out to be a total waste of time. The judge was Gerard Butler and he seemed much better than lovable old Magistrate Bruce. We had more witnesses and the added bonus of no Regan, as he was locked up for the armed robbery. Regardless of all that, Judge Butler still thought we were all lying and was bluffed by the police. He waved the appeal off and gave us the same sentence. It was farcical really, and a waste of a couple of hundred thousand quid. What pissed me off most were our briefs.

The solicitors got us all barristers, as it was in crown court. I didn't like mine from the beginning of the trial: his name was Fletcher and, as a keen follower of *Porridge*, I thought that was a bad omen. He was a black bloke and, with his wig on, looked like a pint of Guinness, so that's

Two pictures of the unbelievable riot on the pitch against Southampton in an FA Cup semi at Highbury in 1984. Over 100 people were arrested and seventy-odd needed hospital treatment after some of the worst mass brawling I have ever seen.

©Press Association

'Munich' jibe starts Soccer riot

By John Alley

VIOLENCE flared when Everton supporters unfurled a blue banner saying "Munich 1958" at Manchester United's ground a court heard yesterday.

The jibe about the air crash in which eight players were among 23 dead resulted in 22 United and five Everton fans being arrested.

Eighteen were fined a total of £3,650 after Trafford magistrates heard that Saturday's match saw the worst the trouble. It angered the home fans and they started to throw various objects into the Everton section.

"Eventually there was a pitched battle which the police had difficulty in controlling," he said.

The highest fine — £250 — was imposed on a Rochdale guilty to using threatening behaviour.

A deaf and dumb youth from Scunthorpe, who is alleged to have thrown a meat pie at an Everton supporter, did not appear and a warrant was issued for his arrest.

Five fans denied charges and were remanded for trial. Three others were remanded

---

Above: The unfurling of a banner saying 'Munich 58' sparked a near-riot at Old Trafford and led to years of hatred between Manchester United and Everton.

Right: The slashing of Man United fan Jobe Henry in 1982 further fuelled the bitter rivalry between the hooligan elements from both cities.

The savages won't keep me from soccer, says slashed fan

SOCCER - MAD Jobe Henry, who needed 200 stitches after a horrifying knife attack, said yesterday: "It will take more than this to keep me away from football."

Amateur boxer Jobe, 19, a Manchester United fan, is still in hospital following the attack by a mob of Everton supporters three nights ago.

But despite shocking wounds to his back and head, he vowed: "I'll be back shouting for United as soon as possible.

"They are the greatest team in the world.

"I have travelled all over Europe with them and I'm not going to let a bunch of soccer savages put me off.

Fists

Jobe was pounced on by a gang of screaming knife wielding louts outside Old Trafford

---

Below: Everton's so-called County Road Cutters became notorious as the worst gang of knifemen in football. This weapon was used in an attack on Middlesbrough, one of our biggest rivals.

The knife used in the attack.

City knifeman hunt

DETECTIVES from Middlesbrough arrived in Liverpool yesterday hunting the knifeman who seriously wounded a local football fan after Everton's FA Cup defeat on Saturday.

The distinctive knife be used is German made with a black plastic handle, a leopard motif and the number KSSK. It has a 3¼ inch blade.

The stabbing happened as 16-year-old Kevin Sawdon and a friend walked away from the Ayresome Park ground and were confronted by about 100 chanting, angry Everton fans.

Kevin told police: "They shouted 'There's the Boro ... get them'."

Kevin's friend scrambled over a wall, but when Kevin tried to follow the knife was thrust deeply into his bottom.

The blade passed within an inch of the spleen and Kevin needed emergency surgery and seven stitches.

Afterwards Kevin's father said: "It's only by good luck that he was not killed. Anyone who carries a knife to a football match is a potential murderer."

Mirror Sport

Saturday, March 25, 1978 (No. 23,060)
Manchester (STD code 061) 832-3444

Newcastle face FA probe after attack on fans

BAD FRIDAY!

GOOD Friday became BAD Friday yesterday when Newcastle United hit double trouble.

They plunged nearer to the Second Division with a 2-0 home defeat by Everton and will be reported to the FA following fan violence at St. James's Park.

The trouble broke out in the 48th minute following Everton's second goal. Geordie fans at the Gallowgate End immediately attacked Goodison supporters who were in a separate enclosure.

Battle

One Everton fan was taken to hospital with a broken leg and another suffered a fractured wrist after a pitched battle which held up the match for six minutes and during which several children were also injured.

Referee George Flint, of Kirkby-in-Ashfield, took the players to the centre of the pitch while police reinforcements with dogs sorted out the trouble and made six arrests.

But the St. James's Park club found no ally in Mr. Flint last night—despite the fact that he will...

BAD FRIDAY! Battling fans get to grips on the terraces during the Newcastle-Everton match yesterday.

Above: Newcastle away in 1978 and my first taste on the receiving end. Hundreds of Geordies attacked us on the terraces and took no prisoners

R.I.P.

REMEMBER
KENSINGTON
HIGH STREET?
WE MUST 'AVE
REVENSE
KILL THE
CHELSEA
GERRY GARDENS
1·30 PM

Above: Leaflets handed out urging Everton fans to mob up in Gerard Gardens to take revenge on Chelsea for a notorious attack at High Street Kensington, when Everton were ambushed on a Tube train.

Mob ambush plot foiled

by Brian Roberts

EVERTON Football Club chairman Philip Carter last night joined police chiefs in condemning a mob of fans who plotted a bloody revenge ambush and attack on rival Chelsea supporters.

The fans were incited to meet on waste ground less than two hours before Saturday's game kicked off, to pounce on the London supporters.

Leaflets had been circulated before the match with the chilling message: "Remember Kensington High Street. We must have revenge. Kill the Chelsea."

And about 500 Evertonians turned up for the planned revenge mission at Gerard Gardens, Liverpool — only to be dispersed by squads of police officers acting on a tip-off.

Last night a police officer said: "It's amazing that there could have been what can only be described as an organised attack.

"It is frightening and Saturday's incident could have had a serious outcome."

But police managed to...

The deadly armoury recovered at Goodison Park.

Left: Weapons seized before the same match at Goodison. They ranged from pickaxe handles to darts and even a lavatory chain.

...but eight ended up in hospital

Even though police prevented the confrontation on Saturday, eight Chelsea fans ended up in hospital, seven with facial wounds and one with a fractured skull.

My good self posing near Everton's ground. The alleys and back streets around Goodison were our stamping ground.

Above: Me (left) with Everton hero Andy Gray and a fan called Edgy at the game in Dublin against UCD.

Above left: With Peter Beagrie on that riotous night in Balsthal and *(right)* holding the FA Cup with Barry Horne. Players at Everton have generally been very approachable and happy to have a laugh with the fans – with a few miserable exceptions.

Above: Joining the England team for the National Anthem before an international in Sweden. Steve Hodge doesn't look too happy but is Trevor Stephen trying to suppress a smirk?

Above right: On the subs' bench at the same match. My services weren't required but I did get to share a laugh with then-manager Bobby Robson *(inset)* afterwards.

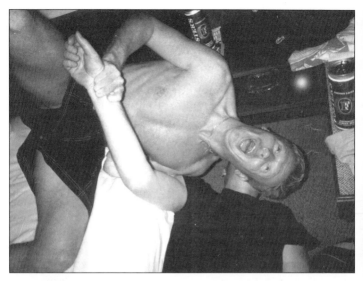

Fun-loving Maurice Johnston on a night of excess in a hotel in Balsthal, Switzerland, shortly after swallowing a lump of dope.

The Balsthal flag, for which we were held at gunpoint by the Swiss Army, has passed into legend.

FURY ON FERRY

Patrick Hannon

'The captain panicked'

EVERTONIAN Patrick Hannon (27), of Hotel Terrace, Tranmere, said: "The B. & I. people just said that no more were getting on even though everyone was very orderly.

"The crew on board cut the ropes to enable the ship to sail but two steel hawsers were still attached and they whiplashed back amongst us as we stood on the quayside.

"I don't know what possessed the captain — I think he must just have panicked thinking that we were all Rangers supporters again."

By Alf Bennett

HUNDREDS of Everton fans arrived back in Liverpool today under police escort after the third night running of angry confrontation on the Dublin boats.

The supporters were put in the charge of Irish police officers and officials from the British Embassy after trouble on the high seas early this morning.

The ship, hours late in arriving at Liverpool, had gone back to Dublin after its captain had radioed he had a "riot situation" on board.

And as they set foot on land again at Bootle's Brocklebank

Everton fans arrive home under Irish police escort

Dock, they were met by three coachloads of Merseyside and Port Police. Coaches were also laid on to disperse the fans quickly.

The latest angry scenes followed rioting by Glasgow Rangers supporters as they sailed to Dublin on Monday night — two people were seriously injured. And on Tuesday night, five were arrested and later fined in court for being drunk and disorderly after rowdy scenes and glass smashing in the bar of

the M.V. Connacht.

Last night's trouble was sparked off as Blues fans arrived at the Dublin Ferry Port after seeing their team play a disappointing goalless European tie with Irish part-timers University College

Earlier in the day, 17 stewards in charge of the 350 fans and B&I officials spent three hours locked in talks in a bid to avert violence on the return trip to Liverpool.

As a result, they agreed that each Evertonian would be

screened to ensure they were in a condition to travel.

This process so delayed the sailing that at midnight, an hour behind schedule, and with 700 other passengers on board, Captain Neville Spurling decided to leave with 50 fans on the quayside — only a handful of them deemed unfit to travel.

It appears that the 6,800 ton Connacht was only 40 minutes out into the Irish Sea when news filtered through to sup-

porters on board that some of their colleagues had been left behind.

Emotions overflowed to the extent that the ship's skipper radioed to Irish Port authorities that he had a "riot situation" on his hands and was turning back.

The ship reached Dublin again to be met by squads of Irish Garda. Some of the Everton stewards went back into negotiations, which eventually got all but two or three unpalatitated fans onto the ship.

But as they set out a second time, four hours behind schedule, Irish Police were taking no chances and put ten constables and two sergeants on board along with two officials from the British Embassy in Dublin

By the mid-Eighties, fans were routinely running amok. An Everton mob actually forced an Irish Sea ferry back to port (see above) after it had left some of thier mates behind in Dublin. In Belgium, events took a more tragic turn when disorder in the Heysel Stadium led to the deaths of thirty-nine people (below). Many left belongings on the terraces as they fled.

©Steve Hale

what I called him. He didn't see the funny side. When we got the same sentence, Guinness said, "Well, it was worth a try, you've lost nothing." Lost nothing? Except another job, as three weeks off to attend court was not on according to my new boss, and three weeks' expense of living in London was a waste of the best part of a grand. Also the holiday camp that was Melton was a goner, as the prison officers had gone back to work and we ended up getting sent to Brixton Jail. It was a bit on top and we had loads of threats from all the Cockneys but nothing happened worthy of a mention. We were all put on the same wing and after ten days got released.

That was the end of it for me but I got roped in on the last-chance appeal, which meant trying for a Royal Pardon. Some of the lads' parents spent a fortune trying to get it and it was well publicised in the press and on TV. We even went live for a *Rough Justice* programme. I went for a nose and did an interview, which was played on national radio. To some people it was important to clear their names for work and career opportunities. Personally, I was in it for some compensation and so were some of the others, as everyone I knew had seen the *Liverpool Echo* and *Daily Post* and had read I had been to prison. So what use is a letter from the Queen's Secretary saying it was a mistake, or a miscarriage of justice? I was hardly going to go around the houses showing it my neighbours. I got sick of it in the end, all the meetings and phone calls were a load of bollocks to me and we had done the jail, so in the end I sacked the whole thing and let the others get on with it.

To their credit they never gave up and a few won in the end. I never heard if my name was cleared and definitely never got a fat cheque, so I wasn't arsed, but I was glad for a few of the lads who saved their jobs or went on to become teachers and social workers. I still see a few of the remaining Everton 29 and, like me, several are still bang at it. One of the lads, Mark Duvall, was sadly killed. Another went missing and hasn't been seen for years. Regan was released after serving eleven years of the eighteen he got for the armed robbery. A week after he came out I met him for a beer and we had it with Boro later that day in the battle on Scotty Road.

Jail as an answer to football hooliganism? I don't think so.

playing the joker

Our sentences for Arsenal were accompanied by eighteen-month bans from all grounds in England and Wales, although very few took any notice. I still went but gave some matches a wide berth. Others went everywhere and one or two got nicked and did a bit more time for breaking the exclusion order. Over the next few years I got a few small fines for breach of the peace, usually against Liverpool, as most of the violence had stopped for various reasons, including the advent of the rave scene. When eventually it started up again, the authorities had had enough and the rules had changed, big time.

An arrest and major court case at Aberdeen followed. That is a story in itself, and is related in the next chapter. By the time I had also been arrested at home to Man Utd and away at Boro, it had became obvious that the police wanted me out of their hair. They didn't give a tiny fuck if they had to put me away to achieve it. Worse still, they didn't give a big fuck if you were guilty or not, and the Man United sketch was a farce.

By this time I was doing well for myself and had a top job, nice car and house, but was still likely to mess it all up, as I believe quite seriously that I was born naughty. I went to the Manchester Utd game with my insurance broker, Billy, who was also one of my best mates. He's a dancer, not a fighter, so no chance of trouble there. I also got tickets for my boss Cally and his mate, who were, by the way, Man U fans. Both were in their forties and, though ex-Red Army members who smashed up Norwich and Saint-Etienne in the Seventies, they had long since packed in the footie violence.

I had executive season tickets by now, so we went for a meal and had a few drinks before Billy and I went to our seats, while my merry Manc mates went in their own end, just in case. No surprise, we lost the game and I left a few minutes early to meet the lads and get out of the way. There was a chance of hassle, as United were on the up and had started to get a decent-sized mob together. I'd heard they had fronted it before the match, and when I came out, Everton had the biggest firm I'd seen at home for years waiting by the back of the Park End.

The bizzies were trying to keep the Mancs in but loads had been locked out and had spent the game in The Arkles near Liverpool's ground. It went off straight away and one of their boys, Joe Brown, took a dig and got nicked for his troubles. I thought I'd have a little mooch and see what was happening and told Billy to meet me by the club shop, as he was looking a bit uneasy.

Man U came out and it got a bit tasty right outside the ground, a rare occurrence by now. They were on one side of the dual carriageway and we were in front and alongside them. A few of them broke out and came behind us and it went off as a load of kids came from the Blue House and started lobbing glasses and bottles at everyone. No-one knew who was who. It was Hallowe'en but trick or treat was not on the agenda.

I decided to get off, as any promotion at work would be looking bleak if my boss caught a glimpse of what was going on. Twenty years earlier he would have been in the thick of it but, unlike me, he had grown up. The bizzies were trying to control it and charged the Everton mob back towards Goodison Road, while others rounded up the Mancs and attempted to escort them back to Lime Street Station. I found Billy (looking paler by the minute) and he said Cally and his mate had gone down to The Oak and would see us later.

I had promised to get a shirt for a mate's young lad, so told Billy to stay put while I went into the club shop. I asked the security guard where the queue for shirts was and he pointed to the right-hand counter and I walked over and joined it. I'd been in there about a minute when two OSD (Operational Support Division) bizzies bounced in and dragged me out. I thought the guard had pointed me out, so as I went past I gave him a bit of a gobfull, but in fairness he told the bizzies, "He's only come in to buy a shirt." It made no difference. They gave me a few digs, took off my leather gloves, searched me, threw my gloves on the floor and me in the back of the van. I was well gutted but had to laugh when they sat me next to Joe Brown, who had been nicked for getting slotted by one of ours.

The drive to Bridewell nick was a hooligan's dream. A film of it would have sold for a fortune. What should be a ten-minute journey took over an hour as the van was employed as part of the escort and we had a boss view of footie violence that was a throwback to the Seventies. United had about 200 and Everton at least that but spread out all down Scotty Road. It went off at every corner and crossing. There were flares going off and charges from both mobs until the Mancs reached the town centre. Even then there was odd scuffles as little mobs from both sides clashed. The van by now was full, with a total of eighteen lads from both sides crammed in. Joe and I had a good laugh and agreed that there was nothing to choose between the two mobs. Respect.

We all got locked up and fingerprinted and photographed

– all the usual bollocks. I was made up when I got put in a cell on my own. Most people prefer a bit of company but I'd rather do a few press-ups or have a kip. Unless you know the person you're with, it can be a right pain in the arse, listening to some whingeing bastard harp on about police brutality or what he's going to say to his bird for being late.

I got my head down and was woken up at about eight. They took me to the desk sergeant, and he gave me the charge sheet. Section Five threatening behaviour. Fair enough. I'd have preferred breach of the peace but as the outcome was ninety per cent certain to be a fine, it would be a waste of time arguing with it and would only add costs that the legal eagles usually rip you on. I collected my money and other bits and asked the old guy at the desk if they had let Joe go, as I was going to wait for him. It may have been a bit on top for him out there and I'm not into seeing one lad get done in on his own by a load of pissed-up Toffees who had been hiding in The Winslow when it was going off earlier. He told me that I was the last out and, as I signed my bail sheet, I asked him how many I was in court with, and were we all on the same charge? He gave me a look of total embarrassment, and told me that seventeen had been given a caution and I was the only one charged. I asked him why I hadn't had a caution and he admitted that it was not possible to caution me. Every time they had tried to process my information the computer was rejecting a caution and then the Football Intelligence Unit had come in and told him to Section Five me.

I went and saw my brief on the Monday and he said it was unusual but not to worry. Don't worry, when you're being set up for a bit of jail. Times had changed and it was a case of one law for football hooligans and another for the general public. To me a fight is a fight. I still can't see how two gangs of lads on a stag night in Mathew Street can have a brawl and get £200 for Section Five, yet do it at the match, get the same charge and end up inside for eighteen months. Should be a law against it!

I went to court suited up, having changed my mind and intending to plead not guilty. I had a chat with my brief. He was sure I was worried about nothing and asked how much money I had on me. I told him three ton and he told me to get some dinner and have a couple of pints, as the worst he could see was a £200 fine. I wasn't convinced, so took his advice on the food front but passed on the ale. I walked back up to Dale Street a bit early and he was pacing up and down the entrance of the Magistrates Court, looking a bit worried. I nearly did one there and then. My brief told me things had changed a bit and the prosecution were not playing ball, wouldn't plea bargain and, worse still, had a big file portraying yours truly as a Category C football hooligan. I already knew this, as that year we had been to Barnsley and, when we got off at somewhere like Wakefield, the bizzies let all the lads go to a boozer in town but told me, Steve and Kelly that we could only drink in the station bar, as we were Cat C hooligans and weren't allowed in their town. The brief still said not to worry, as Cat C wasn't that bad: if I had been Cat A or B, then a spell in Walton nick was a possibility. I tried to tell him that Cat C was actually the worst, but he told me how long he had been in the law game and to trust him.

We went into court, threw a not guilty in and got a trial date. The prosecution asked for a banning order as I was in the worse category of hooligans, gave a speech about organised gangs and said I was a leading member. In fairness, my brief knew his days at my side were numbered, but argued that I was in a top position in work, had executive tickets and entertained work clients, preventing a banning order and getting me unconditional bail. I still sacked him though, and to be honest I think he was glad, as shoplifters and drink-drivers were more in his league.

My new brief was a diamond. He was honest and said I was in the shit. He knew it was a set-up due to my past wrongdoings and record, and confirmed that as a Category C hooligan the only place I was going if I didn't walk at trial was Walton Jail. He spent hours going through the evidence and in the end admitted things were a bit grim. It was my word against the two OSD, whose statements said I was "the General" leading gangs of Everton into battle. Both claimed that they had seen me kicking and punching Mancs who were being escorted from the ground. I even toyed with going guilty and the hope of a bit of judicial leniency, but he made me see sense, and reminded me that I'd probably used up all my luck at Bradford and Aberdeen.

As the trial approached I still went to the match, which was a bit daft, as it was plain to see I was a marked man. It didn't help that old Paddy Cook had been moved sideways and a ploddess called Gill was in charge of hooligan affairs at Goodison. She had had it in for us since the time it went off at Derby's new ground and she fell down a bank and split her police kecks. "A woman in a man's job," one of the lads commented. "A woman in a size ten when she's a size fourteen," I added, as she stood there with her knickers on show.

She got all the credit for ruining our mob and I believe she got a promotion to London looking after England. I'm not sure if that's true but she did fuck all to split our mob up. After Aberdeen we had decided to give it a rest, and one of the top lads went into door security and took a few of the boys with him. We'd been everywhere in the previous two years and done everyone, so how she got the credit I don't know.

A week before the trial, my brief phoned me and told me that if I was going to the match, to pop in the club shop and use my charm to see if any of the sales girls would vouch for me having been in there for a couple of minutes waiting to be served. The two OSD said they had me in their sight after the alleged fight and had seen me run into the shop trying to escape. Maybe they had mixed me up with somebody else.

I left the game early, went into the shop and had a word with the girls at the counter. The Man Utd game had been months earlier and only one of them could remember the incident. She was only young and seemed scared, but told me to have a word with a bloke who was in charge of security for the club shop. She gave him a call and he came down. I couldn't see someone in his position being prepared to give a statement but this bloke was a hero. It turned out that he was the bloke I'd spoken to on my way into the shop, and he could not believe the shit I was in. I gave him my brief's number and he said he'd bell him, but in all honesty I didn't think he would, let alone make a statement.

The trial was on the Thursday, and on the Tuesday my brief called and said that our man had called and not only had given a statement backing my story up, but was coming to court as a witness. Billy was also saying his bit but the evidence was only that I wasn't pissed and he hadn't seen me doing wrong. My boss agreed to come and say I'd got him tickets and that he was a Man Utd fan, so why would I do that if I wanted to cause trouble? I appreciated their help but the only one who could save me was the security guard.

I'm not usually nervous before court cases, but this one was different, as it was purely and simply wrong. Some people may say tough shit, you deserve all you get, others may say stop cry-arsing over six to twelve months. Fair points. I've been a bad one over the years and, yes, the sentence wouldn't be too long, I'd do that standing on my head. But that's not the point. It's frustrating knowing you've been set up and people who are supposed to be the most honest and trustworthy in our society are not.

The trial went to form. The two OSD said what they allegedly saw, which was bullshit. The prosecution made out Billy to be a liar, which was out of order. He is the most honest person I know. In fact I would have preferred him not to give evidence, as he's too honest and could have dropped me in it if the questions had taken a different angle, because he will not tell lies. One time he was pissed in a club on New Year's Eve and fell off the balcony, landing on a woman in the coat queue. They were both rushed to hospital with bad injuries and when it went to court, all he had to say was that he got pushed and he and the poor girl could have got some coin off the Criminal Injury Board. He wouldn't say it and he wasn't even on oath. He said it was all his fault and had to pay her eight grand out of his own pocket. So he was hardly going to lie on oath for me.

The prosecuting brief dismissed my boss, saying he wasn't at the scene. Then he gave me a right going over. He actually called me a liar in the dock, knowing I could say nothing or he could bring up my previous. The trial was before a stipendiary (full-time) magistrate, which I preferred as, although I had a bad result at Arsenal with one, they do know the score and can't be bluffed. Not like some of the silly old twats you see sitting on the bench wondering what's for lunch before they give you twelve months, having not listened to a thing you said and believing that police do not tell lies.

As it stood I was going down, but the security guard had turned up and was raring to go. My brief called him, and he walked to the witness box in a full-length Everton club coat like the managers wear. You'd swear he was leading the team out at Wembley. It was like *It's A Knockout* when a team played its joker. As much as the police brief tried to trip him up, he got more and more stubborn. They tried to say I had run into the shop and had only been in there seconds before getting nicked. He was having none of it, told it as it was and kept reminding the magistrate of his position with the club. Everyone watching the case was amazed that he was a witness for the defence.

The magistrate didn't even bother with the summing up and dismissed the case as soon as the security guard left the box. I thanked him, then got a rollicking for doing a "wanker" sign to the prosecutor, not for giving me a hard time but for calling my mate Billy a liar, the cheeky twat. We went for a Chinese in town to celebrate and asked the security guard to join us but he said no. I shook his hand, thanked him and offered him a good drink. He again declined and said he was just telling the truth. No matter what he thinks of me now – and I don't really care – I can assure him that on that day he did tell the truth.

monday or tuesday

As the captain of the *Titanic* once said, "It never ceases to amaze me how the quietest days or trips can end in disaster." Everton's trip to Middlesbrough a couple of seasons ago was one of them. Now we've had some of the worst violence I've witnessed against Boro but that year, for whatever reason, the hooligan element decided not to go. Even if the firm didn't go, I would usually still attend, so I bummed a lift and went to the match without any intention of causing trouble. Boro is bad enough mobbed up and I'm no hero, so the last thing I wanted was any hassle. Some hope.

We got there nice and early, had a few drinks out of town and got to the ground about five minutes before kick-off. Sometimes you have to do it that way, and anyone who reckons they haven't played out a low one on the odd occasion is either a liar or a Cockney. I was just going in when a tidy little firm of them showed and called me over. They were all right; over the years I'd got to know a few of their faces and them likewise. It was a chat full of the usual bollocks:

"Where's your boys?" "Where were you after the game at Goodison last year?" "Tell the lad who stabbed Fred in 1984 that if we get him he's dead," etc. Yawn. As I was on my own, they said to fuck the game off and go on the ale, but much as I like a drink I decided that, after years of battles with them, it was a kind offer I would pass on. Just in case.

The score was 1-1 with a few minutes left and I had walked down to the front ready for a flyer when Franny Jeffers scored with the last kick of the match and ran to our end. Now I get a bit excited at the big games, and many a time have invaded the pitch, but three points at Boro is hardly shoot-your-load material. Still, a load of Everton pushed forward and, with there being no barrier, about twenty of us ended up on the perimeter – not on the pitch, just the bit behind the goal.

I helped some kid up and lifted him over the advertising board, when this heavy-handed steward pushed me and started gobbing off. I told him to fuck off or he'd get a belt and that was the end of it, as far as I was concerned. We made our way to the doors and Boro kicked it off with the first few out, not with Everton lads but with blokes who were up for it all the same. The police then gassed every fucker and it was getting a bit on top. I was waiting by the exit, as that gas is not the best, when this copper nicked me. That was it. Hand on heart I never raised my voice, never mind a hand.

Usual routine down the station, banged up again for nothing. I was distraught. The charge was breach of the peace, a nothing charge but again no sign of a caution, so it was all the way back up there on the Tuesday, which was going to be a pain in the arse, as the petrol strike was just starting and Boro from Liverpool was a good few gallon, which was not in abundance. They let me out at half past nine and the lads I'd had a lift off had waited for me, so a drive home was a top bonus. They were well pissed up and the journey made me realise what a load of shite the drivers had to put up with every week. Could I not do that job.

The fuel crisis was crippling Britain and the country was at a near standstill. Nothing stops you getting a bollocking off the beak though, so me and Lieutenant Pud got the train from Lime Street at half seven. We changed at Manchester and York, getting to court nice and early for the formality of a £100 fine and a ticking off from a retired school teacher who, if he had his way, would have preferred to give me the cane. We walked from the station and got a bit lost, so I gave Pud my charge sheet and told him to ask a taxi driver the way while I went into a pub for a quick piss.

I came out and got the old saying off my trusty lieutenant: "Do you want the good news or the bad news?"

The good: "The court is five minutes that way."

The bad: "You should have been here yesterday."

To this day, I don't know how I fucked that up, but there it was in black and white on the charge sheet: MONDAY.

I went into the court and made out I didn't know that I was a touch late. The duty solicitor was called and he told me there was a warrant out for my arrest, but he would try to sort it. They kept me there till all the sittings had finished, then put me before a special court at half six. Magistrates and prosecution briefs are bad at the best of times but hungry, tired ones with no petrol are a fucking danger to society and these twats turned out to be no exception.

The duty brief asked for it to be dealt with there and then with a fine, as several lads charged with the same offence had got a maximum £200 the day earlier. The prosecution said they were waiting for a file on me and asked for an adjournment. Mine disagreed but got nowhere, as usual, and then the magistrate tells me to he can't deal with it, and that I'd have to come back. *Here we go again*, I remember thinking, seconds after musing that if I had the last gallon of petrol in the world I'd burn this shithole court down with it.

My man, who was doing this for nish, by the way, as he was only the duty brief and could have finished at five, then asked for a couple of weeks' grace. With the current situation and the difficulties that we were all having getting about our daily business, it was a fair call. The beak thought about it for? Well, it wasn't long, and told me to come back on fucking Thursday! My brief went bonkers, to his credit, but got nowhere again, so Thursday it was to be.

I went all the way back up two days later to be told that the file wasn't ready: soul-destroying, case adjourned for a month. The banning order was not on the bail sheet, so I could still go to the match. Big deal. The one major plus was the duty solicitor. He was that pissed off about the bench making me come back up for fuck all that he said he would see the case all the way through for me. I ended up going back another three times. In the end the secret file was a couple of moody pictures the Boro plod had snapped when I was talking to their lads. But the charge was so poor it made no difference and I was bound over, which was a result of sorts. I worked out though that the trains and time off work cost me a grand over the six months it took to get bound over.

This story is an example of how the authorities can make the rules up as they go along, with regard to alleged football thugs. I'll tell you, it's fucking wrong! However, as they say, there is a moral to every story. This one has two:

1. Always read your charge sheet to see what day you're in court.
2. Never get nicked when some tight-arse farmer is bringing the country to its knees over the price of a gallon of diesel.

By the way, if you ever get nicked at Boro, use: Simon Walker, from Appleby, Hope & Matthews solicitors, telephone 01642 440444. He is the best around. I hope that this publicity earns him a few quid, as I forgot to pay him.

guilty

You need a little bit of luck in court, but you also need another two things, or all the luck in the world won't help you.

You need a good brief. The couple of times I have had crap outcomes in court have been the result of being lumbered with a defence lawyer that would be more suited arguing in a divorce court over who has the microwave and who has the video. Some are just not up to the task of keeping you out of jail, mainly because they are from a totally different background and are not on the same planet as you. If every time I was told to plead guilty by a brief, I did, I would still be in jail now. Some want an easy day and like to be sipping gin and tonics with the prosecution brief by lunch while you're on your way to The Scrubs. They are easily spotted and over the years I have sacked a few within minutes of them reading the charge sheet and tutting before saying, "If I was in your shoes …" Well, you're not, so fuck off, you're sacked.

You also need balls. The bigger, the better. It is not nice standing in the dock being called a liar by a fat bastard whose suit looks like it is about to explode at any minute. It is also very difficult to look at twelve jurors who swallow everything they read in *The Sun* and believe from the kick-off you should be publicly hanged. It is even harder to not jump out of the dock and shake a bizzie by the throat for telling a pack of lies. You just have to switch off from all the crap and convince an awful lot of complete strangers that you are innocent. Whether you are or not.

There are times, though, when despite all your hopes or worries, you do have to hold your hand up and say, "It's a fair cop." I know lads who will never plead guilty to anything. Many have done well on this strategy, but there will always come a time when your luck runs out and then you get the book thrown at you. Make no mistake, if you get a guilty in the Crown and you have pleaded not guilty, you will get double. For one, you have wasted an awful lot of money, and two, you have been called a liar by the jury, plain and simple. They haven't believed you, so in the judge's eyes you are no more than a barefaced liar.

Twice I have been caught between the devil and the deep blue sea and, after changing my mind a thousand times, have thrown my hat in and gone guilty. The first time was after a stupid incident with a motorist outside Leyton Orient's ground; the second, and most serious of all the times I have been to court, was after we went to Aberdeen for a pre-season friendly, and I was charged with mobbing and rioting. On both occasions I was told to plead guilty by my brief, and in each case I took no notice. But like I said, sometimes you have to be realistic, and these two trials were not suited to courtroom amateur dramatics. While you can chance your good fortune with a bet on the Grand National, the odds on me walking away from those two courts if I got a guilty were non-existent.

The stakes were high: twelve months at Leytonstone Magistrates if I was found guilty, and a little higher again before the Sheriff at Aberdeen High Court, where we were told by every brief we met that we were having a seven-stretch unless we came clean and pleaded guilty. It was a hard decision and, had I not been bang to rights on both charges, it would have been even harder!

orient

You just know sometimes that it is a bad idea to go somewhere, but we have all done it and gone, later rueing not following our first instincts. This was the case when I woke up in a cell in the middle of London six hours after being arrested for punching a mouthy Cockney by the name of Colin Walter Read.

It began after work on the Friday night. Me and two mates, Falco and Shaun, went on a bit of a bender that ended with us in the chippy with the usual mixture of lager louts looking for a fight and pissed single mothers hoping to meet Prince Charming. As watery curry sauce was spilled over the last chips from the bottom of the fryer, we saw a couple of lads we knew heading for the train. They told us they were off to London with blag rail tickets on the midnight to Euston. It sounded like a great idea, so we were on board as it pulled out of the station. I had no idea what the intention of the journey was, and still haven't.

We drank from the buffet car all the way down there and then went to the fruit market, where the pubs are open at dawn for all the traders. We had no trouble blending in with them and by ten in the morning were bladdered. A vote of two to one was taken in favour of going home, Falco losing out as he fancied the full day again, as was usually the case. He had the belly for more ale but not the money, so he was forced back to Euston with us.

As we were waiting, a load of lads came through the concourse and I knew a few of them were Wrexham. They were at Orient and we ditched going home as we had an excuse to stay now, and there were a few more mugs to keep Falco in ale. By half two I had no idea if I was at Leyton Orient or the Asian Orient, and foolishly walked from the Tube at Leytonstone towards the ground. It was a daft idea but I had never been there and it was before all-day open-ing, so three bells was closing time anyway.

Although I get in some right states, I still know right from wrong and was dismayed when, at a road crossing, a bloke two cars back started sounding his horn and then bollocked some old lady for taking too long to cross. As he drove past, I called him a wanker and was shocked when he stopped, lent out of the window and spat at me. Not as shocked as he was though when he stalled his crappy Cortina and I knocked him clean out with a right hook straight through his open window.

I got to the ground and was arrested on the spot and taken to the local nick. A patrolling police car had been following the Wrexham lads and clocked me just as I sent the road rager for a little sleep. Bad luck, but I wasn't that both-ered, and once locked up, slept for six hours before they could wake me for an interview.

They tried to put it down as a football assault. This bloke had been in and given a statement that we were all chanting in the road and that he had stopped only when we kicked his car, resulting in him being slapped. It was unreal but I said nothing and my complete interview sheet was one "no reply" after another. I was let out at ten o'clock, just in time for the last train home, and was glad to see Shaun had been nicked as well; not that I was being a sly bastard but it was company home and for the return to court. My joy was shortlived, as he had been nicked again for trying to pinch a knife out of an amnesty bin in the station while waiting for me. He had only been cautioned, so I had to go back the week after on my own, and pay for his train ticket home, as our blag ones had been confiscated.

The case was the same old story, all the way back to court a few days later just to plead not guilty, a few other adjourn-ments and a load of money wasted even before you get a trial date. The charge was ABH and criminal damage to his car. He was a typical Cockney, trying to claim a few hundred quid for this and that I had supposedly damaged. Cheeky bastard, the car was a wreck, you could have petrol-bombed it and struggled to cause £200-worth of damage.

My main worry was that I had been out of jail for only a few months, and if they put two and two together and got five as regards it being football-related, I was going back for at least twelve months. This is what made me change my mind and throw my hand in. If I pleaded guilty, the bloke would not need to go to court and give evidence, which was a bonus, as he seemed likely to lay the shit on for a few extra quid compensation, if his valuation of his trusty Cortina was anything to go by. Also it would leave his missus out of the equation too, as by now she had come forward and said she had been sick in the car such was the sight she witnessed, and was having flashbacks and couldn't sleep.

So I went back to court and shocked everybody with a guilty plea, providing they dropped the criminal damage charge. I was not arsed about the thing, it just made me feel better knowing he would not get my money. My brief was a cracker, both in the flesh and at her job. If I was going down – and with my release still only weeks earlier she told me to expect six months – at least I could think of her in a little, tight, pinstriped suit while I was banged up. She spoke brilliantly in court, football never got a mention and she made the driver out to be a demented road rage lunatic. But for my previous I would have been okay for a fine, she said. I wish.

The wish came true. The judge gave me a bit of credit for being honest, frowned upon the driver for his behaviour and said spitting in itself was an assault and said I should have filed a complaint against Colin Walter Read. The best, though, was when he asked for my previous to be read out and was told a few drunk and disorderlies from years back, a couple of breaches of the peace, and then I waited for the grand finale: "Twenty-eight days' imprisonment a few weeks ago up the road your worship." But it never came.

I was overjoyed. He gave me a bit of a ticking off and told me that while he understood people's need to deal with the fat bloat that was Mr Read, one – they always say "one", don't they? – must not take the law into one's own hands. One has a point, I thought. By now I could sense that one would not be needing all the books and shite one had packed in one's holdall to take to one's cell later that night.

One was correct. He gave me a fine of a couple of hundred and I had to pay the Cockney just fifty quid for the punch. I contemplated asking if I could have another fifty quid's worth but thought better of it. I was made up outside the court and even had a little kiss off Miss Pinstripe. I asked her out to lunch but she declined. It was a great day and that would have capped it; still, at least I was going home … just a pity is was not with her.

8 ABERDEEN

WHILE OVER THE years I have been to blame for too many fights at the match to remember, there has been the odd occasion when I was not totally to blame. Aberdeen away in the pre-season friendly in August 1996 was one of them. Due to continued problems we were causing abroad, the club decided to cancel the annual pre-season trip to Europe and replace it with a series of "friendly" matches across Britain. They must have lost the plot though, as the games planned were away at Aberdeen, Wrexham and Birmingham, all in the space of seven days. Now it would not take one of those professors in football violence at Leicester University to suss out that Everton, who were regarded by many as the most active new mob in England, and Aberdeen, who were always looked upon as one of the best firms in Scotland, would probably involve themselves in fisticuffs if we played each other. So instead of a trip to Europe, they set it up. Better still, they set it up for a Saturday. They must have been on drugs. It was 100 per cent certain to be a weekend of pure violence, and that it was.

By now we had got ourselves a little night club in town that was Everton Only. The Vaults was a top place: a couple of girls ran it, our lads did the door and anything went. It was boss and ideal for our activities. We met there on the Friday night and stayed till about three in the morning before setting off on the long trip to Aberdeen. We had a full turnout with sixty-odd of the main lads on board. Quite a few others flew up and, in total, Everton took a couple of thousand up there. There were not many scarfers on the trip, and it was a top mob that assembled in the bars in the city centre half an hour after dumping our bags and freshening up with a wash and a line. The complete mob was beaked up and it was not even midday. I remember Shaun Mac coming out in shorts and flip-flops, saying that if it came on top he could not run in them and so we would all have to stand. It was a madcap idea, but theoretically a good one.

The city was full of shoppers and before the game the only trouble was when a few lads fronted Mick in the high street and one got banged while his mate ran into a sports shop looking for imaginary trainers. We walked to the ground with over 300 lads and never saw a single member of the notorious Aberdeen Soccer Casuals. It looked like another bluff about the Jocks having a firm to match English clubs, but I knew better. I had seen Aberdeen at Euro 96: they had lads and they were game lads too. They just were not about but would show later, of that I was sure.

As we got to the ground, I went for a mooch and saw Onion coming around near the first aid room, having been clacked over the head with a chunk of wood. He is not a pretty sight at the best of times but with a bandaged head and blood trickling down his face did not look clever at all. I always thought they called him Onion because he has a little tuft on his head and does look a bit like the said vegetable, but found out recently that it is because of a misspelt tattoo on his belly. Around his navel he has the fine script: "Born an Evertonian." Only he did not agree with the tattooist's spelling and convinced him that it was spelt with an "ion" not an "ian", so his tattoo reads: "Born an Evertonion." Hence the nickname Onion.

Anyway, he tells us that they had a mob of about thirty who steamed his little gang as they were by the ground picking up some tickets. I soon clocked them and recognised a few faces that had walked to the ground with us; I had thought they were Everton but they had been Jocks. I had a chat with one of them and he made a lame excuse that all the main lads were at an Oasis concert at Loch Lomond. Maybe they were but it was a poor show if all they had was thirty, and he agreed the mob we had was as good as anything they had seen up there for years. He said that if we went to town later he would get a decent mob together and we could have it by the Harbour at eight that night. I wished him luck, as he was going to need it. We shook hands and I went into the ground with a sorry-looking Onion. That brief chat and handshake was to come back to haunt me.

We won the game but, having heard that they did have a mob, all we wanted to do was get out and have it with them. The Jock bizzies were on top and we had a huge escort back to the city and again never saw a single lad in opposition. By now our firm was massive, too big really; that is how we'd had Jocks in with us earlier. We should have kept it tighter as, if Jocks were in with us, the bizzies could be. I was correct on that count too.

We set up camp in two pubs and, after an hour, a mob of Aberdeen had gathered on a bridge about two streets away, clocking us. Before long one came around and I went into Burger King with him. He explained that they still didn't have the numbers but they were getting it together and told me to get the lads to sit off and keep to the original plan, the Harbour at eight. He went on his way and I went back to the boozer, but was pulled by a bizzie as soon as I got there. He searched me, then a van pulled up and they sat me inside. For twenty minutes, I was quizzed about our plans for the night. I blanked them until he said, "Read this, Andrew."

I had not been asked or given him my name so knew they must be intelligence officers. Correct again. They gave me a file with all my details inside, convictions, pictures, even a couple of nicknames that had long been forgotten. I was a bit shocked, as none of our spotters were there. They said that, having taken my picture earlier in the day, they had sent it down to Merseyside and less than an hour later had the full report on yours truly. They told me we were welcome to stay the night but only in this side of town. Should we move to the Harbour, I would take the rap for it. They showed me a detailed plan of all the CCTV cameras and wished me well as I went back to the boozer. Basically, if any of the lads farted in town, I was nicked.

The Aberdeen lads had seen me get a pull, and when the van went I was called over. As usual I went on my own, but another lad followed, as he did not trust the Jocks. The pair of us going to meet them fucked it all up and was the end of the weekend for me from that moment we crossed the bridge. The lad I had spoken to earlier met us and introduced Davie Reid as one of their main players. He was a skinny young lad but looked like a fighter and seemed sound enough. Again we had all the Oasis bollocks but he said older lads were soon meeting them and not to do anything daft, as the Harbour was the only place not installed with CCTV.

As we shook hands, a lad came out who I thought was pissed and started rambling on about Scouse wankers, so we just laughed at him. He went mental and threw a bottle at me from about three feet away. He missed, which was lucky, as from that range I would have been a goner. Reid told him to cool it and there was a brief skirmish as the lad was bundled back into the pub. A couple more bottles came out as we walked off. It was bang out of order on their part, as the two of us had only taken the piss out of the lad, and the pub turning on us was not in the code. We let the lad Reid know it. He followed us to the end of the road and told us that the lad we laughed at was once a member of their mob who was not pissed but brain damaged from a kicking he had taken off a gang of Hearts fans. That explained the frosty reception we got, but there was no going back and we fucked him off and said to make sure they were at the Harbour for eight, unless they had a Slade concert to go to in Falkirk.

We made our way back towards where the Everton lot were drinking but were met halfway as about 150 steamed towards the Jocks' boozer. They had seen bottles flying over our heads and thought it was going off. It was a total disaster and before we had time to explain, the familiar battle sounds were already up, and this time it was off.

As the Jocks tried to hold the boozer doors, we annihilated them. Poor old Davie Reid was caught outside and although he did himself credit with a fine combination of kick and shadow boxing, he was eventually knocked unconscious and copped for a broken jaw. I saw him go down and pulled a lad away who was ready to slash him; he was a game lad and did not deserve that. They held the door and blocked it with a huge sandwich board. We were trying to get over it and for their numbers they did well not to get badly hurt. There was a lull then all of a sudden it would go off again as they tried to back us off with missile attacks but they just didn't have the numbers to bring it outside. A lesser mob would not have done as well though, and they deserve credit for it, and will always have my respect as a football mob, particularly the boy Reid, who never once moved an inch until he was stretchered off, thankfully just for his jaw to be re-wired, not to be stitched back together. He was yet another who was lucky that not all Scousers are the knife maniacs they are made out to be.

We got off when eventually the sirens made themselves heard amongst all the bedlam. I walked down a side street and was kicking myself knowing I should have left it, but that is what we were there for and it was like a drug that I had to have. Football violence is a drug and a bad one to be addicted to, as I found out an hour later. We split into different mobs and my lot made their way to the hotel. We all agreed to meet up in the same bar as, if we did not stay together, this could come right on top. We knew their main player was in a bad way and their boozer was smashed up and that usually results in sly attacks on stragglers. We were wise to it, but I knew there would be Everton in town getting had off, as payback often doesn't reach the real culprits.

We got ready for the night and Franny and I sat outside having a beer and waiting for the rest of the mob to clean up and have a blast of armpit spray with the one tin of Lynx that had been packed between the sixty of us. Ask someone on our trips for a line of charlie or a blade and you would have offers from the complete mob; ask for a spray or after shave and only one or two would ever remember to pack them. Priorities were always right with the Snorty Forty.

It was a sunny night and as we chatted over a beer, I remember Franny saying, "Imagine getting nicked here, they keep you all weekend till court on Monday, you know." Some lad had been nicked at an England v Scotland game and had tasted harsh Jock justice. In the back of my mind, I knew I would soon have a similar taste of it. I just knew it.

We mobbed up, all smelling the same, and made our way to the boozer, getting about ten yards from the hotel before it went off. They had a tidy little mob and panned across the road, but it was again small and we were straight into them, leaving another couple of casualties in our wake. They were lucky, as earlier we had dismantled a metal fence and had four-foot spears on board before agreeing they would be difficult to get into a club with.

As we hit the main road, a bizzie van pulled up with a load of plain clothes behind in an unmarked car. I was immediately lifted and we sped off to the local jail. They just grabbed me, asked no questions and we were off. That was the last daylight I saw for forty-eight hours. I was thrown in a cell and did not even have to give my name. I knew that despite their lack of interest in my personal details, soon they would throw a very large book at me. When it duly arrived it was like *War and Peace*.

I never have much trouble getting to sleep and after being on the ale for over a day was soon fast asleep in my new home. I woke up and asked for a drink and was amazed to be told I had missed my tea and was entitled to fuck all until the morning. Every so often a few would look in through the cell hatch and wake me up, but I thought, *bollocks, all of it*, and drifted in and out of sleep before being told to get up at seven the following morning.

Thinking I was going for a bit of greasy bacon and sausage, I perked up but was taken to an interview room full of plain clothers and a desk sergeant. I was shown a load of stills that had been taken of me at various times during the day. The main bizzie congratulated me and said I was the star of the show. They were loving it large, and it then dawned on me that although the coach was leaving in a few hours, my chances of being on it were slim to non-existent. I was charged with mobbing and rioting and informed that the coach was indeed leaving without me, as I was booked in for another night's B&B.

The lads on the coach had a whiparound to pay for a flight home. The Jock bizzies refused to take the cash and said that as far as they were concerned, I would not be needing any money to get home, as I was staying put for at least a few months. Of course, I never knew any of this until later when I was given a pile of newspapers. The lads had slipped a note in with them telling me what was going on. I had a couple of visitors in the morning but they were sent away and told I was being remanded in custody. They brought me a big bag of McDonald's to last me the day and were told to leave them at the desk. They were told not to leave money and all I could have was newspapers. When one of the lads came back with the papers the bastards were all eating the takeaway. It was like the Middle Ages. The only rule for prisoners' welfare was that there were no rules.

It was the longest two days of my life and it did my head in. When I was in jail in London and abroad, at least you had a laugh and a bit of exercise; here it was pure solitary confinement. I read every word in six newspapers ten times over to kill the time and did hundreds of press-ups and sit-ups, which hopefully would make me tired enough to sleep. There was no chance, as it had dawned on me that I was in the shit, and the cesspit I had landed in might as well have been on the other side of the world.

Scotland is a backward place, years behind in everything in my book, and but for the football casuals up there it is like watching UK Gold every minute of the day. But the jails were beyond that and I don't believe they would be out of place in Turkey or China. In the morning I was given dry toast and tea, at lunch they brought me a big deep dish with a bit of stew in. Towards the bottom of the dish the colour and taste changed and you were eating your pudding. They put it in the same dish and poured your dinner on top of it. Now I know the old Fairy Liquid is a bit pricey nowadays but come on.

On the Monday, I was again locked up until two in the afternoon, when a couple of CID came into my cell. Briefly they told me I was responsible for the riot, they were oppos-ing bail and I would be taken to a special court at five o'clock. I asked for a phone call but was fucked off and was told there would be a brief for me in the special court. They would not tell me how many had been locked up. I was eventually let out for a wash at about four o'clock, when I saw another two Everton lads and about five ASC.

I knew both the Everton lads. One was a hooligan, the other wasn't. The fan was frantic and looked worse than I felt. The other lad, Bernie, was a good mate of mine and was glad to see me. Personally all I would have been glad to see was a road sign saying "South", so Bernard's cheery smile did little for my depression. We all got washed and were chained, not handcuffed, and walked the few hundred yards to the High Sheriff's office situated in the same complex as the cells.

We were introduced to our briefs and they told us that

there was some arguing about the charge, as mobbing and rioting was unheard of in this day and age. Although serious, it very rarely reached the courts, as it was a complicated ancient charge, which summed the whole place up for me. The laws in Scotland are nothing like England and Wales, even though we are all supposed to be Great Britain. I would let them have Home Rule and fend for themselves. They might suss out you have your pudding on a different plate by the year 3000.

We had to face a Sheriff who was sat in a big room at a massive table with a few solicitors. It lasted a few minutes and he simply gave us bail. It turned out he was not accustomed to the charge and needed further legal advice, so we were free to go. I was made up for about five minutes, until they nicked me again. As we left the jail, the CID pulled me and said they wanted to question me on a conspiracy charge. The other two lads waited and for another hour I was shown pictures and given all the usual crap.

"Tell us who these lads are and we will do our best for you, mate."

"I don't know any of them. Now piss off. I'm going home, mate."

They then showed pictures of me talking to them all, which looked bad for us, and I was shocked they had so many photos from the complete day. But for the pudding incident I may even have helped them with their inquiries. But I managed to keep them guessing and straw-clutching and was eventually let out.

Seriously, they were wasting their time, as there was no way I was going to point out any of the lads. I knew, however that my mates were in the shit, as the pictures of four of them would not have looked out of place above the fireplaces in their homes. They were not your usual blurred action shots from half a mile away but were blown-up glossy numbers, and I knew that if they sent them down to our spotters, there would be a few doors going in during the next few days. It was another sketch I should have had a wager on.

We got to the station and had missed the last train by minutes, so had to get a National Express to Preston that stopped at every bastard bus stop on the way. A taxi ride later, I knocked my girlfriend's front door at ten past six Tuesday morning. I had left at five Friday evening. She was not pleased but I had a copy of the Aberdeen paper to prove my story and, fair play, she stuck with me for the duration of it all.

On the Wednesday we played Wrexham and I went, to see the lads more than for any interest in the game or trouble. They told me the Saturday night had been mad and it had gone off in pubs and clubs until two in the morning. Aberdeen had regrouped and attacked the hotel and smashed the coach windows. To cap it all, Everton had gone into Carlisle on the way home and fronted the famous hooligan Paul Dodd's favourite boozer, but England's Number One was not playing. I warned a few of them about the pictures and left the game at half-time. The last thing I wanted was a row with the Wrexham Frontline lads, who still had the hump from a few years earlier when I had taken a moody little firm through the back streets of their town and ambushed them with a flare gun after a Littlewoods Cup match.

On the Saturday, we played Newcastle, and in the morning it was on the radio that a few houses had been raided over the fighting in Aberdeen and three local men were being taken up there to face charges. Three was a poor result for the bizzies as, if the pictures I had seen were anything to go by, at least eight could have been on their way back up. It took months to go to court and when it did we pleaded the customary not guilty. It was moody the first time we went there, as a few older ASC were about and were not too impressed with us. As is usually the case, though, we soon got talking and I am, to this day, mates with a couple of them.

The worst bit was when we all had to watch the video of the trouble on a big screen in court. Before it, my brief had asked me to change my plea to guilty and then the clips of me would not need to be shown. He had seen the film and was not impressed. I refused and we all watched a seven-minute film of the day's violence unfolding. I was gutted. I was on about six and a half minutes of it. Franny was sitting behind me and was trying not to piss himself. They had me shaking hands with their lads, looking at my watch, going back into the Everton boozer, coming out, meeting the ASC in Burger King, then the whole fight from when I met Davie Reid to him being knocked out. They then had me walking back to the hotel and coming out Lynxed up ready to rock and roll before kicking off with them again. It was a nightmare and Franny said he watched the sweat patch on my back go bigger and bigger as the video played.

By the time it had finished, I was suicidal. There was some bad violence on that video and, to make it worse, it looked like I had set it all up. My brief pointed out that I had, and I couldn't argue, so he set up a private viewing to see if I could get out of any of it. I had to sit there with my brief and the prosecution fella and watch it frame by frame. I argued the toss that it was not me and they blew the picture up so big that the badge on my Ralph Lauren polo shirt was the size of a real pony. The prosecution said that if I did not throw my hand in I was looking at seven. If I went guilty on a lesser charge I would get eighteen months. It was not a difficult choice and I was one of four lads to change my plea.

One was a lad nicknamed Monkey. He was off his rocker and was on film as long as me. They even had him fighting then changing his jumper in the high street before going into another row. Davie Reid had a bit of common sense and threw his hand in, as he was bang to rights before being banged out, and another lad who was older than the rest of them, called Corbett I think, eventually followed suit. Out of the blue, a new film appeared of him fighting with a load of Everton outside a boozer later that night. He was on his own and kept getting put on his arse, but just jumped up every time and waded in again. He was proper, and I mean proper. He would not move and in the end I think everyone got fed up of him and went into the pub, so the mad bastard ran in with a stool and off it went again.

The stupid thing was that even though we pleaded guilty, we had to go back for the trial of the others so that we could be sentenced together. It cost a fortune. We went three times just to give our names and surrender to bail: in and out, shake £200 about, good money wasted, bargain. Two of our lads got off with it in the end and another three changed their pleas after finally seeing sense. I was made up for the lads that got off. Franny was one of them, and he came to all the hearings with us after, right up to sentencing. The other lad never, and stopped going to matches. He was well known on the England scene but lost it after that. That's how it affects some people, makes them go all soft and get married, as happened in this lad's case.

We had to have social inquiry reports and mine were great but the bloke did mess up by recommending a fine or a bit of community service. The judge asked me how I had got to the court and I told him I had flown. He asked me did I have a return ticket and I thought, *this is looking good*, until he ordered me to fly home, make a new appointment to see the probation officer and tell him to report to the judge why I should get six months, not two years.

That is all you need, a nark between the judge and your probation officer and I was well pissed off as I had to fly back and return in a week for certain jail. That was a great week – like being on Death Row. I went to see our man in the probation office but he was adamant that he could not change his report. So I flew back to Scotland with a one-way ticket to jail. I even said my goodbyes to my girlfriend and family and left a letter to work asking them to keep a job for me.

Outside the court there were loads of reporters and I thought we were main news, but it turned out that the night before had seen the biggest drug and underworld raids in the city's history, and special courts were dealing with and remanding Aberdeen's finest. The brief said it was good news, as it put our fight into perspective, so we went on the ale for a few hours, as our sentencing was put back till four o'clock. We went to Willie Miller's bar and had a top time banging the bottles down until one of our briefs came in and told us we were up.

We soon sobered and even Willie wished us luck. He must have been our fairy godmother. When we got to court, we were put up before a lesser judge, as the top Sheriff was dealing with all the real bad bastards. Our charges were read out and he asked to view the film, but they only had one tape, of Monkey playing up. The prosecutor asked for an adjournment but it was refused and was told that he'd had over twelve months to sort it out and that we would be sentenced on the evidence the judge had before him which, apart from Monkey's, was very little.

Things were going too well and all the Aberdeen CID who had been gloating minutes earlier were now looking pissed off. First up was Monkey. He was given a great testimony by his brief, family man, takes his daughter to the match, got involved by mistake, all that crap. Then his previous were read out. I kid you not, it took about twenty minutes. He had been at it for years and I said to Mark, who was up with me next, "Three years." The judge gave him 200 hours' community service. I swear the bizzies were nearly crying.

I was next, and got a bollocking for "bringing your gang

up to my country and spoiling people's enjoyment." He emphasised "your gang" and "my country" as if he had just watched *Braveheart*, before ending with, "I am not accepting it, Mr Nicholls." I thought, *Go on you soft bastard, get on with it, six months here and I'll take it as a result. Just get on with it.*

"I fine you four hundred pounds," he declared. "Maybe that will mean you won't have the money to attend football matches."

The next hour was a blur. All that worry and I ended four ton down. I felt like kissing Willie Miller's arse, but thought better of it. I ended up outside, and one by one they all came out laughing. It was not right. The police were gutted and when we all went for a beer they parked outside hoping we would kick off on each other. It was never going to happen; we had been mates with Monkey and Reid for months and even the nutcase Corbett was speaking to us by now.

As I left the bar to go to book a flight home, the main bizzie pulled me and I thought, *Here we go*. To his credit, he said, "You lucky bastards have had a right result there," and admitted they had screwed up by thinking it was sorted and not having all the tapes with them. He then shook my hand and I was amazed when he told me that he had enjoyed the day of the battle and thought I was a sound lad. He may have been suckholing but I think he meant it. We flew home and I got pissed for a week, as I had booked it off thinking it would give my mate time to sort my notice out with work when I got sent down.

They say never look a gift horse in the mouth, but me and Mark did as we never paid the fines and months later were raided and had to pay on the spot or go back to Aberdeen. I was at the speedbank in minutes, as I had seen enough of the place to last me ten lifetimes. Still, £400 is £400, so it was worth a try.

9 HEYSEL

ON 29 MAY 1985, Liverpool played Juventus in the European Cup Final at the Stade du Heysel in Brussels. At around 7.30pm that night, football violence as we knew it was finished. Just the word "Heysel" is enough to convey some of the most shocking scenes ever broadcast on live television. The images that night, transmitted to millions of viewers all over the world, resulted in all English clubs being banned from European football indefinitely. The knock-on effect and changes in the laws and control of football supporters and hooligans alike was frightening.

Heysel also rankles with many Evertonians. They blame the tragic events for the sad demise of our beloved club, and they have a point. I agree that had Liverpool not played in Belgium that night, Everton would still be one of the top club sides in Europe. However, I cannot join in the "Murderers" and "Thirty-nine Italians can't be wrong" songs and chants that can be heard at Merseyside derby matches, because on that fatal night, I was there with them.

A lot has been said, written and rumoured about what happened that night. People were eventually brought to justice and jailed for their part in it, and even to this day some so-called eyewitnesses or experts like to have their "ten penn'orth". Much of the stuff thrown around about the events, had they not been so tragic, would be laughable though. Some accounts are fairly accurate and some plain bullshit. My view of what happened is honestly unbiased and I take no pleasure in telling this story; indeed I initially had no plans to write it. Nevertheless, this is my honest account of the tragic events of that day.

Having been on the sick for a few months, allowing me

178

to follow Everton's conquest of Europe (see Chapter Twelve), it seemed silly to go back to the grim reality of factory life without one last trip abroad as the greatest season in my life-time drew to a close. We had one more game left to play, away to Luton, but the Championship had been sewn up weeks earlier, so when a few Reds suggested the trip to the European Cup Final instead of watching our reserves play at Kenilworth Road, it was not a difficult choice. A mate called Roger, who was a big Red, had organised the trip and it was a bog standard, cheap and cheery little number.

Of all the Reds I knew, Roger was up there with the very best. He would spend weeks organising trips for the lads and never make a bean out of it. He died aged just thirty-three and is sadly missed. I will never forget him after Heysel, he looked a broken man and was one of the few people who told the tale as it was. He was not a thug and would do anything for Liverpool Football Club, or their supporters, except lie for them.

We travelled on the Monday night and it was the usual Scousers on Tour: card schools, ale, rob the duty free, smoke the odd spliff and round the night off with a scuffle with your best mates, great days. It sounds like stereotyping at its worse but that is how it was, and always will be. Harry Enfield has made a fortune out of the sketches mimicking Scousers. I bet it was the easiest money he ever made, as the research into it could have been done in one night away with Everton or Liverpool in those days.

We got to Brussels early on the Tuesday morning and it was full of Liverpool fans, or what were supposed to be Liverpool fans. There were thousands in the main square and it was a friendly atmosphere, very similar to Everton in Rotterdam, but there were a lot more accents around. Although Liverpool have a worldwide fan base, there seemed to be a bit of an England v Italy rivalry. There were relatively few Italians around, but when they did show the main chant aimed at them was the annoying "Ingerland, Ingerland". It suited me, as the last thing I wanted in my earhole all day was the more annoying "Liverpool, Liverpool" or even worse, the wrist-slashing Kop anthem "You'll Never Walk Alone". So, annoying or not, I was happy to drink a Stella or two and watch a load of pissed-up whoppers get sunstroke for their team or, as it seemed to me, Queen and country.

There were also loads of "grafters" out and about and every five minutes gangs of Urchins would be in the square selling off the latest fashion accessories, and there were plenty of takers. It was an education watching them. As far as lifting went, the Reds were the masters. I never fancied the buzz of putting your freedom in a strange city at risk for a few Lacoste polo shirts. If a jeweller's was planned to go in I would have a tickle, as the rewards were so high, but for a few quid ale money I always preferred to blag tickets. Everyone to their own and stick to what you are best at.

By evening the place was chocker, and many Italians were on show. The main Juventus following would be on club trips, in and out on the match day. As is always the case though, when an Italian club side play in any country in the world, the ones who have fled their homeland to seek fortunes elsewhere turn up, and there seemed to be more Italians in Brussels than there were Belgians.

There was the inevitable fighting between various groups. That will happen regardless of who is playing, but one nasty mob of Liverpool lads seemed more determined than most to have it with the Italians. They were a proper mob of Liverpool Urchins and it was rumoured a couple of them had been slashed the year before at the European Cup Final in Rome. By all accounts, Liverpool fans were picked off that night and loads were stabbed or slashed. This group was out to settle a score.

They were taking no prisoners and I gave them a wide

berth, as their antics were going to lead to a major kick-off, and at the time I knew very few of their heads. Loads of English and Italians alike were ready to have it with them after they smashed a bar to pieces and battered the few people in there, which caused bad feeling, as the victims were a mixture of all sorts. But the Urchins were on a revenge mission after what had happened in Rome and, whether it was right or wrong, it was gaining momentum. By the time I left for the solitude of our hotel bar, their numbers had swelled to a couple of hundred and they had begun looting shops. I heard the next day that I had missed out on the customary jeweller's going in, which disappointed me somewhat.

On the morning of the match, me and my roommate Pat, also an Evertonian, were awoken by a Kop choir in the street bar directly below our room, singing their dreaded anthem. I quickly filled a carrier bag with water and lobbed it out at them. Seconds later there was a right commotion going on, so I took a sneaky peep and saw a bloke fronting the Kopites, soaked from head to toe, with his bird sitting soaked in an open-topped Mercedes that had mounted the kerb. My shot had gone astray and landed on the lovebirds and the driver had lost control and nearly run all the Kopites over. They wanted to batter him for his bad driving and he thought they had thrown the water bag. It was very nearly the perfect start to the day. We got dressed and went for a bacon croissant before the Reds saw us smirking and put two and two together and for once in their lives got four.

We went with the main group of fans in the square, as there were odd tickets flying about and many Italians who were after them. A ticket for the Liverpool end was 300 francs and we were getting double that for any spares, sometimes treble. This is what I believe caused the disaster, and yes, I accept that people like yours truly played a part in it by selling tickets to Italians, but that goes on the world over and needs sorting at the root source, not the Scally end of the process.

The tickets for the Liverpool end were for blocks X and Y, while the remaining third of the vast terrace, block Z, was supposedly reserved for neutrals. This meant that a third of the tickets for the Liverpool terrace were sold to home supporters, the Belgians. All the tickets had on them were the date, a map of the ground and X, Y and Z, depending which part you should have been in. The other block had simply been blacked out with a marker pen. They were a forger's dream and must have been the easiest tickets in the world to blag. There was not even a watermark on them and, indeed, the market was flooded with forgeries.

By mid-afternoon everybody was slaughtered, and bars that had earlier welcomed the Liverpool lads with open arms were now regretting it as tills and stock were removed in snatches across the city. I was with a gang that stole a delivery wagon from outside one bar. A lad simply watched the driver pull up and go into the bar cellar, then jumped in and drove the wagon down an alley. We emptied it of its load in minutes; it really was that easy, such was the dominance the Liverpool army had in town that day.

I spoke to lads from numerous other firms. I had a drink with lads from Chelsea, West Ham and Birmingham, but they were not in any real numbers, just small groups on a jolly having a nose. But Liverpool did have a barmy, pissed-up following and once a small scuffle broke out in the square, it went off, and any Italians who decided to have a go were dealt with. The word on the street was "remember Rome" and anybody that had been there the year before seemed determined to give the Italians a bit back.

We made our way to the ground early, as we had sold our tickets and were on the lookout for a cheap way in. In all my years of watching football at home and abroad, I have never seen anything like the sight that greeted us when we got to the Heizelstadion, or Stade Du Heysel, whichever you preferred to call it. Some of the lads had been there in the night and knocked a massive hole in the wall surrounding the ground. All you needed to do then was push past the gateman – there were no turnstiles inside – and you were in. This is not Accrington Stanley or Rhyl FC by the way; we are talking about the national stadium of a major European country hosting the most important club final in the world. It was a disgrace, but beggars can't be choosers. We pushed our way past the Scouse "doorman" trying to charge us 100 francs and were in by six o'clock.

Inside was worse. Immediately you could see that there was going to be trouble. The so-called neutral section Z was nearly full of Juventus fans and there were also loads of Liverpool in with them. The atmosphere was moody and it was only a matter of time before it went off. A shitty wire mesh fence separated the sections along with a thin line of Belgian bizzies, who looked fresh out of police academy and were obviously cacking their police-issue undies.

When it went off, it went off in seconds. There was no real build-up as such and all the bollocks about Liverpool kids being attacked in section Z is exactly that, bollocks. There were a few skirmishes in that section and they were caused by Liverpool fans who were on the wrong side of the fence and who tried to get in amongst their own fans in sections X and Y.

Loads of dickheads who were shouting abuse at the Italians across the divide started to pull at the flimsy fence and it eventually gave way. I was about 200 yards from the fence when the roar went up, and I thought it was a proper battle and joined the masses to have a go. All I witnessed was the Italians running down, and to the right of, the goal and loads of Liverpool fans piling into section Y from section Z. Very few were actually going the opposite way to chase the Italians. I bet if you re-ran the complete film of the trouble you would see about twenty punches being thrown. For a start, all Liverpool's main firm were still outside the ground, while the Juventus "lads" were all in the other end.

No doubt the Liverpool fans' fence-ripping and subsequent mini-charge caused the Italians to run, the wall in the corner then collapsed and the tragedy occurred. Thirty-nine people lost their lives. That is what happened and they are the facts. There is very little dispute about that even from the powers-that-be at Anfield. They say that there is blame apportioned to all sides:

Liverpool fans for causing the initial panic.
Italians for travelling to the game without tickets, thus ending up in the wrong section.
Touts for selling tickets on the black market.
UEFA for staging such a major fixture in a crumbling stadium not fit for a Connect 4 championship.

So twenty-five per cent of blame each, then. Well, I don't know about that. I do know that this is what you often hear when the word Heysel is spoken on Merseyside:

"It wasn't us, it was Chelsea."
"It wasn't us, it was the National Front."
"It was the fence's fault."
"It was the wall's fault."

Then there is the old chestnut: "If they would have stood and fought, it would not have happened." Why don't those involved just hold up their hands and say, "We were to blame because we kicked off?" Even as I was finishing this book, a TV documentary called *Football's Fight Club* interviewed a self-appointed Liverpool top lad who was still blaming it on every man and his dog nearly twenty years later.

Liverpool do admit, in a roundabout way, that some of

their supporters share the blame. After the initial commotion, nobody realised that people had been killed and indeed were still dying and many Liverpool fans spilled into the empty section. The area was littered with discarded belongings. All the police were on the pitch trying to help out in the corner and stop the Juventus mob at the other end getting across the pitch. Before long it was apparent that things were not well and people on their way into the ground told tales of how a makeshift morgue had been erected in the car park outside. At first nobody believed that people had died. Similar battles had gone on for years and nobody had been killed. Soon, though, the facts filtered through and it dawned on many that they had been responsible for the worst sporting tragedy for decades. I saw Liverpool fans crying, and many left the ground. Their manager, Joe Fagan, came to the terrace and pleaded with the fans to stop fighting. It was too late, the fight was long gone and I told him so. He was that badly affected that he retired after the game.

I could not believe it when they announced that the game was still going ahead. It was an incredibly insensitive decision, but no doubt one made with money in the minds of the powers that be. I watched from the section where the Juventus fans had previously stood and it was eerie. It was still unconfirmed that anybody had died but you could sense that people had. The players must have known, as they were half-hearted, and Juventus won with a dodgy penalty.

At the final whistle, Liverpool kicked off again outside, smashed up the souvenir stalls and went on a bit of a rampage. That is also a fact. It was a pointless exercise that just wound up the already irate bizzies even more, and quite a few lads took a beating for the sake of a free bobble hat. In town it was confirmed that scores of people had been killed and the place was like a ghost town, with most bars shut. The reporters were out in force looking for some knobheads to oblige with a tale of the attack. There were plenty about and for a few francs souls were sold to the devil himself.

The next day, the full horror of it all was plain to see as the TV and papers carried images of people taking their last breath. It was horrible and I felt sick. It could have been anybody dying, your dad or even your kids. It was not what my notion of football hooliganism was about – two mobs of consenting males looking to take each other on – and I still feel remorse, not so much for playing a part in it, because I didn't, but for being there. It took over a day to get home, as no ferries would take us and the port turned into a media circus. We eventually got a boat and, on arriving in Dover, had a police escort all the way home, as people were waiting on the roadside and motorway bridges to brick the coaches carrying Liverpool fans.

That is a true account of what happened at Heysel. The truth hurts, but I am certain the outcome would have been the same had any other big English club been in Liverpool's place that night. The only difference might be that those clubs would have accepted responsibility, and not, as in some cases, blamed everybody bar themselves.

10 GET INTO THEM

THERE IS A saying that everybody will be famous for a day. I cannot work that one out, as I have been alive for forty years and there are loads of people I know that have not even had their names written on the bog walls in school, never mind made national or world headlines in the press or on television.

However, I have been fortunate, or unfortunate, to have made quite a few columns in the local papers, mainly for my antics off the football pitch and the resulting court cases, but also for quite a few performances on it. I played a fairly decent standard of local football and was a successful player and manager, particularly with the mighty Feathers FC, who I led from Division Four to the Division One championship in consecutive seasons, the first time that had ever happened in my local league's history. That is hardly being famous though, as the odd headline in the *Daily Post* or *Liverpool Echo* does not exactly reach the global audience needed to achieve fame.

My claim to fame occurred on 10 May 1990, after I had produced and edited a wind-up fanzine about football hooliganism. The magazine was called *Get Into Them* (*GIT* for short) and it made the front page of *The Sun*, was covered by ITN and BBC news and was immediately banned by the Government. It caused me so much hassle that it was binned by yours truly before it made me a fiver, never mind the vast fortune I had hoped and budgeted for.

Five years later, after an incident involving myself and the German footballer Jurgen Klinsmann at Elland Road (see Chapter Fifteen), there was also a headline on the back page of *The Sun* about me allegedly attacking him. So really

I am one of an elite group of people, including soccer greats such as George Best and Gazza, who have made front and back page headlines in Britain's most popular tabloid newspaper. Those two have made a lot more money out of it than I have, I suspect.

The idea to produce the magazine came after I had been writing for the Everton fanzine *When Skies Are Grey* for a couple of years and they went a bit soft and thought my work was way over the top. I got some bad press from them and I accept that they had the club on their backs and had already been threatened with legal action, so they had good reason to want to tone their publication down. I disagreed at the time, as a fanzine is exactly that, a fans' magazine and an alternative, especially in those days, to the boring official club programme. I realise now that they were in it for the money and I imagine they do very well out of it, so they had a point. It just pissed me off that a lot of the articles I wrote would end up filed under BIN, so I decided to bring out my own magazine.

Initially it was going to be an alternative to *When Skies Are Grey* but then I was shown some of the snotty letters the club had sent them. I thought that if I put my mag under an Everton theme, there was only one place I was going and that was the launderette, as the Everton legal team would take me to the cleaners. There were many independent football fanzines on the market, such as *When Saturday Comes*, and they were even worse than *Shoot* magazine, so I decided to call it an Independent Hooligan Fanzine, as a lot of the material I had was of that nature. It also meant that, as it had nothing to do with any particular club, there was no way I could get into trouble with a club for writing, producing or selling it. That belief would prove to be somewhat off the mark.

At the time, I knew very little about computers and printing, so a mate called Ernie agreed to come in on my get-rich-fast scheme. We calculated that the ninety-two Football League clubs and a few in Scotland we could hit each had about 100 hooligans, and we were being very conservative with our sums, as some clubs had a couple of thousand thugs in their ranks. We would need to sell to only ten percent of this market to make a grand a week.

It seemed as simple as that, so a makeshift office was set up. We borrowed a computer the size of a washing machine, and it was all systems go as we began our careers as editors and publishers of the UK's first independent hooligan fanzine. I came up with the name, as it was a famous terrace chant when the boot went in: "Get into them!" Abbreviated, it was great, *GIT*, short and sweet and a bit wicked. It was perfect and should have made us the money we hoped for. However, all get-rich-quick schemes have pitfalls, usually costs or marketing. Ours was the Conservative Government and the gutter press.

I had enough material for the first issue already typed up (my rejects from the Everton editor), so all we needed to do was get a few cartoons drawn and add a few controversial newspaper cuttings with headings, write an editorial and issue one was complete. Neither of us fancied using our home address for mailing, for obvious reasons, so we asked a lad, George London, who was in a rented house, for his. For a couple of beers he agreed to open a P.O. Box number from his place and we were sorted in less than a week.

I put it together and it was a bit flimsy, so we made up a load of letters, supposedly from fans and hooligans all over the country. We called the first one "issue two" to make out the letters were in reply to a request in issue one, which never existed. It was a masterstroke and we had as many pages as most of the other fanzines on the market. We then set about finding a printer daft enough to run a few hundred copies off for us. I knew a bloke who would print most things thrown at him, as he had previously done snide tickets for both the football and the races for me. He agreed and we had 200 copies of *GIT* ready for an away game at Chelsea, with a further 1,000 ordered if they went well.

They were the proverbial hot cakes; even the specialist London bookshop Sportspages took 100. I came home on the train that night thinking I was Enid fucking Blyton. My mate Ernie had gone to the Racecourse Ground at Wrexham on the same day with fifty copies and they were gone in minutes. He said the complete hooligan following in the ground were reading it all game in the Main Stand, which at the time was the Wrexham Frontline's patch. The local police had been trying to keep this lot quiet for years and within minutes we had succeeded!

Things were looking good, so we approached the printer, who by now had read it and back-heeled it, as he thought it was a bit iffy. However he gave us a number of somebody more crooked than him, if such a person existed. He did indeed, and by the following Saturday we had the 1,000 copies we believed we could sell at the Everton v Aston Villa game. Villa were going well that season and were sure to bring thousands. They have a big England following, so I thought they would buy it on the strength of that, and I knew everybody at Everton, so they would buy it regardless. I was not wrong and we did about 200 in half an hour in The Crown at Lime Street when the first train load of Villa arrived.

I really did believe I had made the big time. The only pain in the arse was the selling. I was sure, though, that I could get a little army around the grounds doing all the spade work while I concentrated on the writing and publishing side of the *GIT* empire. You don't see old Mrs Blyton in the streets selling her *Famous Five* books, so I thought, *what's good for Enid will do for me.*

The following Saturday was the FA Cup final between Manchester United and Crystal Palace. I got a Man United lad to take a pile down there, as I was not that well in with the United lot at the time. It was our first backward step, as a load of Mancs tried to have him off. The lad, Ben, pulled a blade on them and was nicked at Euston. It was a hooligan fanzine and the lad selling them was a knife-wielding hooligan, so it did not take Sherlock Holmes to decide it was a dodgy publication that needed looking into.

By this time, we had been to the post office and returned with stacks of letters from all over the country. I had sent a copy to the hooligan professors at Leicester University and John Williams, who was always on TV commenting on hooligan issues, replied and sent a cheque for future issues. Somehow a copy had got into the hands of a news agency and I had a letter from an Italian TV station asking for my views on potential problems at the forthcoming World Cup, which was being held in their country in a few weeks' time. It was mental and in my wildest dreams I did not anticipate just how well the magazine would sell.

To be honest it was a load of shit and a total wind-up. It was bottom of the range and could have been produced on a school photocopier, such was the poor quality. There were only two or three articles in it worth reading but it still went well so there must have been a market out there for it. I was working in the airport at Manchester and all the local lads had bought a copy. We had a plane in from London and a bloke called Paul bought a copy from me. He was a smarmy fat bastard and it turned out his brother was a freelance reporter. What happened next was beyond belief.

I woke up on the Thursday morning to the sound of the phone ringing. I thought I had overslept but ignored it when I saw I had a good hour left to get over the ale consumed on the increasing profits of *GIT*. It kept ringing and I eventually pulled the plug out and went back to sleep. When I got up, the answer machine was full of messages. Before I could play any of them, my wife-to-be phoned up crying. I could get no sense out of her apart from, "Read the papers, you're not nice," or words to that effect, so took the short walk to the newsagents to see if I could see what she was worked up about.

It hit me like a cannonball the minute I walked in the shop. The huge headline on the front page of *The Sun* said it all: "THIS EVIL MAG." There was even a picture of *GIT* to accompany the headline and I ran back to the house half-laughing and half-panicking about the contents of the article. I then dropped a bollock when I phoned my girlfriend, soon my wife-not-to-be, and told her not to worry. She knew about *GIT* but I had convinced her it was nothing serious. I didn't realise she had read only the local *Daily Post* that morning, so when I foolishly mentioned *The Sun* and told her it was full of crap, she nearly passed out. I had not seen the *Post* so did not know what they had said, but telling her about *The Sun's* headline freaked her out and it was a case of cancel the church.

I went to work and it was crackers, the lads had copies of it everywhere and I soon had to take the rest of the day off. I went to see my brief. I took a copy of the magazine and a copy of *The Sun* and we went through each article to see if what they were saying had any substance. The "exclusive" carried a sub-headline of "Soccer thugs stir up fans to riot" under the EVIL MAG headline and picture of *GIT*. It read:

A VICIOUS "hooligan bible" glorifying soccer riots is being sold to fans on the eve of the World Cup.

The 24-page magazine is packed with PHOTOS of bloodstained victims, CALLS for violence and TIPS on dodging arrest.

It has a cartoon showing a rival fan's throat being cut with a craft knife.

Police have already raided the offices where the 50p rag …

And so on. Some of the so-called exclusive, especially about us giving tips on how to avoid arrest, even made my brief cringe with embarrassment for what was Britain's favourite daily paper. We had written a list on one page entitled "Ten ways to avoid being nicked at the match". It went:

The Window Cleaner Method.
Always carry a bucket and rag with you and after it has gone off and the bizzies start nicking everybody start whistling and give the nearest window a wipe.

The Tourist Method.
When you are about to get nicked always put a massive camera around your neck and shout "English Hooligans" in a funny accent.

The Rope Ladder Method.
Do a Milk Tray-style escape on a rope ladder dropped from your dad's private helicopter, only applies to Cockneys with more money than sense.

And so on. It was so obviously a piss-take that I cannot believe *The Suns'* reporters managed to get it published. But they did, and the nation would have read it and thought that *GIT* was as bad as they made it out to be, as very few follow the old saying, "Don't believe everything you read in the papers."

Although some of the article was in context, the vast majority of it was utter rubbish. The bottom line was that they believed we were inciting fans to riot, and were racists. We had got a bit close on a few issues. We had reproduced a news picture of a huge wagon in South Africa full of black people hanging off it carrying weapons, and I had entitled it, "Nobody is left behind as the Zulu tour bus leaves Birmingham". It was meant to be a joke, not racist – Birmingham's mob call themselves the Zulus because of their large black contingent – but it was pointed out by my brief that in the politically correct society we lived in, I could be perceived as saying all black people carry spears!

He suggested that I lie low for a day or two to see if it blew over. Under no circumstances should I speak to the press or the police, and I should forget publishing another issue. I agreed with him on the first two points but thought that, with the publicity we had had, we ought to milk it, and I already had plans for the next one with reversed roles. *GIT* had been on the front page of *The Sun*, now I wanted *The Sun* on the front page of *GIT*.

I got home and the phone was on fire. I had a message from George saying that the police had got his address from the Post Office and had raided his house looking for a printing press. Of course they did not find one, but reporters and cameramen then besieged the place and he was forced to take off for the day. He was even followed for a while and his brief had to go to his house and make a bit of a statement. The police believed that he had nothing to do with it and after a few hours it died down, and only a few reporters were left outside. They offered him a few quid to tell who the editors were but he fucked them off. One bloke from *The Sun* left him his card and said to give him a call to put over our side of the story. We did call but I asked for a grand up front and was told that it was now yesterday's news and there was no money in the story any more. They were bastards. They'd had their story and now were not even interested in our side of the proceedings. In the end we told them that we were nutters and were going to cut up the reporter if he came back to the house, but he just laughed and told us to fuck off.

The next day there was a little follow-up story about police raiding a scruffy house with anti-poll tax posters in the window, and the reporter claimed he had been threatened by a six-foot skinhead who sped off in a Ford Cortina. Even twenty-four hours later they were bullshitting about the whole thing and worse still we never got a shilling! By now the local papers were also on our case. Radio Merseyside, in fairness, took a copy of *GIT* from us and slated *The Sun* for bad coverage, telling everybody not to buy the gutter paper. I think they were still on their case after the bad press Scousers had from the paper after Hillsborough, when *The Sun* claimed the dead were robbed and bizzies assaulted as they tried to revive dying victims. The paper is still the most hated on Merseyside. Many shops refuse to sell it, and rightly so.

By now the Sports Minister had sworn to track us down for inciting fans to riot, and the magazine was officially banned from public sale. I immediately set about producing the next issue. We even got a load of T-shirts printed with the front-page headline on. But after that day, mysteriously we did not get any mail through. We thought it was because people were scared to write in. Although they say the Queen's mail is safe in the hands of the Post Office, I set up a trap which blew that theory out of the water. A mate of mine was a long-distance lorry driver, so we gave him ten typed letters and asked him to post them from various parts of the country. Some of them were requests for 100 copies to sell, others were made-up letters about fights and others requests for interviews from blag reporters. After two weeks, not one letter had reached our P.O. Box, which means the Royal Mail are thieves, end of chat.

We produced the next issue, but wherever we tried to sell it they were confiscated and sellers were locked up but never charged. I ended up having to pull the plug and was left with about 2,000 copies. Financially it was a nightmare and although we lost only about £500, the potential profits had gone down the drain. I still believe that had we managed to get the second issue out before it was banned, we would have cleaned up, as the *Sun* front page was the best publicity we could have hoped for. It was fun while we were doing it and was a shame that we never made a load of coin, but at least for that day we were famous and not many people can say that.

When I was doing some research for this book I found the original two master copies of *GIT* and the newspapers from the 10 May 1990, and had a good read. I cannot see what the fuss was about. Today it would not get second-column space on page forty-seven of *The Sport*, never mind front-page headlines in *The Sun*. But in 1990 Mrs Thatcher was on the warpath and had to be seen to act. *GIT* was just one in a long line of so-called sensational hooliganism stories that, if the truth be known, were not worth a second glance.

Later that year, I went to Italy for the World Cup and did at times think if I had been a bit more switched on, *GIT* could have earned me a few quid. Nowadays the likes of Cass Pennant and my mate Steve Cowens from Sheffield seem to be on the box more than Trevor McDonald and they must be getting a little drink out of it. I know Steve well and am sure he is getting a good drink out of it, as you know what they say about Yorkshiremen. I found a box of *GIT*s when I recently moved house and I have sold loads on the Internet to Americans who love to read about us English football hooligans. I get up to £10 for a copy from them. Now that would be nice: how many people are there in America? Divide by ten percent, times by £10. Happy days.

11 ARE EVERTON WHITE?

three non-blonds

Over the years Everton have had some serious bad press for being a racist club. I don't think we were as bad as was made out, but only Billy Liar would deny that we did have a problem. In the Seventies and Eighties, if you were anything other than white you could be in for a rough ride when you came to Goodison. It didn't matter if you were player or fan, you got shit, and plenty of it. It didn't help the club's reputation that, for about the first 110 years of its history, it had only one black player. He was a winger called Cliff Marshall, and it also didn't help much that he was shite. It was also evident that black or brown faces, particularly in the hooligan mobs we had over the years, were few at Goodison. I can only remember three of any note.

Joe Blackie was one of the main lads in the late Seventies and early Eighties. He was a game fucker but fell out with everyone when he thought he was the Nelson Mandela of Goodison and started preaching and slagging everyone off. He used the race card to his advantage though and ended up as a social worker or something similar. He denies ever being involved with us all, which is a letdown, as a lot of good lads backed his corner when things got a bit nasty with our own fans and other mobs. I've seen him on the telly a few times talking shite, but I suppose he's earning a few quid. The thing is you can't change the past or the colour of your skin, so I don't know why he doesn't just hold his hands up and admit he used to be a thug. It's not as if he could claim mistaken identity, as he was the only black lad in the ground for about twenty years, except when Marshall was given the odd run out.

Carlos was a proper thug during the casual era and was

as game as they come. He didn't give a fat toss about black, white, pink or purple, he was just like the rest of us when it came to football violence, and he loved it. Unlike Joe, who was always having run-ins with Evertonians about racism, you never heard any of our lads call Carlos names and people would be comfortable in his company. He got killed in a car crash at some rave. There was a load of rumours going around about what happened, let's just say he died in suspicious circumstances and is sadly missed.

We also had Jimmy the Indian. Now to be an Indian and follow Everton took some doing but Jimmy had another serious flaw to his character: he was a Cockney. How he ended up supporting Everton was beyond me, but he did and was well respected. I went down to stay at his once when we played Crystal Palace. I had been to London only for matches and the odd school trip, so it was an eye-opener wandering around the place on a Friday night. It was so multi-racial and multi-cultural that it was like being abroad. Not being used to it, I was a bit on edge and asked Jimmy if he got much hassle. Just as he said, "No," a stone hit him on the head. If I hadn't been so nervous I'd have pissed myself laughing. It was a black guy who chucked the stone and called our Jim a "fuckin' Paki!" It was the one and only time I stayed at his house, and I didn't see him for years until a recent charity do at the Adelphi Hotel in Liverpool. I was amazed when he told me he was still a season ticket holder and travels from London to every home game.

Apart from those three, I don't remember any other black lads even going to the match, never mind being in the mob.

"niggerpool"

I never thought the club itself was racist but many people did. I think that Liverpool as a city in general is, so I suppose that with not having any black players to warm to, the mood of some of the Blues fans was: fuck them, Everton are white. Football fans like to be contrary – if someone labels them thugs, they'll play up to it. Look at Millwall, for example. Everton fans were called racist so many of them started to act it, even though most really didn't give a toss. Liverpool were no better, and some would argue worse, until they signed John Barnes.

That really did it for Everton. The Red enemy had something we didn't, a quality black player in their team. Overnight that gave thousands the excuse to become Saturday afternoon racists. Before Barnes came to Merseyside, there was always racist chanting, but it was ignorant banter, not the vile hatred that Barnes suffered. Clyde Best was the only black player in the early Seventies and he used to get a bit of grief. I can also remember Man City having a black goalkeeper, Alex Williams, who got a load of stuff thrown at him when he came over to the Street End, but it was mainly the Urchins having a bit of a "laugh". I don't think most of them really cared about race one way or another, it was just one of those things English football fans do to torment their opponents. He got the same at other grounds.

I do remember one time when there was a minute's silence for Harry Catterick, our ex-manager. We were playing Ipswich and the whole place was silent, hear-a-pin-drop material, when a shout of, "Get out of our ground, nigger," went up. Everyone looked and amongst the away fans was one black face that someone had spotted. That was the end of the silence. Although some of the insulting was essentially light-hearted, some of the shit Barnes got was merciless. How he didn't do one back to Watford I will never know. I think the twenty grand a week had something to do with it.

The first game he played against us was a League Cup match at Anfield and he got slaughtered. We had about a third of the Kop and for the whole match the chants of "Everton are white" and even "Niggerpool" echoed around the ground. The fruit and veg shops made a mint as about two tons of bananas were chucked onto the pitch every time Barnes got the ball. Everton made a public apology to him the next day, and our chairman had a right go at the so-called "minority" who had shamed the club. Minority, bollocks, about ninety percent of Evertonians were at it that night. The moan in the papers if anything made it worse, because we played them in the League days later. Although we didn't get so many tickets, Barnes got slaughtered again. In a book about Barnes called *Skin Deep*, it reports that someone got arrested for trying to smuggle a live monkey into Anfield to throw onto the pitch. I'm not sure about that; those people might spend a quid on a bunch of bananas but a monkey would set them back at least four giros.

The instances with Barnes were well documented, but things happened off the pitch that were far worse and didn't get the same media attention.

west ham

I have already told the story of Jobe Henry, who got badly cut up in Manchester, but that wasn't a racist attack. He would have received the same treatment if he'd been white, as he was believed by those who did it to be one of United's boys. The story of the West Ham lad, Peter Lawrence, who got seriously damaged, was a different matter though (see Chapter Two). We played them on a Wednesday night at the end of the season. When the tickets went on sale, both Everton and West Ham had a chance of the Championship and the game at one stage was a potential title decider, so it was a sellout. In the end, Liverpool had already clinched the League so it turned out to be a nothing game but the East Enders still brought a few thousand up, including a good number of the Inter City Firm. Before the match they had a bit of a show, the usual story with them, front it, all flash but without making much of an impression. In the front was a black kid and I remember thinking, *you'd better shut the fuck up, because if you lose Bill Gardner and your gang after the game, there are not many black faces to blend in with around here.*

As sure as night follows day, at the end of the game the ICF came down County Road, which very few firms did. Mr Gardner and his boys showed but got chased back up and the black kid who was giving it so much before the game got left behind. He was cut from head to toe. It literally took all night to stitch him back together. Such was the ferociousness of the attack that the police got him to make an appeal on the telly asking the people responsible to give themselves up as they needed help.

I honestly don't believe he would have taken so much punishment if he was white. The pack around him wanted him dead and I was a bit disturbed by it, because if the plod hadn't turned up, I reckon he would have been killed. A lad called Larry got seven years for slashing him but it was a bad call by the jury, as every man and his Stanley knife knew who had done it and it wasn't Larry. He was that pissed off with Everton that when he came out of jail he had started supporting Liverpool. I never realised how bitter and twisted a seven-year stretch could make you.

There were loads more incidents like Jobe and the West Ham kid, but they were the two that the papers covered and I think it was propaganda to go with the racist tag we had. If every time someone was slashed at an Everton game it was put in the paper, your scrapbook would be filled every month.

politics

After Liverpool signed Barnes, we were forever being linked with black players who the club hoped would rid Everton of its racist tag. However, many had started to believe they were not welcome at Goodison and they were always turning the club down. Viv Anderson, Paul Parker, Mark Walters and even Stan Collymore gave us a "thanks but no thanks", the latter two joining Liverpool instead, which did for race relations at Everton what Fred West did for patio installation.

The more black players turned us down, the more the press made of it and in turn the "Keep Everton White" campaigners increased. We eventually managed to convince a black player to sign for us but he wasn't a star name that might have kept the majority happy. He was a bloke called Daniel Amokachi. He was pretty dire but scored a few important goals, especially in the FA Cup semi when we battered Spurs 4–1. There was a bit of a moan from some fans when it was announced we were signing him. The situation reached a head when one of the lads ran on the pitch and tried to attack him when he was paraded to the fans on the day he signed. The lad got a not guilty when he said he had run on to welcome him to the club and the judge believed him. How he got away with that is a mystery that Arthur C. Clarke would have trouble explaining.

Amokachi scored on his debut against QPR and loads of the diehards claimed they never cheered. Maybe they never but I bet they did when he scored the goals that took us to Wembley the following year. Later that season, we played Newcastle and someone got a few thousand National Front stickers printed with, "Everton are proud to be white. Keep it that way." A lad went into the Upper Gwladys Street Stand and let them go like the Argentineans did in the World Cup. They were blowing all over the ground and the pitch for about two months, they were everywhere, and once again Philip Carter, the chairman, was on the television saying he was going to ban the culprit for life. The way we were playing, he'd have done the lad a favour.

The next home game brought a mini invasion of Anti-

Nazi League protesters, such was the bad press we received after the sticker incident. They got a good slapping and were not seen again. Organised politics and football have always remained separate at Goodison. It's funny really, because although Everton were regarded as a bad racist club, we never had a big National Front or BNP following like some of the London clubs. A few of the lads joined Combat 18 when they started up but it was hatred of the IRA more than of blacks and Asians which sold memberships, particularly after the cowardly Warrington bombing which claimed the life of a young Evertonian named Tim Parry.

On that year's pre-season tour, someone had a few hundred of the Keep Everton White stickers and some fans stuck them on their baseball caps. When we played in Hamburg, I asked then-manager Mike Walker to have a picture with me. He was dead arrogant, so I grabbed one of these caps off someone and plonked it on his head just as the picture was taken. We sent it to an Everton fanzine, *When Skies Are Grey*, who were on a anti-Nazi campaign, with a letter spoofing that the manager was a racist, but the editor claimed not to have received it.

super kev

By now we had had a steady flow of non-white players at the club. None of them made much progress and some continued to get as much stick wearing the royal blue shirt as they did when they had came to Goodison as visiting players. One in particular was Earl Barrett. He somehow got a few England caps but I'll never know how, because for us he was utter rubbish.

When we conceded a goal, we used to chant, "Don't blame it on Southall, don't blame it on Hinchcliffe, don't blame it on Watson, BLAME IT ON BARRETT," to the tune of "Blame It On The Boogie". I swear I saw Southall and Watson laughing one time we sang it. In the end I think everyone got bored with the Everton are White theme, and the signing of Kevin Campbell finally meant we had a black player deemed worthy of wearing the famous royal blue jersey. Some believe that the club made him captain as a race relations exercise – that is bollocks. At the time, he single-handedly kept us in the Premiership, and for that alone he will have the respect of Evertonians for life.

A recent incident with Alex Nayarko at Highbury, in which a fan clambered onto the pitch and asked him to swap shirts claiming that he could do a better job, resulted in Nayarko stating he'd never play another game for Everton and again raised the issue of our so-called racist element. I know the lad concerned and he is not arsed what colour the player is, he just hates lazy arses. We still, however, continue to get bad press for minor incidents which would not be worthy of a mention at other clubs. The Muzzy Izzet one is a prime example. We played Leicester City a few days after two Leeds lads were murdered in Turkey, and every time Izzet got the ball he was booed. Big deal. It was going to happen whoever played them after the murders, as Muzzy had made a song and dance about his loyalty to Turkey. Rightly or wrongly it made him an easy target for those who wanted to air their anger at the slaying of two of their coun-trymen. Did it really warrant headline news, an FA investi-gation and a club apology?

Even in the 2001/02 season, we hit the headlines for the wrong reasons. I could not believe the press we got after a bit of banter at Leicester and yes, racist chanting at Fulham. The one at Filbert Street was sheer mischief-making. Leicester fans sang the highly original "Sign on", a tedious reference to all Merseysiders allegedly claiming the dole. Everton sang back, "You'll be working for the Pakis all your life," an equally silly reference to the large number of Asian businesses in that area. Both crap chants, agreed, but front-page news again? All it did was give a few whoppers an excuse to jump on the bandwagon and slag Fulham's black players off at the next away match – after two of them had assaulted our captain David Weir, by the way.

Later in the season when we played Leicester at home, a few of us were sitting in The Legends Bar at Goodison when a bloke in his fifties called Uriah Rennie a "useless black bastard" after he had awarded the visitors a dodgy free kick. For years, all referees have been called black bastards for the colour of their kits – that is why they now wear green, I believe – but Mr Rennie is, of course, black himself and you could argue the comment was made about the colour of his skin. A bloke sitting close by heard the comment and offered the old fella out. It seemed harsh, as this bloke was a bit of a monster and the fifty-year-old was out of his depth, so we told the bloke to behave. Next minute his wife turns up, a lovely-looking girl of half-Caribbean origin, which explained her husband's actions. We calmed it down and offered them a drink but this bloke was having none of it and continued to offer us all out. He was well pissed and even more pissed off but kept throwing in the race issue, which to us never existed.

The old bloke who made the first comment apologised but to no avail and eventually the angry meathead was slung out. It was a totally silly situation that too much ale and one daft comment had caused. End of the matter ... not at Everton Football Club. There was a full inquiry set up, with deputy chairman Bill Kenwright promising to ban the culprits for life. It made the TV, was on the radio and was covered by the Liverpool newspapers. All I can say is that either the club is looking for scapegoats for its previous fail-ings when racism did exist at Everton or the media are desperate to stir up the issue again. It's naughty.

Still, instances like the Nayarko, Izzet, Leicester and Fulham sketches give the press the ammunition to tar us with the racist brush, which is unfair because, apart from the Barnes years, which I accept were bad, I believe Everton was no worse than most other grounds. The club in general could have done more to rid us of the racist tag, but maybe the powers above were as ignorant to the issues as the fans? The transfer of Abel Xavier across the park was the cause of more bad feeling. However, the problem was the same with Nick Barmby when that greedy Judas did the same thing. He received death threats and hate mail and was slaughtered when he played, then scored, against us. That was down to hatred between the two clubs, and that was all that got mentioned. It was very unpleasant for him, but in fairness to the little louse he kept his mouth shut. I suppose the forty grand a week was worth it. But if any bitterness had been expressed on the terraces about Xavier, you will find the press and the authorities claiming racism, mark my words.

To the club's credit, we now have a couple of coloured lads who work for the Everton in the community scheme, training the kids and visiting schools. They are great blokes; I have been to one of the sessions and the kids love them. Had this been done years ago, we may – and it is a big *may* – have been spared the bad press and rejection by several black players who would have improved our mediocre teams. One thing is true though: you will still find it hard to spot a black face in the crowd at Goodison, unless Campbell is injured and sitting in the Main Stand. Maybe it's coincidence or maybe we still have the reputation that prevents black people watching Everton. I would not bet a large sum of money on the reason. It's far too close to call.

12 THE BLUES IN EUROPE

(This chapter would be much longer had Liverpool fans not caused all English clubs to be banned from Europe. We were ready to rule the Continent in the mid-Eighties and now have to resort to trying to get in through the Intertoto Cup.)

IF ANY LIVERPOOL fans out there have bothered to buy this book, I bet you this week's giro that you are now thinking, *this will be a short chapter.* Ho, Ho, Ho, Kopite wit at its best, now piss off and read Tommy Smith's page in the *Echo*. Had I attended Everton games only in competitions abroad, they would indeed be correct and this section would be only a couple of pages deep. However, since 1979, when the Blues went on a pre-season tour of Antwerp, I and a good few others have had some of our best days at the match watching Everton warm up on foreign soil for another season of disappointment.

In all, I have seen The Blues play at fourteen different grounds abroad, ranging from the superb Feyenoord Stadium in Rotterdam to the less impressive Sportsplatz Moos in Balsthal, Switzerland. Collectively, events on every trip would fill a book alone, but many of the things we and the players did quite honestly cannot go into print, as I am sure several of us would be extradited and certain men who once were professional (?) footballers employed by Everton Football Club would no doubt send me a writ in a poor attempt to clear their names.

Apart from the pre-season tours, I have watched Everton play in two European Cup Winners Cup campaigns, in 1984/85 and 1995/96. In the 1984/85 season we went on to win the trophy days before Liverpool got us banned from Europe. During that season I went to every game apart from Inter Bratislava away. The club refused me a visa to travel to that game on the cheap official tour, three days before departure, making it impossible to get there off my own back. During the rest of the competition though, I had a ball. The police did not really know me and you could get away with virtually anything once you had waved goodbye to the white cliffs of Dover.

By the 1995/96 season, when we finally won a cup at home and English clubs were allowed back into Europe, two things had changed: the team were crap and unlikely to progress very far in the competition, and I was by now a marked man. The two games I went to before Everton's inevitable elimination were as enjoyable as itchy piles in the cinema.

Of all the pre-season tours I attended, I have covered only one in detail, the trip to Balsthal. The rest are told as one, as they were all seen through an alcoholic haze and, although the venues and countries were different, the outcome was always the same: drunken, thieving behaviour and a row with the Everton officials or players. The odd battle with the locals did happen but was rare, and not worthy of mention. Several photos accompany this chapter and I thank all the lads who supplied them and more importantly those who are on them. If any cause embarrassment, tough, particularly if you are a player.

Following Everton abroad was my greatest summer pastime. You can keep your Benidorm or Ibiza.

pre-season education

The first tour I went on was to Antwerp in 1979. I was sixteen but had been to loads of aways by then and a trip abroad was a natural progression. The casual era was also taking off in Liverpool. This trend made millionaires out of two-bob shopkeepers, well, the ones clever enough to jump on the bandwagon and get into the casual clobber, anyway. In Liverpool, Wade Smith was a market stallholder who bought gear from the lads when we returned from foreign lands. He then started travelling himself to buy gear and re-sell. He recently sold his shop for eight million quid. Fair play to him.

By the time we went to Antwerp, most lads were into the gear and I mean the smart sports gear, not the brown stuff with needles that wrecked the city a few years later. Although I went to watch the match, most of the lads were just on the ale and the rob and it was an education I will never forget. From that trip I learned that if you came home with less money than you went with, you'd had a bad time. I met some great lads over there, Evo, Colin and Chris, Harry Collins, they helped me grow up fast and I owe them a lot for making me what I am today, a hooli-gan! The club were baffled why we took 1,000 fans to Antwerp for a game against Beerscott. Well now they know: it was not the sight of Mike Lyons or Peter Eastoe trying out the new kit, it was a business venture and a very good one too.

We were booked into the Holiday Inn and it was too good for us, to be honest. They were foolish to let about 200 Scousers stay in there at the same time and should have demolished it after we left, as it already had been partially dismantled by our good selves. All the rooms had false wardrobes and if you took a panel out you were in the next room. In an hour you could go through the whole floor and empty the contents of the mini-bars and have anything away that was lying about. It was paradise for the lads.

We had a bit of bother in Antwerp with the local Jewish population. I had never seen orthodox Jews before and they were everywhere with their black hats and beards. I have no problem with them but loads of lads ended up fighting with them every night. On the day we were leaving one lad sprayed, "EVERTON ARE MAGIC" on the hotel wall in five-foot letters. Years later when I went to Antwerp it was still there, and the place was a dump. I doubt if it ever recovered from the invasion of '79.

After that, I rarely missed a foreign trip and always remembered what I had been taught on my first one. I found Switzerland the best place to visit, dead classy and easy pickings. Germany was always a bit moody and Holland had too many other things going on to take you away from the shops. In the end, the club stopped going abroad on pre-season tours and I am sure the hassle we caused was one of the reasons they made that unpopular decision. By the time they stopped them in about 1992, things had changed for the worse anyway. The blag railcards that were the main form of transport had been sussed. The "ramp" for dodgy Visa cards was a distant memory, and had been replaced by electronic anti-theft devices. The players also had been briefed to give us a very wide berth.

Of all the players and officials I met on tour, Howard Kendall was the best. He often bought a round of drinks for the lads and was always giving us shirts or getting gear signed by the players. Dave Watson and Neville Southall were also diamonds, but there are always a few who were anti-social. The worst was a toss-up between Mike Walker and Martin Keown.

Walker was arrogant, pure and simple. He came from Norwich and thought he had made the big time as manager of Everton. He forgot that, unlike Norwich, at Everton the fans were the most important part of the club, not him, and no-one was impressed by his job title. One example of how far up his own arse he was came when we were in Germany for a friendly against St Pauli. We were in the club bar after a game and we had just signed Vinnie Samways. He was our record signing, so I asked him for a photo. He agreed but the camera flash was a bit dodgy and Walker shouted, "Hurry up, we've been travelling for hours to get here." I replied, "How do you think we got here knobhead, in a fucking Tardis?" He was shocked that a fan had dared speak to him like that and told Samways to fuck us off. I was glad when we got shot of Walker and even happier when I read he was working for a skip hire company, as that was his level.

Martin Keown was another. It was customary before the crap games at even crappier grounds for the lads to go on the pitch and have a kickaround with the players. Not very professional, I know, but it was a laugh and not many of the players minded. Keown was an exception. We were at some shithole place and were blasting shots at big Nev when Keown shouted, "Get these cunts off the pitch," to Colin Harvey, our manager at the time. One of the lads, Gino, walked up and booted him right up the arsehole: not a side-footer but a proper toe-ender, and Keown went crackers. It took Southall and a few other players to hold him back and later Dave Watson told us that Gino was lucky because Keown was a real hard bastard. Hard bastard or not, he was cheeky and was another I was glad to see the back of. Unlike Walker he did very well career-wise; he was crap at Everton, though, and is remembered more for giving Kevin Sheedy a hiding in a Chinese restaurant during a team-building meal out than for his football ability.

I suppose that stories like those above contributed to the club stopping the pre-season jaunts, but I think that it would be impossible for us to get away with the same things now, so if Bill Kenwright is reading this book, bring them back. Although if he is reading, this next tale may well make him decide that it is safer if we play the likes of Wigan and Preston North End.

balsthal

I had a job in Frankfurt that was paying good money, but to be honest it was a pain in the arse, so I phoned a mate to see if any of the lads were going away on holiday. His mother, when she knew who was calling, seemed reluctant to give me details of her son's absence, so I guessed that she didn't want her youngest mixing with the likes of yours truly. That meant one thing: the mighty Blues were on tour.

An hour and few phone calls later, I handed in my notice, sold a few tools I had acquired and, with a pocketful of deutschmarks, headed for the station and bought a single to Balsthal, which I was told was somewhere in Switzerland. Four trains later, I was waiting at a station in the middle of a mountain range seriously wondering if this was a wind-up, as Balsthal was only two stops away on the map and as far as I could see there wasn't a field flat enough for a game of marbles, never mind football. A single-carriage train pulled up and the passengers, some of whom were accompanied by a range of animals, including a bloke with a very angry goat that kept butting anything in sight, got on and we set off.

I was convinced that there must be two places of the same name and that I was on the way to the wrong Balsthal when a horn sounded and I looked out at a road that ran parallel with the train track. The sight of fifteen Scousers packed into a Leasowe-hired minibus was not a pretty one but a lot better than the other option that included the even angrier goat. So I bid my farewells, disembarked at the next stop and fifteen became sixteen on the remaining five-mile trip to Everton's tour camp.

It was the first time I met the lad who was driving and who was the self-appointed tour operator, Steve. He was not a thug, a thief or even a bit naughty, and I often wondered what he was doing with us, but without him everybody was bollocksed, as he knew everywhere and could speak a few languages, which was a help with some of the scrapes we got into. He does a lot of charity work for the old Everton players and is well respected at Goodison; if he was a Red, he would earn a fortune doing the same things across the park.

Balsthal was a nice little town with a very small football ground, about ten shops, three bars and just the one hotel. Right in the centre of the town was a little square with a statue of a local war hero and a flag flying at half-mast. A nice touch, I thought, although what war they were ever involved in I still have no idea. I had never seen a place as peaceful as this and I was sure they had never seen a little mob of Scallies like us either. *Very soon*, I thought, as we unloaded our Head bags into the hotel lobby, *they are going to wish it had stayed that way*.

We were given rooms in chalets on the ground floor, which were basic but good enough for us to crash in and store any goods likely to be collected over the next few days. As is the norm, we headed for the bar and had to do a double-take, as congregated around it were the Everton players. Two things were certainly obvious: the cash problems that have crippled our club must have started, as the hotel was okay but not one you would expect flash-arse footballers to stay in; and if this was the idea of a pre-season warm-up we were sure to be in our usual relegation dogfight, as it was only about eight o'clock and half the squad were already pissed.

The majority of them were a good laugh and had the crack, but as is certain with any group of young males on the ale there is always a nark who deserves a slap. The Everton players were no exception to that rule and the customary arsehole was Mark Ward. It was not as if he was a world famous star, or even one of our better players. So when we let on to them, Ward's reply of, "Haven't you pricks got anything better to spend your money on?" did not go down well. Dave Watson was his usual top self and bought a round which just about kept the peace, as even before a drink had passed our lips the first fight was brewing and it had nothing to do with opposing fans, just a jumped up mouthpiece with no manners who thought he was a superstar. We had our drink and left, as one lad wanted to follow Ward into the toilets and knock him out, which would not be good for team morale, and even in those days our squad was a bit weak.

We settled in one of the few bars and they foolishly gave us the customary bar tab. Needless to say it got battered before we left, with all drinks on the house. A local told us that there was a bit of a lap dancing type bar in town, so we ended up there. It was one of those seedy clubs that, to try to make it a bit posh, wanted you to sign in before being shown to your table. The bloke in charge asked us if we were with the Everton party and, thinking nothing of it, we agreed and went in. All I can say is that it is no surprise that Everton have got no money, as the sight of four senior club personages being entertained inside would finally lay to rest the notion that Peter Johnson was the only person to waste the fans' hard-earned cash. We are not talking players here, and don't think for one minute they were paying out of their own pockets, as the names in the guest book were not the four blokes enjoying fine champagne, cigars and the friendly attentions of some rather fetching Swiss ladies.

Our arrival resulted in glasses down and a swift exit, leaving us to finish the drinks and order some more by the bucketful. In a roundabout way it was our money anyway, as most of us were season ticket holders. Before long we were joined by one of the players, and it was no surprise that the individual was Mo Johnston. He was plastered and stayed for the duration, buying rounds and having a laugh. You would not have known whether he was a player or a fan, he was top class, and "Nark" Ward could have done with taking a few tips from him, and not for the horses either.

The bar shut at about two and we headed back to the hotel. There was not a mention of payment, proving that it was a deal with the club, and I am sure the next day the bill was settled in full, with no questions asked, by one of our fine board members. We made the town square and within a minute one of the lads had scaled the pole and cut down the flag for us all to have a photo with. It was dead smart, blue and white and had a big snake across it. We held it up and Mo Jo took a picture, then he had a few with us. Top bloke.

We got back and had a party in our room. Mo Jo joined us and grabbed a chunk of dope a lad was using for skinning up. We all thought he would have a moan about the grief drugs cause, but this was Everton, not Liverpool or Manchester United: he tossed it into the air, not the bin, and swallowed it in one. I don't know whether he knew what it was or not, but he was soon off his barnet, and it was no shock when he later went to bed a funny shade of green. When we ran out of ale, Mo Jo took us to his room to empty his mini-bar. It was a classic: he was sharing with Nark Ward, so we all piled in and jumped all over him in his bed. He was not so clever by now and sensibly shut up.

Peter Beagrie came in and had a beer but took the hump when a lad called Ray took the piss out of him. The previous year in Spain, Beagrie had made the papers when he rode a moped through a bar window. I always thought it was paper talk but after just a few hours with this lot I was not so sure, as they all seemed wilder than us – and we were Everton's thugs. Anyway, Ray offered out Beagrie when he was bulling up Middlesbrough's mob, and they went out to have a go. Garry Ablett got involved but was fucked off, as he was still regarded as a Red. It all got out of hand and it was a pity, as both Beagrie and Ablett were sound blokes. I was pissed off with some of the things which were said to Garry, as they were bang out of order, and in the end he snapped and was ready to have a go as well.

It took the usual calming presence of Dave Watson to sort it all out. He brought the contents of his mini-bar to our room, prevented any major punches being thrown, tucked the players up in their own beds and wished us good night. His gift of ale helped but also what "Waggy" said went. I don't think there would have been any takers if he'd have got involved and started swapping a few digs. He's a top bloke and a hard bastard, make no mistake. As I've said before, it is no wonder Harry Enfield does his Scouser sketch as, except for the muzzies and shellsuits, we were as bad as he makes out, and that includes many of the players.

We got to bed at five o'clock. There were now eight in our room. Me and my good friend Barry, who was in Brixton nick with me, had a bit of a scuffle over a pillow and I won, which he still contests to this day. It is of no interest, I know, but it will wind him up seeing the official result in print. We'd had only a couple of hours' kip when the door nearly came in with a cry of, "Open up, police." We thought it was a wind-up but after a dozen "fuck offs" the door did indeed give way under the force of several Swiss flatcaps, led by a very angry "general" waving a loaded pistol at us, screaming, "Where is the flag?" He was off his head; seriously, he was frothing at the mouth and going ballistic about the where-abouts of this flag. He was still pointing this gun at us and we all had to dress and were marched out into the hotel garden. A few were handcuffed. He asked for our papers and one soft twat went back into the room and brought the *Daily Mirror* out. He was not amused and the culprit joined us in cuffs spreadeagled against the wall.

Just as it was going off, a taxi pulled up and Neville Southall got out. He had arrived on tour late due to a family bereavement and was his usual cool self. The sight of several armed police and a load of handcuffed yobs did not bother the big man. He took his bags from the boot, walked past us and, without a second glance, said, "All right lads, was breakfast crap?" He was a legend and we were all in stitches.

This made the top bizzie worse and he came over still waving his gun about, shouting and bawling in what I think was German. In the end the hotel manager came out and calmed him down and told us that they were taking our camera to get the film developed and everyone on the picture of the flag was going to jail. Chief Plod then got angry again and made a speech, which I will never forget. He said, "The flag of Balsthal has flown for eighty years in this town and has survived two world wars and many storms. You have been here for only one day and it is now gone." *Fair point*, I thought, as I tried my best not to wet my Calvin boxies.

Big Nev must have told the players what was going on, as within a minute Mo Johnston was looking very sheepish and pleading with us to return the sacred item. He explained that he was on borrowed time as it was and should Mr Kendall see the photos, his imminent exit from Goodison would be a step closer. He had been sound to us, so Sandro, who was in his car and had the flag in the boot, drove around the car park and slung the thing in a bush.

Minutes later it was discovered and all the flatcaps shook hands with each other, leaving us still cuffed while the hotel manager poured them all a whisky. I do not believe the British police made as much fuss when they caught the Yorkshire Ripper, but obviously this flag was pretty important to the town and I was glad we were able to oblige and keep foreign relations intact. Mo Johnston thanked us and Howard Kendall told us he had made a deal with the police, and that if we left the town straight after the game we would not be arrested. We agreed, and then went and did a few hours' shoplifting, with a promise from certain players that they'd buy any decent gear off us – and that is God's honest truth, by the way.

I have no idea what the result was but that night we left Balsthal never to return. I was quite happy about that, as if nicking an old flag nearly got us shot, in the morning when the hotel manager saw we had cleaned out his safe I would not have been surprised to see public hanging reintroduced to the old town.

hamburg

The red-light capital of Germany was another place I had worked and grown to enjoy. I preferred it to Amsterdam, and spent over a year there in the late Eighties. I watched the lesser-known football side in the city, St Pauli, so years later when Everton arranged a pre-season game there it was one I could not miss. The main problem was that it fell on my first wedding anniversary. It was not even a close one and off I went. It was the only wedding anniversary I missed – I was divorced by the next one.

The place was full of all the usual suspects, the anoraks who never miss a game and the rest who never miss a European game. I know lads who would not watch Everton if they were playing in your backyard nowadays but would be at a pre-season game anywhere else in the world. They hate the crap football we play but the crack on the tours is too good to miss.

I went with one of my oldest mates from the match, a lad known as "Austin from Mostyn". He really lived in Greenfield in North Wales and his name is Ian, but nobody had ever heard of Greenfield, so as it was near Mostyn, Bruce decided it was easier to call Ian from Greenfield, Austin from Mostyn. One year we were abroad and a few lads were nicked who shared a room with him. They honestly thought his name was Austin, and when the police went to the hotel to get their passports they asked the manager which room Austin from Mostyn was in. It caused murder and everybody was nicked again for allegedly giving false names.

Another time, Austin wanted to watch Wales play in Hungary but booked a flight to Bucharest instead of Budapest. Geography was not his strong point, and he ended having to get a taxi from Romania to Hungary. It cost only about £80 but took nearly all day and when he came out of the ground the driver was waiting for him in a bar to take him back. Austin was crap at languages as well and it took him an age to make the driver understand he only wanted a lift one way.

The first night we were in Hamburg we all went to the Reeperbahn, which is the main nightspot and has the biggest red-light area in Germany. There is a Thai transvestite bar called Monica's, and unless you know the score you can be misled into shagging a man, such is the professional job some of the "she-men" have had done. I have known a few lads who have paid to go with one of them and been suicidal a day later when they have been told they have been up a tunnel that used to be a funnel.

We had been in there about an hour and Austin was in his element, giving the things a bit of a rub and getting a rub back. A couple of YTS trannies came in, the ones who are halfway there and have had their bits done but still have a bit of stubble and talk like a docker with a forty-fags-a-day habit. One of them headed for Austin and whispered something in his ear. Austin drained of colour and came and stood by us. "It's time to go," he whispered, "there's a bloke dressed as a fucking woman who wants to shag me." It took us an hour to convince him that all the others who had been pinching his arse and feeling his bollocks were men. He was in shock for hours and it ruined his holiday.

The game against St Pauli was spoiled by Mike Walker, who was not fit to lace Howard Kendall's boots on the pitch or wipe his arse off it. Every time we had a drink in the players' company, Walker was sticking his nose in and belittling us. It was a pity we couldn't get him pissed and take him to Monica's. I gladly would have paid for him to shaft one of the trannies in the hope that he got a dose, or worse. Walker spoiled that trip for me, but at least it was not ruined by having your balls rubbed by a bloke like Mr Austin from Mostyn did.

iceland

It had been ten years since Everton Football Club won the European Cup Winners Cup on that famous night in Rotterdam. Thus a return to the competition to face Icelandic Cup Winners Reykjavik in 1995 was a must-attend match for us all.

Such was the interest that one of the lads, who used to sort the coach for us to away games, tried to hire a plane. He found it a bit harder to get a Boeing 747 to Iceland than a fifty-two-seater bus to Newcastle, as the club had it all boxed off, and in the end we were forced to join the Official Everton European Travel Club. We were pissed off, as we did not see eye to eye with anyone involved with the club except for a few of the stewards, who were old school lads anyway. We had no choice though, because the boat over there took days and there was no "ordinary" out of Lime Street. We were not happy but far happier than the club was by the time the plane took off on its return to Merseyside later that night.

Everyone travelling was sent information telling us that the trip was alcohol-free, and any individual deemed unfit to travel would be nicked at the airport. The flight was leaving at half seven in the morning, so where you were supposed to get pissed I don't know. Still, rules were rules. Pity the pricks running the club were too thick to tell the airport or the airline. We had to be at the airport for five and, as I thought I might get some grief off the bizzies, I made sure we were the first there, apart from the check-in chick and a couple of cleaners. We booked on and went into the departure lounge and for a laugh I asked the bird serving coffee if she could get the bar open. "No problem, love," was not the answer I expected, but was the one I got and at quarter past five we had our first pint of the day. Things were looking up.

By the time the bizzies coming on the flight had arrived, led by our favourite Sergeant Cook, the bar was full with a good 200 lads and the place was buzzing. The authorities were not amused and the shutters on the bar were soon closed. However, the duty free shop had been well visited and the vodka was now flowing. Soon we were boarding the plane and, to the disgust of the club officials, the only people on it sober apart from themselves were the pilot and the plod – although Paddy Cook was spotted having a sneaky pint before he ordered the bar to be closed, ten minutes after he had told us to fill our glasses, bless him.

We drank all the way there as a blind eye was turned to our antics. One of the lads did get a bollocking from a trolley dolly stewardess for not locking the bog door when he was having a line of charlie. It was a fair call, as anybody could have seen him and tried to blag a snort! We arrived on time in Reykjavik and were met by a pretty big police presence. It was a bit over the top really, as I had never heard of Icelandic football hooligans, and we were on the ale and not looking for trouble – unless it found us, of course. The chief spotter of the British football intelligence was there with the main Icelandic bizzie. The English cop was called Shakespeare – I don't know if that was his real name or his nickname because of his daft beard – but he was red hot and soon pointed me and Vic out to the local chief. We were taken into an office as soon as we cleared customs. I thought that we were on our way back home. Instead, they explained that they did not expect any trouble from the locals but would prefer it if we drank in three allocated pubs. They assured us that they would be open from now until when we were to be taken to the ground by coach. Again it was a fair call, so we agreed and were let out to rejoin the lads.

The drive was only about half an hour, so by twelve we were back on the ale, although at four quid a pint it wasn't going down as fast as in Liverpool Airport. Before long, some lads had robbed the offy, so we sat in the pub drinking cans, which the barman okayed as long as we bought one round every hour. We agreed, drank all the cans and fucked off to the next pub we were allowed in. Bargain. We had a few beers in another bar but a local camera crew turned up and were trying to get everyone to look angry and chant for the television, so a few of us left and went on a bit of a lifting spree, which would help pay for the trip. Iceland was a grim place and I found it hard to believe the hype that it was a top night out in Reykjavik, it was dead grey and so were all the locals. It was like watching a black and white television. The shops were easy though, and we headed back to the boozer and sold all the clobber within minutes. The film crew had gone and the fans were in good spirits when all of a sudden it went off between two groups of Everton. Harry Enfield again, I'm embarrassed to say.

One lad was singing when he noticed a huge black wooden statue in the bar. He put an Everton cap on it and started singing, "Amo," the chant for our striker Daniel Amokachi. Loads lifted the statue up and half the pub joined in. It was quite funny and only a fool would have thought it had a racist slant, but there are plenty of fools about and one knobhead called another lad a racist bastard and a bit of a scuffle broke out. In the melee that followed, Amo was lifted a bit high and hit the fan on the ceiling, causing it to shatter and a big chunk to be severed from Amo's wooden head. One of the lads, who had been on the Peruvian marching powder, thought it was great and just as the police and the camera crew returned, grabbed the remains of our decapitated mascot, shouted, "Everton are white," and slung it through the bar window. He was hand-cuffed and loaded into the police van with a damaged African statue as Exhibit A.

The bar was shut and we were put onto coaches to take us to the ground. On each bus were a couple of local police and a club official. We had the good fortune of our "club rep" being a bloke called Andy Watson. Everton had poached him from Leeds Rugby League Club to be our new commercial manager, but I'm afraid he was not on the same wavelength as a load of dishonest football hooligans, and that description is being kind to us. The poor bloke looked terrified. We'd had off a sunglasses stand and half of us were wearing designer shades even though it was a dull evening, and even through them he looked as white as a ghost. We asked him about match tickets, as they were part of the package, and he foolishly told us he had them all on him.

One by one, four of us went up to him and asked for our tickets. To each of us, he said, "How many in your party?" Answer, "Ten." Next. Same sketch. By the time we pulled up at the ground, I had thirty tickets worth £20 each in my arse pocket. I went around the ticket office and started tout-ing them. There were loads of locals who would rather be in with the Everton fans and within half an hour the tickets had been done in. One lad was holding some more, so I went back to the Everton end to find him but there was a right commotion going on. By the time the third bus had pulled up, our new commercial manager was ticketless and fifty pissed-up blokes were ready to kill him. I did a swift one into the ground and met the lad with the other tickets. He told me he had been slung into the ground by the police. All his life he was used to being slung out and now he was being slung in. It's a funny old game.

I went to the tea bar and Everton were by now steaming the gates, so the police opened them and let the bus-full in. As they came in, I went back out and I got a few funny looks when one of the Everton stewards asked me where I was going. I replied, "Two-nil down to these cunts after five minutes, I've seen enough!" A few believed me and were that pissed off that they came back out as well. It was still an hour to kick-off.

I should have been happy with the day's profits but was a bit of a greedy bastard and went back to the ticket office to do the rest of the briefs in. I had sold one when I got a baton across my back and was cuffed and thrown into a police van. The main bizzie had watched me come back out and had me followed, and I was rumbled for the stolen ticket scam. There was no way they could nick me for stealing them, as I was given them by the whopper Watson and they knew it, as he was brought around to the van by Sgt Pat "Paddy" Cook to point me out. They decided to nick me for touting. I argued that I was selling them for face value but it didn't wash and I stayed cuffed. The main bloke in charge went into the ground as the game had started, and after about ten minutes Paddy came back out and they let me out and took me into the ground as well. Paddy said he had convinced the local bizzie that I was okay and they just agreed and let me go; I think Sgt Cook wanted me where he could keep an eye on me.

I sat down just as a fight broke out between two lads called Jimmy and Barry. Jimmy had a top dig on him and

Barry was dreaming of going back to Rotterdam by the time the police piled in and broke it all up. The fight was over a serious matter though; Barry had sat on Jimmy's programme, so it needed sorting. Harry Enfield would have loved it. Before I could shout, "Calm down, calm down," I was hit over the head with a baton, dragged backwards over the seats and thrown over the wall by the riot police. It turned out that the bizzie Pat had sorted my release with was a no-mark and the main bloke had seen me near the fight and thought I had escaped. Even poor Pat Cook, with all his connections, could not help me and, along with Jimmy and Barry's cousin Mick, I was nicked again and taken straight to Reykjavik jail. Do not pass go and no £200.

We had all the usual bollocks, picture, fingerprints, shoes off, door slam, nice cell though, proper bed and, after a fourteen-hour bender, no problem dropping off. I didn't give a hoot about being nicked, as I was sure they would want us out of their hair at the end of the night, and as it turned out I was spot on. I got woken up and interviewed. They wanted to know why I had six pairs of Armani sunglasses and two Lacoste jackets on and for once I could not talk my way out of that one, so they were confiscated. I had to sign a declaration handing my money over as a fine. I had about £800 which went west and Mick only had £60, so it was a bit unfair. Still, it was a fair cop and we were going home, so I wasn't too bothered, as a single from Reykjavik to Liverpool on a Thursday afternoon was sure to be a bit pricey.

The bizzies were winding us up saying Everton had lost 3–0. We didn't care really, which annoyed them, as they must have been rehearsing it. It turned out we had been locked up for five hours and the police had ordered one of the three planes to be delayed until we got on it. A bizzie van took us straight to the plane where Pat Cook was waiting for us. We were taken on still handcuffed and Jimmy was going mad, booting out at the police. We nearly got refused by the pilot but we calmed Jimmy down and he agreed to let us on.

As we walked up the aisle to our seats at the back, everyone at the front was booing, and one of Everton's big knobs from the boardroom announced, "It is no wonder we have been banned for ten years with animals like you following us abroad." I told him to fuck off and reminded him of his attendance in the seedy Balsthal nightspot. He sat down and shut up. All the lads at the back gave us a good reception and Foulksey cracked open a bottle of Bacardi for the flight home.

I didn't have a penny to my name on arrival at Liverpool Airport, but spotted Neville Southall in the car park and asked him for a lift to town. He was sound and took me to my front door, which was a bit embarrassing really, as all the way home he kept asking me about the game and said how badly Everton had played. I realised I still didn't know the result. For the whole flight home nobody had mentioned the game, just the boss day and laughs we had had. Nev said he'd had no chance with the goals he had conceded and I started to believe the Icelandic bizzies' story that we had lost 3–0. I thanked him for the lift, went into the house and turned the Ceefax on. We had won 3–2. Brilliant. A 1–0 defeat in the second leg and we would still go through on the away-goal rule.

I put Sky TV on and waited for the goals on the news. It was six in the morning and my girlfriend came down and couldn't get her head around the fact that I wanted to see the goals again. I didn't have the heart to tell her I had been on a twenty-four-hour trip to see my beloved Everton, spent £250, lost £800 and had not even seen a ball kicked. I pretended to nod off as she asked me where her duty free perfume was. She was in work when I bought some later in the day from the local chemist. Got to keep them sweet for the next round.

feyenoord

We managed to avoid a two-goal defeat in the second leg against Reykjavik at Goodison despite going a goal down. A 3–1 win saw us go through 6–3 on aggregate and the draw the following day paired us with Feyenoord of Rotterdam. It was a tie that was likely to be a lot tougher than Reykjavik, both on and off the pitch.

Everton had played them once before, in 1979, and there had been big trouble home and away. Feyenoord were one of the first foreign club sides to bring hooligans to England and had it with Tottenham as well as us on home soil. The Yids, to their credit, twice went in the home end in Rotterdam but quite a few got stabbed. I saw a video once when I was working over there and it looked like the Cockneys took a good kicking. Feyenoord were great wreckers too and were dubbed the Leeds of Holland, smashing up grounds and towns wherever they went. Until a couple of years ago "FC Feyenoord of Rotterdam" was still sprayed on a wall in Liverpool and that was from 1979, not 1995.

By all accounts in 1979 the away leg was mental, with both sets of fans climbing over fences to get at each other. The story of a police dog being set loose into the Everton fans and being thrown back dead is one often told after a few ales by some of the forty-plus mob. I had just started my first job and couldn't go, so cannot confirm it. So any members of the RSPCA, please save a stamp and don't bother writing to me complaining of cruelty to animals.

Their reputation was big and we knew they would be coming over for the first leg. What they brought still surprised us. I got into town for about one, and met Steve, who had been there from opening at eleven. He told me that the Feyenoord fans had been in town since breakfast and as soon as the boozers had opened started smashing up bars around Mathew Street. By all accounts they had a couple of hundred boys as well as a load of scarfers who were bladdered and ready for a go. Our mob of thirty did not look too clever or confident as we toured town looking for the Dutch boys. I wish it had taken longer to find them but, as is usually the case when you have a small mob looking for a big one, we bumped into them within minutes. If it's the other way around and you have a massive mob you can spend all day searching and get nothing. Still it makes you a stronger mob in my book, as if it goes off you know the thirty-odd with you will be having a go, as any wasters or hangers-on, if they are sane, would have made their excuses and blended in with the shoppers.

We walked down Mathew Street past Lennon's Bar, and across the road in Flanagans was the sound of singing and chanting. As Everton have only one song and it isn't in Dutch, it did not take a scientist to suss out that the mob inside were Feyenoord and the two lads on the door were their spotters. There was no time to mess about, as if this lot came out tooled up we were for it, so I ran to the door and dropped the doorman with a flying headbutt. It was a classic and he flew through the door and over a load of tables. The rest of the mob were in the left corner, and as Steve and I turned into them we were bombarded with glasses. The bloke I had nutted was history so we picked up a table and, as every one piled in behind us, Steve and I walked slowly towards them as the bottles, glasses and stools bounced off our makeshift wooden shield.

There was about fifty of them, which gave us a good chance but it was all their lads, no pricks, just pure boys. We motioned for our lads to get closer to us as only a few feet separated us and their boys and it would soon be time to throw the table into them and have it. Bottles were now coming over our heads as Everton returned fire but it was a pain as the odd missile bounced off Steve and me. We dropped the table and the Dutch were huddled in the corner. I think they were another firm who overestimated the size of our mob as these were big lads and, had they known how many we had, I think they would have shown more bottle. As it was, they looked scared, so we slung the table into them and traded punches with the few at the front of the firm as the rest cowered behind each other. The bottle- and glass-throwing from behind had stopped but it was down to the police arriving, not due to me and Steve telling them to pack it in before they took our heads off with a stray shot.

The fun was over before it had begun. The police piled in and we made a sharp one for the doors. There is only one way out of Flanagans and the police blocked it, so we had to stand there while they took stock of the situation. We had been at it for only a few minutes but the bar was in a bad way. Apart from the furniture damage, there were a few Feyenoord with cuts and the lad I done in by the door was still in a heap. Yet the police didn't seem arsed about us and gave a few of the Dutch a slap when they started to get a bit clever once the odds were back in their favour. I thought we would be okay until the barmaid starting screaming that I was the ringleader and had attacked fifty Feyenoord hooligans with a table. The police told her to calm down and I had to sit on the floor while they listened to her tale of woe. I knew I was nicked and had no complaints really. The police came over and confirmed that I was indeed nicked and I didn't even bother with the usual "I've done nothing" bollocks. I just hoped the place had no CCTV, as in court I would plead guilty and if there was no film I was sure no Feyenoord would come over to give evidence and an acting-in-self-defence story should result in just a fine or bit of community service.

I was handcuffed and put in the van. The police were OSD and that was a plus, as they patrol all over the city and very few of them know the football lads. On a negative point, the vast majority of them are ruthless bastards and think nothing of giving out a good kicking if you get a bit lippy. Over the years quite a few of us took hidings due to their less-than-zero-tolerance approach.

With that in mind I decided to say nothing. As they drove off, all I was worried about was the thought of CCTV. We had only got the few hundred yards up Dale Street when they pulled over into a small car park and I got ready for a kicking. The one who nicked me asked what had happened and I said, "No comment." He said, "Fuck you then," and told the driver to reverse out of the compound. His attitude surprised me, as he didn't sound like he wanted to put his size tens into my ball bag. So I said that I was walking past the boozer and a lad on the door had slung an ale over me, I'd gone in to see what the fuck he was up to and then all hell broke loose. I claimed I didn't even know they were Dutch until I had been nicked. The officer said that they were off duty in half an hour and had had a belly-ful of the Feyenoord fans for twelve hours, undid my cuffs and told me to go home. I got a taxi to the ground and thought I had won the lottery.

I went into the Red Brick where all the lads were meeting and they could not believe I was out. After five minutes the footie intelligence officer, Shakespeare, who was now becoming a regular at our games, came into the pub with Frank Flatcap and took my picture, warning me that if they saw me within a mile of any Feyenoord lads I would be nicked. I did not have the heart to tell them that I had just been released after attacking their main lads with a table. They were spending thousands of pounds of taxpayers' money trying to arrest me every week and some of their colleagues had let me go because they had had enough of the Feyenoord mob's antics and couldn't be arsed with all the paperwork that would hinder their early finish. For once I was not moaning at the attitude or heavy-handiness of the local bizzies but I was a bit disturbed that my taxes were being spent on such a poorly organised shower!

We mobbed up and went to the ground but the police had put most of the Dutch into their end early. The game finished goalless. At the end, sixty of us mixed in the Feyenoord escort but got spotted and the police chased us into Stanley Park. There was a tidy mob of Everton in the park and, as we got level with the coaches, we broke through a gate and for a few seconds the police lost control. Respect to the Dutch, they didn't budge an inch but a load of police vans steamed into us and we got chased through the bushes and trees, with anyone unfortunate enough to get collared getting a good whacking from the police.

Most of the Dutch were on coaches that went straight to the airport or ferry but two buses went into town with fans that were stopping the night. We mobbed up again and had the best crew I had seen for a home game in years. We stayed in the Big House (a local nickname for The Vines pub), then went into Mathew Street and straight away had it with small mobs of Feyenoord. They were not organised and did not know where to go and it was a bit of a farce really. We were expecting a huge mob of them but for whatever reason they were all split up and quite simply got knocked everywhere. We ended up outside Flanagans again, where a small mob of boys were inside. We knew the lads on the door and didn't want to bring it on top for them, so I went in and told Feyenoord to follow us out. They wouldn't move and soon the police came and took them out of the back door, as the street was full of us. I felt embarrassed for them as they were escorted back to their hotel. The night was over as far as violence was concerned and was a bit of an anti-climax, as I thought the Dutch would have had more of a go. At least Leeds wreck towns and grounds and can have a bit of a fight, so to call Feyenoord the Leeds of Holland is a little unfair on the Yorkshire boys.

Still, there was the away leg to come and I was sure they would be up for it on their own patch and would want payback for the few slaps they got at our place. All the lads were going and I was hopeful that it would be livelier than the home leg. I was also hoping that the police were as keen to turn a blind eye if I got nicked over there.

We had more luck booking a flight for Holland than to Iceland and about forty of us got the same plane to Amsterdam, and were booked into a couple of hotels close to each other. It was just as well, as I had received a letter from Everton saying I was banned from travelling abroad with the club again following my arrest in Reykjavik. It was on top at Manchester Airport, as the police were on our case as soon as we got there. At one stage me and a lad called Keith, from Helsby, looked like we were getting turned back. In the end they just made travelling a pain. On arrival at Amsterdam I shot through customs on my own and did not get a single tug. I took the train into the city centre and waited for the rest of the mob. As it was, plain-clothes police followed them to the hotel, and when we checked into the rooms they were in bushes outside the hotel taking pictures of us. I bet the chief of Merseyside Police did not have as many volunteers when we played Newcastle on a Wednesday night in January as he had for this little jolly.

We had a few drinks in the hotel, then went around the town. I have never been keen on the Dam. I think it is a shithole and unless you're a big pot smoker or haven't had a jump for a few weeks, there is no great attraction. I was no Bob Dylan and was sexually active, so all I wanted to do was get to Rotterdam and have it with Feyenoord. Others were not so keen to give up the delights on offer, so we stayed and I had a lousy time. It is always dodgy in the red-light district and this trip was no exception. A few lads got mugged and at one point I thought it was going to go off when a pimp got slung in the canal. A massive mob of blacks and Hells

Angels were on our case and, as good a mob as we had, I don't think we fancied it too much. It's no good giving it the big one; these fuckers are bang at it 365 days a year and a football mob would not get near them. We have blades, they have shooters; that sums up the difference between the mobs and anyone who has been there and said it's not an iffy place is either a liar or has smoked too much pot.

I was glad when we got back to the hotel but even then it was on top. One lad got pestered by a couple of Turks to buy some charlie, and he asked for a sample line. They gave him the package and he did half of it in off a key. He said it was top drawer but then said he had no money, and thought it was hilarious until they pulled a huge blade on him. He got chased all the way back to the hotel and came through reception like a train. The Turks couldn't get into the hotel and had a barney with each other. It ended up with one of them stabbing his mate in the bollocks. We were all on the balcony pissing ourselves but word got around that we had done it and the police had to cordon off the road to stop them steaming the hotel doors. A few lads who came back late had to wander about for hours until the crazed mob of Turks got fed up and went home.

The next morning, Amsterdam was full of Everton and we told everyone to get the four o'clock train from Central Station. We had a good drink; it was a lot better place by day. Frank Flatcap and Paddy Cook traced us in a bar and we were followed all day. It was a mistake to leave so late, but the theory was that if we got to Rotterdam too early we would get put in the ground. As it was, a few who went early got no hassle from the police but had murder with Feyenoord. They were steaming anyone, blokes with kids, scarfers, normal fans, and the few boys that went into Rotterdam early got annihilated. Maybe it would have been different if we had gone but I doubt it, as the firm we had was too big and there was no way I could see the police letting us loose.

We got the train about 400-strong and it was no Muppet firm, nearly all lads. An Arsenal face was on and said to me it was a firm that would do damage anywhere, but like I said it was too big, and once at the station the place filled with riot police. We decided to get off at Den Haag but that was also a bad move, as the same thing happened. The lads that stayed on got done coming out of the station by Feyenoord's ground. Typical Everton really: great mob, bad organisation.

We took a small train to Rotterdam Central and came out of the main doors to the most police I had seen since the Miners' Strike. You'll remember that one, the sketch when they were all doing loads of soft overtime in their short-sleeve shirts until it got a bit tasty and the disgruntled coal diggers got stuck into them. They never seemed as happy, boiling hot, in all that riot gear with bricks and chunks of coal bouncing off their helmets. We tried to get past the local plod and about thirty of us made it out into the street. Feyenoord were nowhere and we soon got picked up and put on a bus to the ground. Anyone without a match ticket was nicked and put on a separate bus and loads had to sit there until the game finished. We got to the ground and it was easy to wander off. Loads didn't even try, which was a shame, as we walked around the ground and had a few minor scuffles with little mobs of them. We reached the main concourse and they had hundreds. It was hard to see if they were all boys but if they were, it was a scary mob. If we had all got down there it would have been a top battle but once again we had messed up by not staying as one. We were put in the ground, which was a right result, as if they had spotted us we would have either got legged or killed.

Inside, Feyenoord were mental. They were to the right of us, and it was like a throwback to the Seventies. They were all scarves and club shirts and spent the whole game trying to get over the fence and into our section. One bird even had a fight with a police dog and for the first half I don't remember seeing the match, as the entertainment was so good from the lunatics in red and white.

We went downstairs at half-time and there was a fence and big gate between us. Again it was mental. There was a different mob downstairs, all boys and all casuals, and they were trying to pull the fence down. Everton were on the other side doing the same. If the gate had given way there would have been deaths, without a shadow of doubt. They had lads on the other side showing us six-inch blades. Our bizzie came over in plain clothes, took one look, said, "Fuck this," and went. I couldn't blame him. There was CS gas going off and in the end everyone gave up, as the gate was going nowhere. Some said it was a pity it never gave way; I was not so sure. Dutch hooligans with six-inch blades were bad enough but most of these were so demented they looked like they had been smoking crack. Apparently when Man United played there a couple of years ago the police did not lock the gate and the Feyenoord mob simply opened it and it went off big style. A main United lad said it was so on top that no Mancs would go through the gate, and I don't blame them.

We lost 1–0 and went out of the competition. We were kept in the ground for about an hour and I didn't see a Feyenoord fan after. We got put on a train back to the Dam and twenty of us went to a small bar and had a great night. We flew home the next day and to be honest I was glad to get out of the stinking cesspool. The trip was crap and the violence minimal but I will hold my hands up and admit we could have tried a lot harder to get it than we did. Considering the numbers we had, maybe as a mob we did blow it, but I think the amount of blow being smoked by the majority of our lads was the main reason there were no major disturbances. So there it is: after thirty years of different governments and psychologists trying to find a cure for football hooliganism, I've sussed it. Legalise cannabis.

We were out of Europe, which was no surprise, and haven't been back since in a proper tournament. On the flight home I thought back to the last time we had played in the Feyenoord Stadium, ten years earlier, and then of all the rounds we played on the way to the final. Great memories, and the flight seemed to be over very quickly. To me, Europe in 1995 was a bit of a laugh, no more, no less, a massive anti-climax on and off the pitch. Europe in 1985 was the one: quite simply, the best days of my life, and so I have saved that story until now. Off the pitch we did as we pleased and took liberties everywhere we went; on it, the players did exactly the same. As the song that the players made it into the charts with that year goes: "Here we go, here we go, here we go, Everton are the best we all know." Possibly the crappiest lyrics ever written, I know, but if ever a truer word was sung I haven't heard it. In 1985, on and off the pitch, Everton were the best.

sectarian football violence

Although pre-season tours were top of the range, the chance to watch your team in competitive football abroad is just pure sex: it does not get any better. Being an Evertonian and having had to watch the Red enemy win several major honours abroad made the 1985 season even better.

A trip to the Irish capital to play a team called UCD (University College Dublin) was the start to the campaign we wanted. It was an easy place to get to and, barring disaster, there was a fair chance that Everton would be in the draw for the next round. We booked a ferry from Holyhead to Ireland, as all the Liverpool to Dublin boats were full days after the draw was made. We went the night before the game and were in Dublin for six that morning. It was an uneventful journey. The boat was full of Evertonians but they were a pain in the arse, so pissed that the bars and duty free shops got closed down, so there was no chance of an earner before getting there.

We got to a pub but the barman told us it was shut. There was a load of Paddies inside, so we pulled him and, after checking who we were – which was a bit weird, as the Irish were supposed to be a friendly lot – he let us in. Once he knew we were Everton he was sound, and at six-thirty we had our first pint of Guinness. His problem was that Glasgow Rangers had played Bohemians there the night before and there had been riots. Our little mob was of mixed religion, nobody gave a toss about it, but it was deemed best not to mention if you were a Protestant, so a few of us kept schtum when the blokes in the bar started calling the Rangers lot all sorts of Proddy names.

One of the lads came in who had been in Ireland for a few days grafting. He had been to the Rangers match and this is his story:

The game was the night before Everton played UCD and a few of us decided to go, as we were in Ireland for the week on the rob. We were all loyalists, and Rangers were our second team, like many Everton lads. Most of the country has us down as a Catholic club but just go on the Orange Day march every 12 July and you will see loads of us. Is right.

We got up the ground and there were loads of blokes selling loyalist and Rangers memorabilia, but the Garda were moving them on and nicking them while letting the Paddies openly sell all the IRA and Celtic crap. We got to the coach park and saw a convoy of about thirty Rangers coaches being escorted in. There was not a window on them that hadn't been put through. They all stopped and, before the Garda could prevent them, they stormed off and went to war. Their only interest was to cause trouble and damage to the Republic. It was soon obvious they were not Jocks but Linfield Rangers fans and they were a right load of hard bastards. I thought we had a good firm but these were battle-hardened from the sectarian wars. They smashed up everything that was in their way to the ground and for our own safety we went in with them, as the Paddies were now going mad to get at them.

Inside it was a nightmare. Rangers had half the end and behind it were tower blocks with IRA flags hanging out of windows. There were blokes with balaclavas on slinging all sorts into our end; people were dropping all around. Our end were picking things up and lashing them into the Catholics. Things like frozen oranges and bags of piss were landing on us. It was evil.

The end was fenced off but two blokes ran on the pitch from their end towards us with the IRA flag and it went mental. A few ran on but got tackled by the coppers, so the Rangers lot set fire to some Irish flags and then used them to light the advertising boards. One Garda copper foolishly tried to stop them but was kicked to the floor. He was attacked for at least five minutes before he was rescued. It was bad, and it only stopped, and saved his life I reckon, when an undercover copper pulled his gun and pointed it through the fence into the gang attacking. One of the mob tried to grapple the gun out of his hand. I had been around but never seen anything as bad as this before.

It was out of control. To the right of me, police were charging up the terraces, but were getting forced back down with bricks, bottles, sticks and even crush barriers that had been uprooted. For the whole first half I never saw a ball kicked and still cannot believe the referee didn't abandon the game. This went on all match until about twenty minutes from the end, when what looked like a pre-planned exit took place. The Prod army all stopped as one and made their way to the exits and a Jock Rangers lad told us we were better off going with them, so we did. It was a bad call. As soon as we got out there was hundreds of revenge-seeking Garda, all with their batons out, and they charged right into us. We had to dive through gardens but there we encountered gangs of Paddies waiting to tar and feather us to lampposts. Coppers were pulling lads out of gardens and battering them but the Rangers fought them back and by the coaches we could see them fighting with each other, even jumping through the smashed coach windows to get at each other: not different gangs of fans, but the Garda and the Linfield Rangers.

We made it to a garage where a bloke was filling up his car with petrol and blagged him. He was happy to get us away from the trouble and gave us a lift back to Dublin. Even the drive was on top; the Paddies were everywhere with roadblocks and ambushes ready for the Linfield Rangers. I always thought going to West Ham was the roughest trip of the season. Compared to this it was like going to your Great Auntie Mary's tea party. I was glad to get to Dublin alive.

I loved football violence, especially in the Seventies and Eighties, but that night had nothing to do with football. It was simply sectarian violence at a football match. They say football and politics doesn't mix; I am no politician, so don't know. Celtic and Rangers is on top but what I saw that night made me realise that football and religion in Ireland took things to a different level and it was out of our league.

It was no surprise, having heard that tale, that the Dubliners were a bit wary of us. There was no chance of any trouble on that scale from Everton, as religion is not prominent at Goodison; we have the tag of a racist, not sectarian, club. We had a good time in Dublin, got pissed, had a few bits and pieces away but nothing major until we went to the ground. We got in and there was a bit of a karate club exhibition on the pitch. A photographer walked over to take a few snaps, leaving the rest of his gear by the barrier. It was not there for long. One of the lads had it away and it was sold in town the next day for £600, which was a nice touch. We also took some nice pictures with it; I'm on the bench with the subs on one of them. We remembered to take the film out before selling and it was quality.

The game was piss-poor. We were expected to hammer them but it finished 0–0. Outside the ground we were herded onto waiting buses and escorted straight to the ferry port. I would say at least seventy per cent of us were totally bladdered, so didn't ask any questions when we were put on the boat. For all we knew it could have been going to Egypt. It turned out to be different to the one we had arrived on, as we had boarded the Dublin to Liverpool, not the Dunlaoire to Holyhead.

It was better for us but soon things turned nasty, as there was nowhere near enough room on the boat for all the fans, around half of whom should have been at a different port. It started to kick off on the quayside as people realised they were not going to get on and all the doors were shut, leaving about 100 still on land. The lads on the quayside wouldn't let the dockers near the device that releases the boat to sail and they started fighting. It was then that a crewman cut the thick wire with a big axe and off we set. The wire flew onto the quayside and, had it hit anyone, would have cut them in half. There were kids on board whose dads were still on land and loads of other people had been separated from companions. Total chaos, and for once we were not the cause of it.

To make matters worse, the captain ordered all the bars

and shops to close. That was the final insult; the whole boat went up. We smashed the duty free doors in and looted it while other gangs raided the bars and compartments. The captain was kidnapped and made to turn the boat around in the middle of the Irish Sea. I know it sounds unbelievable but there is a press report to back it up in one of the photo sections of this book. We had the captain on the top deck, telling him we were going to sling him overboard, and lads were pissing on him. He was demented and must have thought we were going to kill him.

Eventually we sailed back into Dublin and the Everton pirates let him go once all the lads were on. The captain had apparently radioed the port saying that there was "a riot situation" aboard. The boat filled with bizzies and we set off again, arriving in Bootle in the early hours to be met by loads of our own bizzies, the *Granada Reports* cameras and half the country's press. "FURY ON FERRY" was the headline in the *Echo*.

The return leg was not the easy game it had promised to be but we scraped through 1–0. All that mattered was that we were in the next round, and we drew Inter Bratislava. The club ran a trip but I got knocked back, as I have previously mentioned, so didn't go. It was a bummer really as it was the only game I missed and showed that the club was getting to know who the troublemakers were. Still, we won both legs so I wasn't that bothered.

fortuna sittard

We drew the Dutch cup-winners in the quarter-finals and were all going on this one, whatever the club decreed. They tried everything to stop us travelling and even cost themselves thousands by refusing to run a club trip for the decent fans. The blag railcards were in circulation by now and hundreds of the lads made it to the second leg on them, even considering we were virtually through having won the first leg 3–0.

I had never heard of Sittard, which is in the north of Holland. We got there the night before and loads were on the rob, clearing up with tills, clothes, jewellery, anything that wasn't nailed down. I met one firm who were by now professionals: they had all the anti-theft gear sussed out and their haul was unbelievable. They had Rambo-sized scissors to cut through the alarm wires, reverse magnets to take the security tags off clothes and holdalls with the insides covered with tinfoil, which stopped the alarms going off. They were nicking stuff to order and must have made thousands on each trip.

We settled for bits and pieces and had a night on the ale. Sittard was okay but nothing like Amsterdam or Rotterdam and I was glad we were there only for a night. We were befriended by a reporter for Radio Merseyside who was sniffing around for reports of any trouble. He took us to his hotel and bought us ale and we booked in for the night, leaving the bill for the snide bastard to pay the next day. The following year he collared me at Spurs and was playing hell that he nearly got nicked for refusing to pay the bill, before having to cough up for all the rooms. I honestly think he expected me to give him some money back but all he got was a slap. I've seen him on the TV a few times so he must have been good at his job, even though he was a bit soft with his money. There was also a big TV crew around the town and it was the first time I have witnessed reporters buying ale to get fans pissed in the hope of a kick-off. A documentary was on Granada later that month but it just showed loads of barmies singing Munich songs. All the real lads were on the rob and a film crew is a hindrance for such escapades, so they obviously weren't allowed with us.

Everton FC had refused to take any tickets but, as so

many had travelled, the Dutch put a load on sale for us and it was a nice two fingers up to our club for being so pathetic. About dinnertime, a few buses of squaddies turned up and they made a right nuisance of themselves. I have never had much time for them; they get a day off and go daft, all tattoos and spewing up. They are like rugby players – hard bastards but with nothing between their ears. It makes me laugh when old guys preach that National Service would be the answer to the yob culture we suffer today, as ninety per cent of the army lads I have met at football or on holiday have been a right pain in the arse. It got so bad in Sittard that we gave the Dutch a pass and our only bother was with the Queen's Union Jack-clad finest. They can have a fight, squaddies, but are easy pickings when they get so pissed up; fighting wars with guns is the job for the "professionals", fighting wars on the terraces was the job for us. We did loads of them in before they cleared off to whatever base they belonged to. Northern Ireland, I hoped, was their next port of call, as they got right on my wick.

Loads of the lads were still locked out. The funniest jib was when a local brass band entered the stadium and twenty Everton marched in formation behind it, then took their place on the terraces. We won the game 2–0 and all I can remember of it was when a streaker ran on and a police dog bit his arse, then as he climbed over the fence another dog attacked the first police dog, there was a mad dogfight and the streaker got away.

We went to Liege on the way home and had a top night; it was like a little Amsterdam with a big red-light area and loads of bars. Some of the lads stayed another night in Sittard and got nicked for breaking into a train and using it for a hotel, as there were no rooms left in town. Thirty of them were locked up and put in a compound for the night. They lit a big fire to keep warm and the Dutch police threw a huge cannabis plant on it that they had confiscated from a house in the town. They were let out the next morning uncharged, so all in all it was a decent trip, apart from the arseholes who are supposed to prevent any new attempts to take over our beloved Great Britain. On their showing, if a tyrant does decide to attack us my hopes will not be high.

bayern munich

Up to the semis the draw had been kind to us, but then it all went pear-shaped: we drew the German giants Bayern Munich. Everton were by now top of the League and in the semi-finals of the FA Cup, but this draw was likely to be the hardest part of the Treble to complete. We went by coach and it was a journey to hell and back; we were on the thing for over twenty-four hours getting there and longer coming home. In between, though, was top of the range.

We arrived in the middle of the night and everything was shut, so by morning we were ready for a big session and really went for it. If you want a beer, Munich is the place and we got absolutely trashed. The city is boss and I have revisited it many times since. Bayern never had a firm, just loads of barmies, so the chance of trouble was slim but we still had bother in a few bars and had a battle with some bouncers in the Bier Keller after one of the lads was caught trying to have the till off. Years later I had trouble in the same gaff with some lads I was working with and we destroyed the bouncers and the bar, but that's another tale that has nothing to do with football.

We got to the ground and were put in an open end, where it pissed down on us. The place appears smart but was built for the 1972 Olympics and looked decrepit to me. Everton were missing a few stars but the lads played great and held them to a goalless draw. There was a big moat around the pitch but that was not going to stop us and when the ref blew, fifty of us jumped the moat and were on. The problem was that he had blown for an offside, not full-time, and we had to get off. Several didn't make it and fell in the moat. A few were attacked by the nastiest police dogs I had ever seen but seconds later the final whistle went and we were back on, rescuing a few in the moat before joining the players to salute one of the great Everton performances.

The players were made up but we upset the club, as they were fined about twenty grand for our mini invasion. They should have given us that for the risks we took getting on there, ungrateful bastards. Outside the ground there was no hassle, so we had the souvenir stalls off and everyone of us had Bayern hats as we headed into town for a brilliant night. All we needed was a win of any sort in the second leg and we were in our first-ever European final.

On the boat, we met the robbers and again they had cleaned up. They had come via Austria and had had a safe away. The contents were in the back of a hire car but the driver had lost the keys during the pitch invasion the night before. They had gone back up and the groundsman let them in and they found them. We got back and got ready for the FA Cup semi at Villa Park against Luton Town. Things were looking good.

The only naughtiness in the second leg was on the pitch, as the Germans brought only about 100 fans. We went 1–0 down just before half-time but in the second half Everton went mental on the field, and Andy Gray was awesome. Several Germans had to go off injured as we battered them. If the game had been played today we would have ended up with about five players left on, but it wasn't, and the Germans crumbled. The crowd was unbelievable as we came back to win 3–1. As another of the Bayern players was carried off, their manager shouted to our bench, "This is not football," and to a man the complete Everton bench – manager, trainer and all the subs – shouted, "Fuck off!" It was that kind of night. I have never witnessed anything to come near it before or after and I know many of the players feel the same. Although I am a football hooligan I am also a fan and that night was the very best. I never even got pissed, as there was no need to. No more needs to be said. Rotterdam here we come.

goodnight rapid vienna

By now the cost of Everton's success had begun to hit the pocket. I'd had no holidays left at work since before the Sittard game, so had been on the sick with an imaginary dodgy knee for three months. Money was tight and a basic trip to the final was all I could afford, bearing in mind that three days later we were down in London for the FA Cup Final.

We got a boat to Ostend, had the night there and travelled to Rotterdam on the day of the match – very cheap and nasty but it was the only option. In Rotterdam we had thousands, easily about three-quarters of the ground. Tickets were easy to come by and I saw people there that I hadn't seen for ten years. We expected trouble from Feyenoord but they never showed and it was just as well, as they would have been murdered. Every lad that had ever fought for Everton was out and nobody could have got near us. The police presence was low key and as was the norm, loads went on the rob. There was a bit of trouble with the touts and flag-sellers but they got wasted if they tried it on. I heard a small mob of Feyenoord gassed a bar in town but I skipped it, as I didn't fancy getting nicked before a game like this. I got in the ground early and soon a few of us had blagged it into the sponsors' lounge and got bladdered in a free bar. The seats were top drawer and we were a just few feet away from where we hoped we would see Kevin Ratcliffe collect the cup. Everton had done the hard bit beating Bayern and, in comparison, Vienna were nothing, but Everton had a habit of messing things up so I was flapping a bit before we kicked off.

I should not have worried. We went in level at half-time but came out in the second half and destroyed them. Andy Gray and Trevor Steven had us 2–0 up before they got one back with a couple of minutes to go. Instead of hanging on, we went straight up the other end and Kevin Sheedy finished it off, 3–1 and the cup was ours. I have no shame admitting I had tears in my eyes as the trophy was lifted up a few feet away from us. We tried to get on the pitch but there was no chance and I was glad, as the team was allowed to do a proper lap of honour. As they came off we managed to climb down and got into the dressing room area. It was bedlam and the players were boss, opening a window and letting us kiss the cup. Gary Stevens was getting drug-tested and he gave us his medal to hold before we got slung out by the stewards and had to pass it him back through the window. It was what following your team for years is all about. Crap seasons, winning jackshit, cold winter nights at Brighton away, hitching it home from Ipswich, getting kicked in the knackers at Spurs, Kensington High Street, doing jail, paying fines, all this was repaid that night.

After the game it went off outside the main railway station with a load of black lads but they were chased off. Another gang got nicked when they did a smash-and-grab on a jeweller's and two of the lads, including Franny, were jailed when the swag was found hidden outside the hotel in a load of sand. Franny got six weeks, which was harsh as he was only sixteen and had to do it in a Dutch borstal. He did the full term as well, as he banged a few out for giving him lip. He still moans about it now; not the jail, but that he missed the FA Cup final against Man United on the following Saturday.

We had another top night and got the boat home the next day, heading straight for Wembley to complete the Treble. Like I said, Everton had a habit of ruining things and we lost to United 1–0. It did spoil the season a bit. I wish it had been played a week later, as the players looked knackered at Wembley. Still, we had already clinched the League and the next season we could have a crack at the European Cup. If only. The rest, as they say, is history and we didn't play in Europe for another ten years. We lost our manager, best players and millions of pounds through no fault of our own and I doubt if I will see us win a European trophy again in my lifetime.

I will, however, take the memories of winning that cup to my grave and this chapter is dedicated to Neville Southall, Gary Stevens, Pat Van Den Hauwe, Kevin Ratcliffe, Derek Mountfield, Peter Reid, Trevor Steven, Paul Bracewell, Graham Sharp, Andy Gray, Kevin Sheedy, Alan Harper, Kevin Richardson, Colin Harvey, the late Mick Heaton and Howard Kendall, who collectively in Rotterdam, on Wednesday, 15 May 1985, contributed to the greatest day in my life.

13 ENGLAND

no go

Following England did not appeal to Evertonians and the Kopites as much as most other groups of fans, and for those that did go, it could turn out to be a very dangerous pastime. Nobody liked the Scousers much, and mobs from all over the country did not hide the fact. Very few blacks followed England at the time, as all the NF bollocks was about, but those who did were welcomed more than Scousers.

It had a lot to do with the bad reputation Scousers had, and still have I suppose, for robbing. Nobody trusted them. Secondly, and this was the excuse for many mobs' pure hatred of both Everton and Liverpool fans and the shit they received once the Liver Buildings were out of sight, was the amount of slashings they were responsible for in the early Eighties. I think if Everton or Liverpool had shown at an England game in any reasonable numbers they would have been facing England as a mob.

There was always a frosty relationship between the different Cockney firms, although some got on better than others. Once the Mancs started to realise the pickings England trips could offer, they often ended up in lumber with the Cockneys. Occasionally it was a pure North v South battle but in the early days these were few. However, if we went, it was watch-your-back time, as every little firm would be after you, not just the Mancs or the Cockneys. The rules were simple: if Scousers went to watch England, particularly abroad, there was a fair chance that most of the other firms would have them at the top of their hate list. That led to one thing: trouble. So most of the lads I knew gave England a wide berth.

Unlike most of our lads, however, I loved it: not so much the football, but the travel and the crack you could have. This was long before all the police were jollying with you on taxpayers' money. There was nothing to beat it, and I was envious of the British clubs who were in Europe every season at the time, as what could be better than watching your own side abroad with all your mates? It would also be a lot safer, in our case.

Years later, it is easy to get away with going, as there are so many different mobs about that they either all have a nark with each other or form these daft alliances, like Shrewsbury and Newcastle or Sunderland and Man City. It's mind-boggling to me why they do it but seems to work for some. But in the days when I started going abroad with England, the individual followings that main firms like Chelsea, West Ham and, a little later, Manchester United had at internationals were massive. So, shithouses or not, we never made a show as a hooligan mob at any England game worthy of a mention. Bar one.

wales away

Everton played Brighton on the last game of the season in 1980, and loads of us stayed down for the weekend. We met a few lads that watched England who were okay with us. They said they were coming up to Wrexham for what was to be the last Home International tournament, so a few of us said we would meet them. Word got out we were going and soon most of Everton and Liverpool's boys were up for it, as it was only a thirty-minute train journey away and what else was there to do on a Saturday in the summer?

If the decision to stop the Home Internationals was not made before this game, it sure was after. It was totally out of control. Everton and Liverpool got together, as was occasionally the case in those days, and took on anyone that fancied a go – and there was no shortage of takers. We had it with the Mancs, the Cockneys, Cardiff, Wrexham, England and Wales. I reckon it was only the Jocks and Paddies we never fought that day.

We went in the Kop End at The Racecourse and scattered all the Wrexham, who didn't know what had hit them. We walked to the back of the terrace and just poured down, giving it to anyone in the way. The police left us in there and made a line between the rest and us and soon there were about 1,000 in the end. I thought it seemed top heavy, as before the game we were only about 500-strong. Next minute it went berserk as the mob in the middle of us turned and started chanting, "Manchester." We had the advantage as we were above them but they took some backing down.

It was just a mad free-for-all. They had quite a few who had latched onto the casual gear and about half of both mobs had striped polo shirts on. Once it went off, no one knew who was who. If we didn't know, the plod were even more in the dark, so they let everyone get on with it until a bit of a no man's land opened up. To this day I don't know if the mob were Man City, Man United or a mix of the smaller Manc clubs, but whoever they were, they had a right go. In the end the police poured in and made another line between them and us, but it was a poor idea really, as for the full ninety minutes it went off. At half-time there was another mass brawl as Cardiff battered through the Wrexham mob and had a go at the English. They were a bit miffed when the police broke lines to keep them apart, and all the Scousers and Mancs went for each other again. It was that kind of day.

After the match – which Wales won 4–1 – we poured out of the end and fought with everyone in running battles that lasted for a good hour. It was bedlam. The Welsh were fighting each other, Chester and Wrexham were at it, Merseyside and Manchester, North and South, every man and his dog was having a go. It was nothing to do with football, just pure violence, as the least trouble was between any England or Wales mobs. We eventually got stuck on a train home and there must have been hundreds of casualties from all sides.

It amazed me because I got all the papers on the Monday and there was not a single mention of the lumber. Had that sort of trouble gone on today, the Government would have brought back public floggings or reintroduced National Service. As it was, a few lads got a clump from the plod, one lad had the arse of his Lois jeans ripped by a police dog and about ten got nicked and cautioned. Cautions – those were the days.

england united

Some of the worst trouble ever at an England match was at Luxembourg in 1983. It was one of the first times a big Manc firm turned out for an England game. There were still only a few Scousers there but the Mancs had a massive mob, mainly United but quite a few City as well. They had all come on the rob, as at the game previously in Switzerland quite a few had done very well out of the trip, and by all accounts Luxembourg had even easier pickings.

The day before the game, a little firm of Everton had done Bruges in, and on arrival in Luxembourg already had Head bags full of stolen gear. At the first bar they went in, the Cockneys were looking for trouble with anyone who didn't sound like Alf Garnett. One of the Mancs had a word with a main ICF face and everyone agreed that the place was there for the taking, so any club issues should be sorted later. In fairness the Cockneys kept their word; it was an uneasy truce but it worked, as England United took the place to bits.

England as one mob turned the city over. There were

gangs looting jewellers' shops, setting fire to cars, walking into bars, grabbing the tills and smashing them in the street. The army was called out in the end but was chased by a huge mob of mainly Chelsea; no messing, England had the Luxembourg army on its toes. Loads eventually got nicked and a few Mancs did about three months jail. Everyone who had a bag with new clobber in got nicked and had all the gear taken off them. The lads with the gear from Belgium and Luxembourg lost it all: hundreds of pounds' worth of sports clothes, jewellery and leathers.

A Manc escaped from the cells and, while a few plod were searching everyone, he opened some of the other cell doors and a load of lads broke out. Some of them took all the gear that was in the reception area of the jail and just walked out. It was that mental in and around the station, and they were not seen again. They were lucky, as loads had the hump with them that they had nicked the nicked gear!

Later that night, when the army had stopped running and got the city under control, they herded everyone back to the train station. Normal service was resumed as the truce ended and West Ham and Chelsea teamed up and tried to do the Mancs. It was a nasty brawl and City and United stuck together, not because they wanted to but because they had to. It was a pain for the Northerners, as they put all the Cockneys on the first train and the rest had to wait all night for the next one. Loads of the lads were fuming that they ended up going home skint and even lost some gear that had been paid for. That was a rarity at the time, Scousers buying something.

melting

As in Luxembourg, I've seen it go off at loads of England matches between different gangs of domestic thugs as various inter-club feuds were settled. Usually it was between the Cockney firms but also City and United, Pompey and Southampton, and Villa, who were always trying to bully smaller mobs. I even saw Burnley and Blackburn have a right go at Italia 90. There was never really a time when they got it all together as well as they had in Luxembourg, which was a pity. It didn't make much difference to us, though, as the shit we got was still the worst. We got it off everyone too, from Arsenal to York and back. They hated us.

Germany was always a good trip, but in Dusseldorf in 1987 I was with the poorest mob England must have ever had. We got battered by the Germans, totally embarrassed. The one good point was the Cockneys walking around as usual before the match acting like they owned the place, then melting after the game as gas and flares filled the air and the likes of Hull tried to save England's reputation. The Germans were the best organised mob I saw in Europe. They were always tooled up and, because of the lenient laws over there, had a good supply of flares and CS gas. This time they didn't show before or during the match, but ambushed us in a park afterwards. Anyone there would have to admit that England got done good and proper, and quite a few should have slung their "These Colours Don't Run" T-shirts in the bin the minute they set foot back on British soil.

On trips like that, when it was every man for himself, I got to know some good lads from the smaller clubs: Danny from Hull, who had a Chelsea and Hull City tattoo; a lad called Garry from Cambridge who was a game fucker and who got jail for the infamous attack on Chelsea in the Eighties that caused the invincible Headhunters some embarrassment; Billy Plumb of Man City, daft but mad; a mob from Stockport, led by a lad called China, who were always having a go; and small but tasty firms from Oldham, Bristol City and Southampton. They were all easy to get on with but could handle themselves if they had to, and between them could cause as much damage as the rest and back their corner when needed against the bigger firms.

By the time the European Championships came around in 1988, only a few of us could be bothered to go and that was either to do the tickets or the T-shirts. Liverpool's lads went in small numbers on the rob, so there was little chance of any major hassle with domestic rivals. As we were so few, it was only the Mancs that would want to fight you every minute of the day; as long as you kept your gob shut and your hands in your own pockets and out of theirs, most of the other lads left you to your own devices.

I followed England for about eight years, up to Italia 90. By then it was becoming difficult to travel away with exclusion orders and so on, but three trips I had will always be fondly remembered: Sweden in 1986, the Euro 88 Championships in Germany and Italia 90.

sweden

The game in Sweden came about through work. Some of the lads had got jobs in a place called Linkoping, which is between Stockholm and Gothenburg, making metal bits for the car firm Saab. It was 1986 and the money was a tenner an hour, so we forged a few papers – as you had to be a time-served sheet metal worker – and God knows how but we were accepted and were on the next boat out of Harwich. I went with a Liverpool fan, Tommo, who had been nicked with me during the sports shop looting a few years earlier. He wasn't so much a real hard case but I have never known anyone with as much balls as he had. I wished I'd left him at home. He caused murder from the minute we got off the boat, and it was no surprise to anyone when we were deported and banned from ever entering Sweden again.

We started work and soon got sussed, as we didn't have a

clue what we were doing. To make matters worse, Saab also made airplanes, so it wasn't a case of "bollocks, it's only a car panel," we were talking big plane skins and people's lives in the hands of a couple of Scallies who didn't know the difference between sheet metal and heavy metal. Luckily we got on well with the lads and they covered for us and gave us all the easy jobs. I used to drive a minibus and pick up all the shift workers, which meant I was in the factory for only half the day, which I spent tidying up and cutting metal to size. Four hundred a week in your back pocket, it was a dream. They also paid for your flat, which was excellent, and gave us a Saab Turbo for transport.

The first real trouble we had was in a club called Stardust. An Australian lad we worked with asked the DJ for some record. The horrible prick thought he was Sweden's answer to Fatboy Slim and blanked our man, so for the next hour we gave him grief and kept requesting loads of crap songs. In the end he got the bouncers to have a word and a scuffle broke out. Swedes are a funny race: they were a fit lot, but all the time I was there I didn't meet a single person who could fight like we do – no rules, headbutts, poking eyes, the full shooting match.

We had been there only a week so were a bit wary, and got tooled up with a couple of pint pots and ashtrays as we left. Sure enough, they were outside waiting for a Queensberry Rules straightener. As if. We battered them all over the street. Tommo put a pot over the biggest one's head and the rest just flapped and tried to do one. I picked a piece of fence pole up and put a few away as Tommo picked off anyone within his reach and we cleared the street in half a minute. Some bird did have a go and bent a golf brolly over my head, which put the lads to shame. There were bodies in the road and one lad jumped through a hamburger van window to get away, but I caught him across the head and that turned out to be our downfall, because

Above: The front page of *Get Into Them*, my "vicious hooligan bible that glorifies soccer riots," as *The Sun* objectively put it.

Above: An inside feature about how fat Leeds fans are. Anyone with half a brain could see that *GIT* was just a pisstake. Sadly it didn't last long.

My relations with the club have not always been strained. My mate Pud (left) and I with Howard Kendal and Everton legend Alex Young (seated right) at a champagne reception at Liverpool's Adelphi Hotel.

By the mid-Nineties the football intelligence officers were much more on the ball. Their files on me – which I have no doubt are inches thick – contain plenty of surveillance shots, including the following:

1. Nicked at Middlesbrough in 2000
2. Villa away, 2001
3. Boro again, 2000
4. Elland Road v Spurs, 1995
5. Iceland, 1995
6. Leeds away, 1994
7. Nicked at Stockport, 1996

TEAM COACH IS TORCHED

Blues' rivals in arson drama

©Press Association

AN ARSON attack has destroyed the luxury Wimbledon football team coach.

The vehicle was bringing the Wimbledon football team to Merseyside for today's crucial game with Everton.

But it was found blazing in the car park of the Lord Daresbury Hotel, near Warrington, at 5am today — just hours after the London club expressed fears of a hostile reception from Blues fans.

The fire — now being investigated by police — began as the Dons' players were sleeping in their rooms just yards away.

It was spotted by staff at the Lord Daresbury.

Extensive damage was caused to the whole front half of the coach, which was empty at the time. Nobody was injured.

By Val Woan

As fire investigators carried out forensic tests today, a police spokesman said: "We are treating it as suspicious."

The duty manager at the hotel told the Echo: "There has been an incident involving the Wimbledon team coach, and the matter is now in the hands of the police."

He said that Wimbledon's owner, Sam Hammam, was dealing with the situation, and by 9am this morning a new coach had arrived to take the team on the 20-mile journey to Liverpool.

In the build-up to today's game, which Everton must win to stay in the Premier League, some Wimbledon players had spoken of their worries about the reception they would get on Merseyside.

Wimbledon defender Warren Bar-

● **Turn to Page Two**

Above: Self-styled soccer hardman Vinnie Jones stirred things up with his comments before our crucial relegation match against Wimbledon in 1994. The result: the torching of Wimbledon's team coach, a plot to slash Vinnie on the pitch - and victory for Everton.

Above: Joe Royle's 'Dogs of War' took us to an FA Cup final. In the semi we clashed on the pitch with Spurs at Elland Road. The Everton lads are on the left.

Ähangendur knattspyrnuliðsins Everton létu ófriðlega á leiknum gegn KR í Laugardalnum og þurfti lögreglan að skakka leikinn á áhorfendapöllunum. Eftir leik hélt gleðskapurinn áfram og var að lokum brugðið á það ráð að veita Evertonmönnum lögreglufylgd úr landi. KR-ingar stóðu sig vel. Everton sigraði, 3–2.   DV-mynd ÞÖK

Above: My arrest in Iceland, as covered by the local version of *The Independent*. Harry Enfield's comic Scousers had nothing on us when we travelled together. I made it back from this one after a few hours in the cells.

Above: Aberdeen away and, though I didn't know it, this would be my last beer for several days as I was banged up in a police cell minutes after this photo was taken. With me are Big Shaun (left) and Fallon.

Above: Queueing for seven hours in the hot sun for an England ticket in Italy in 1990. That's me sitting down on the right. Following the national team was hazardous for Scousers, as everyone hated us.

Above: With the best England mob I've seen outside the Swordfish bar in Düsseldorf at Euro 88. That's me at the front holding a can in the air.

Above: A couple of Everton lads on a jolly in Japan in 2002. Unfortunately the Government decreed that I wasn't allowed to join them. Some made a killing over there selling merchandise.

Above: Anderlecht, pre-season, 2002. I thought I had seen it all, but this one will stay with me forever. Here an Everton mob are held back by riot police before the game as they try to reach hundreds of Belgians further down the road.

Above: The Anderlecht boys arrive and it goes off briefly before the police fire a gas bomb into the middle of our mob.

Above: Marching through the streets of Brussels later on. Just about every 'lad' who has ever followed Everton was there.

Outside Goodison, contemplating my hooligan past. For me it's probably a case of full-time or do time, so I have reluctantly had to call it a day. End of chat.

©Jayne Walsh

the hamburger man was the only independent witness who gave evidence against us.

We got off and went back to the Oz lad's flat, but soon got the knock and were in the cells by the morning. In the cells, now that's a laugh, they were better than our apartments. The one I was in had a leather couch, colour television and a coffee machine. The police were great with us. They told us that a few of the locals had suffered a bit of a bashing and we were the main suspects. We were the only British lads in the town, our gear was covered in blood and they had about twenty witnesses, yet still they didn't charge us. It turned out they wanted to give us a chance to tell our story, and even arranged an ID parade so the busload of witnesses could check us out in case they were mistaken. Now I'm no detective, but as far as I could see we were bang to rights. Due to their naivety, though, I decided I was owning up to nothing. I really thought we were on a winner and then, as is usually the case, "it all went horribly wrong".

Identity parades are a strange set-up at the best of times. If you're a crook or a thug and you're in one, there is a fair chance you have done the crime, as very few of us volunteer to go in them to help the police. The point is, unless you are cool – and I mean ice cool here – the chances are that you will be marked out as nervous while everyone else in the line-up is on a jolly earning a soft twenty quid. I think they should have all crooks in them and not tell you which crime it is for, then the complete line is on edge and sweating, not just the odd one who is sure to get a hand on his shoulder. The one in Linkoping nick took the biscuit.

The police led us into the yard at the back of the jail, put numbers on pieces of card and hung them around our necks. I was eight and Tommo was six. Now we were about the same height and build and both had short dark hair. The door opened and the other eight blokes walked into the yard and got in the line with us: two Turks and half a dozen

Swedes who were all six foot-plus with blond hair. Tommo and I might as well have been in fancy dress. Every single person that had to pick us out, did. In the end, as they were walking down the line looking at us we were going, "Boo!" and pulling faces at them.

Within twenty minutes, we had been charged with "grave assault" and various public order offences, along with carrying weapons. The grave assault, our brief told us, was GBH and was as serious as it could get. We were going to do about three years, with no chance of being sent home to do it in a prison in England. Locked in my plush cell that night watching a Swedish version of *Stars In Your Eyes*, with every contestant mimicking either the bird from Abba or Elton John, I felt rock bottom. I had a job paying me hundreds of pounds a week, was living in luxury, and once again I had blown it. I remember thinking, *if ever I get out of here, that's me finished with fighting and clubs.* They were ruining my life.

Two hours later, we were getting bladdered in the pub! The police had given us bail, we had to pay no bond and we had no restrictions. All we had to do was surrender our passports and appear in court on October 17, three months away. I must say I suddenly began warming to Swedish justice. The next day we went to work and not much was said; there was a bit of an atmosphere as one of the casualties was working in the same factory, but we didn't give a toss, as the money was the same whether they spoke to you or not. We went to see our brief and he said to carry on regardless. We handed our passports over, signed a declaration that we would turn up in court and went on the ale.

The next few weeks were great. We were stars in the town, the word was not to mess with us and we swaggered around like we were Cockneys. The birds were all over us and we didn't have to queue to get into the clubs, as all the doormen were giving us a wide one. We were as happy as monkeys in a banana plantation.

A few weeks after I had been nicked, Everton played Liverpool in the Charity Shield at Wembley. Now I never miss a derby or an Everton game at Wembley, so I had to get home for the match. I asked my brief could he sort it and the police agreed that I could fly home, as we told them I had a family illness and they were the compassionate sort. All I had to do was leave my bankbook with the solicitor, and if I didn't return I lost the four grand in my account. Also they said that Tommo would take the rap, so it was best if I came back on the Monday.

Not a problem. I got my passport from the police, signed my bail papers and was at Wembley for the game on the Saturday, back in Sweden on the Monday, handed my passport in and got my bankbook back. Happy days indeed, as on the Monday morning before my flight back, I went to the post office with twelve quid and a birth certificate and got myself one of those one-year passports which were around in those days. So now I could go home anytime I wanted but with my money as well.

Freedom beckoned, but before leaving Sweden for good, I decided to earn a few more quid and stay for the England game at Stockholm, which was about six weeks away. Tommo later did the same thing to get a passport but decided against the extra stop or the game, and never returned from Blighty. I have seen him only twice since. I'm told he's running some rough-arse pub, which I believe will suit him, as he likes a challenge and a good fight. I also heard he had made a million quid in the early-Nineties construction boom and lost the lot in two years. That I also believe, as he was a good grafter but hopeless with life's vices, horses and women.

I had the time of my life in Sweden, and by the time the match arrived I had sent a good few grand back home. The trouble was that it was too easy, and had I stayed longer I'm sure I would have ended up doing some serious jail. Some of the scams and jobs we were planning were out of our league, but we were out of control and when that is the case you don't think straight and believe you can get away with anything.

There was one job we planned which was a gold factory. We looked around it and thought, *we'll have this away*. The security was a joke and there was thousands of pounds' worth of gold in there. We were going to smoke-bomb the place, gas the guard and take the gear, escaping on a motor-bike one of the lads had robbed. That easy. But an old Cockney boy heard about it, managed to talk some sense into us and we sacked it. Looking back, it was a daft idea, but that summed us up over there; we were above the law, or at least believed we were.

The game was England's first since Maradona had single-handedly knocked us out of the World Cup in Mexico. The support we had was rubbish and only about 1,000 made the trip. There were quite a few lads out though and I met up with a Bristol City boy I knew. We had a good day in Stockholm with no sign of trouble. There was a good young firm of Chelsea who I thought might want a go, since we had cut one of their lads at Kings Cross the year before, but as luck would have it they didn't like him and were sound with me. It was also the first time I'd seen a firm of Leeds at an England away game; they were only kids but acted like they were "the boys" all day.

Before the game, I blagged a press badge and had access to all areas. It was mint. I had lunch in the press lounge and was on a table with the commentator Brian Moore. He asked me which paper I was with and I told him that I was on a blag, as the camera I had was worth about a tenner and I did not really look like the John Motson type. He was sound, laughed about it and we had a good chat about football. His knowledge of Everton was unbelievable, a top bloke in his profession. He gave me all his drinks vouchers and wished me all the best in life. I was sorry when I heard he had died recently before the England game in Munich.

I made my way down to the pitch and sat by all the other press blokes, then went over to take a picture of the team as they lined up for the National Anthem. As the band played, I thought, *fuck this,* gave my camera to a ball boy and got Trevor Steven to budge over as I mumbled "God Save the Queen" with England's finest. I had to laugh at all the fuss when a Man United lad did a similar thing years later as United lined up for a game in Europe, and got loads of publicity. Typical Manc, years behind! The picture is in the book and the faces on the players said it all; they didn't know what to do or say, and just let me get on with it.

When the game kicked off I went and sat on the bench with the subs. Dave Watson had just signed for Everton and he was sound, Tony Cottee was there and also David Seaman, Stuart Robson and a few others I didn't know. At half-time I caned the free bar and came out with about twenty minutes left, totally pissed. As I sat down, Bobby Robson told all the subs to warm up, so I joined in and did a few press-ups as the rest ran up and down. England were losing 1–0 and Bobby snapped and got the security to sling me out. But I was soon back in the bar and when the players came in after the game, Bobby came over and shook hands and had a picture with me. Dave Watson gave me a programme signed by all the squad, which was a nice touch. It is a bit different today, when they all act like superstars.

The bar shut and, as the rest of the squad made their way to the airport, the sixth sub headed into town. There was the odd skirmish with the Swedes but nothing major, which was just as well, as the firm England had was bottom of the range and the little Leeds kiddie mob didn't seem as up for it as earlier, for some reason.

I made my way back to England with the fans and got home safe and sound. About a week later I received a letter and a video from a girl I was seeing over there and I was on the telly. As the Swedish commentator went through the team during the anthem, he announced the players' names and for some reason was a bit stumped when he got to me. He should have asked Brian Moore, as he knew exactly who I was. A few weeks later I got another letter saying that they had tried Tommo and me in our absence and we had got twelve months. This girl said if I went back I could carry on working in the week, be on a curfew at night and do my jail at weekends. I declined. She was fit but not that fit.

euro 88

After doing quite well in the 1986 World Cup, England were one of the favourites for the Euro 88 tournament. I saw the trip as a chance of a good holiday, sure to be more interesting than two weeks in Benidorm. We drew the Irish in Stuttgart, which was sure to go off, the Dutch in Dusseldorf, which had the makings of a war, and a final group match in Frankfurt against Russia, by which time we would be back home either skint or deported. I was correct on all counts.

We flew to Dusseldorf but hadn't done our homework, as Stuttgart was hours away on the train, and by the time we got there we were knackered. It was a couple of days before the match but there were a few hundred English already on the ale in the town square and by the train station, which always seems to be a major draw to football travellers. There were surprisingly loads of Scousers, though I'm ashamed to admit that about half of them, mainly the Liverpool contingent, were supporting the Irish. I don't know what it is with the Kopites but, like Man United, they seem to get on great with the Paddies, whereas when they and the likes of Celtic come to Everton there is trouble. We were always regarded as the Catholic club but religion has never shown itself at

Goodison for me to see, and if you came there singing either IRA or King Billy songs, you would get a slap and that was the end of it. Once we'd had a kip and a shower, we met one of Everton's top lads at the time, Rozzer. He looked after us well at the expense of someone else's credit account. We were well fed and watered until he got nicked for getting a bit greedy in a sports shop and went over the daily card limit. Still, it was good while it lasted.

The night before the game, we were in a bar by our hotel with a few English and Irish fans, good lads, not the IRA-singing bigots who make a pest of themselves after half a Guinness. We were having a laugh, no trouble, and were drinking out of this big glass boot, a yard-of-ale type deal where at a certain point the beer spills over you. We had decided to go to another bar when this moody mob walked in and the atmosphere changed straight away. This big shot who seemed to be the mouthpiece grabbed me and asked who I was with. I told him we were Everton and he said to stick with his little firm and we would be okay. I would have liked to have told him where to go but they were twenty-handed, so the three of us made an excuse and left.

We hadn't even made the next bar before the sound of sirens filled the air. They had not bothered to buy a drink, just battered the Irish lads for nothing. It infuriated me because those Irish lads did not want to know and didn't have a fight in them. Later we were in another bar when mouthpiece and his cronies came in looking for more hassle. This time his hangers-on got the ale in and it turned out they were a mob of Bradford. Big shot didn't sound like he was from Yorkshire and when I had a word with him later he told me he was Forest. I'd had the unfortunate plea-sure of meeting Mr Paul Scarrott, self-appointed England's Number One. I was told many times that he could have a fight but after that introduction I had him down quite simply as a bully, and his sidekicks were just tossers.

We soon got fed up of listening to his tales of bullshit, so did one again and met up with another of Everton's top lads, Bruce, outside a bar near the town square. I had seen him a week before in Alton Towers when he was in a rowing boat with his bird, and I was giving him some grief for being a romantic bastard, when this lad went flying past on roller skates and slashed an English fan's throat. It was horrible; one minute he was standing outside drinking, the next minute he was squirting claret all over the square.

We all chased after this lad. Someone cut him off with a stool and he went down. There was a pack all around him and he got stabbed. We all got off sharpish and the next day someone claimed it was in the papers that he was dead. I doubt it, but if he was, I bet he never went to heaven. We stayed out of the way all night with a few Southampton lads, who still come up to Bruce's whenever they play at Goodison. Even now after a few ales they say I killed the lad. I 100 per cent deny it, of course, just as Bruce denies ever being in that rowing boat.

The day of the match was a bit strange. The whole place filled with Irish supporters, who must have outnumbered the English by three to one, which amazed me. They had most of the ground while we were all put behind one goal. It went off a bit with the stewards but there was a party atmosphere and I could only guess that most of England's mob were saving their money for the Dutch game. We lost 1–0 and there was the odd fight after but nearly every bar was shut down and I think most of the lads headed up north to the delights of Hamburg or went to Amsterdam for a few days.

Later that night we bumped into a massive mob of Germans. It was the first time they had shown since we had been there. They kicked it off but there was only a few of us and we got chased into a hotel. The police came and had to cordon off the street, as the Krauts wanted to kill us. It was a pity they had left it late, as the numbers England had the night before might have been a match for them, though I would not have bet my ever-decreasing wad of deutschmarks on it, as they were a real firm. Sometimes in Germany you meet a mob that will have a go but are a bit like aled up Geordies, but these were proper, had all the gear on and looked tooled up. For once I was not too disappointed to see the police and admit they saved us that night.

We ended up having a top night in the hotel. It was five-star and the manager let us stay for our own safety, bless him. He even gave us a bar tab, which was the norm over there but had been refused to the English, such was the reputation we had abroad. The sports commentators Frank Bough, Barry Davies and Elton Welsby were in there, and old Frank got ripped to bits, as he had just been accused in the papers of being a bit kinky, so he went to bed early. The other two were sound and we had a right laugh. It was that good we even paid our bar tab before we left – all thirty marks of it! I would like to have seen Mr Bough's face in the morning when he got his, which included about fifty ales and a full round of fine Cognac. Still, I bet the BBC paid his tab and I paid my TV licence, so in a roundabout way we were entitled to it.

dusseldorf

It was a week before the Dutch game, so we made our way to Holland and stayed with some lads I had worked with the year before, in a place called Putte, on the Belgium-Holland border. The idea was to keep out of trouble and save a few quid on digs, as Germany was not cheap and we were running low on funds. Well, there was a chance of saving money, but staying out of trouble was a rank outsider in the local bookies. The lads who put us up were top drawer. They were all on a good screw and looked after us top style: Jeff Burke, a Redneck, Tony Birtwell, a Man Utd lad, and a big angry fucker called Oggy from Hull, made sure we were not short of ale and food while they worked in the day. At night they took us out and we never had to put our hands in our pockets the whole time we stayed there.

We had one bad night when we went into Antwerp and caused murder. When we left Holland I asked Burkey if we needed our passports to go across the border to Belgium, and he laughed and said it was like going from Liverpool to Rhyl on your holidays. He knew best so off we went.

The fight started off as a laugh when some dozy woman driver nearly knocked over one of the lads, Stuey. He made a bit of a meal of it, rolled over the car bonnet and pretended to be dead in the road. This bird got out screaming and he got up and started laughing. She went crazy, booting him, scratching at him, spitting and whacking him with her shoes. Either she did not get the joke or had the world's worst case of PMT. He'd have been better off being knocked over by the silly bitch. Right or wrong, he ended up giving her a slap, and within seconds a nearby bar had emptied and a full-scale brawl broke out. We had to get chairs and tables to hold our own as they were fighters, but in the end we managed to back them off into the bar. We should have left it at that, but we put all the windows in for good measure. They were a game little mob though, and the odd one or two kept running out and having a go. In the end I cut one across his chest and that was the end of it. We went back to the train station but the plod got onto us and searched us all for blades. They found nothing, so nicked us for not having passports. They kept us in for the night and one of the lads' bosses had to bring the passports the next day before we could go back to Holland. All of us got a £50 fine as well. Liverpool to Rhyl, my arse.

We still all went to the game, as Dusseldorf was only a

couple of hours away by train, but to be honest we'd had a better laugh in Holland. There hadn't been much trouble in Stuttgart, but the police were taking no chances and the day was a right pain. As soon as you got there, you were stopped and searched, if you moved you were searched, it was way over the top and makes you realise why some people behave like animals when you get herded around and treated like them all day.

Eventually they saw sense and opened a bar for us outside the station called The Swordfish. Before long everyone was there and I reckon that it must have been one of the biggest mobs England have ever had, about 2,000-strong and all boys. I don't know what happened to all the Cockneys and the rest of the South but that mob was ninety per cent northern. That isn't a criticism of the southerners, it was just strange, as they always show and must have been there somewhere. There was never a better chance for North to do South, but the opportunity was missed. I'm sure if the numbers had been the other way around we would have got steamed, judging by my past meetings with the South of Watford masses.

There was a bit of trouble with the Dutch before the game but nothing like we had expected and built ourselves up for. A few barmies were slapped but, as a firm, they once again didn't show. They are overrated in my book. I have watched a lot of football in Holland and domestic violence over there is as good, or bad, as it gets, depending on which side of the law you are. But as a mob following their country, I don't rate them. They always have it with the Germans but have had many chances to take on the English and never seem to bother.

We got into the ground which, like the game earlier, saw the English way outnumbered, and had a battle with a mob of Germans in the forecourt downstairs. They were big blokes and up for it, but their main lad got done in and slung in a pond, so the rest did one before they joined him with the ducks. Apart from that, it was another anti-climax; the police operation combined with a no-show from the Dutch hooligans ensured there was only the football to concentrate on. Someone should have told the players though, as they were rubbish and lost 3–1. We were out of the competition with a game still to play.

By now we were well borassic, so said our goodbyes and got a flight home the next day. When we arrived at Manchester Airport, the press and police were there in numbers, looking for all the thugs that had once again shamed the nation. I had been there over a week and seen about ten fights. I see that many in town on a Saturday night, and could not believe the fuss they were making. My mate had video-recorded the news every day, and all I can say is that the cameramen must have been following England's main psychos and filmed every incident that had gone off and made it into a major film. As far as I was concerned, apart from Scarrott's bully mob, 1,000 Germans wanting to kill us, 2,000 English mobbed up to take on the whole of Europe, the battle in Antwerp and the roller-skate slasher, Euro 88 was nothing!

italia 90

By the time we set off for the World Cup Finals in Italy in 1990, the authorities had well and truly had enough of hooligans and could even dictate where England would play matches to prevent trouble. Being stuck on an island drinking watered-down ale and living in a tent with a load of whoppers on one of the Football Association camp sites did not interest us, so we decided to give the group qualifiers in Sardinia a miss and watch a few games on the mainland, hoping England would get through and meet us there.

Six of us left Manchester Airport on an Air Italia flight to Milan, and had a right result from the off. At the airport I was a bit wary of being turned back, as I had only just done my short spell in Brixton for the Arsenal sketch. There were loads of lads in the departure lounge but they were all on the British Airways flight. Our top tour operator, Jacko, had got us tickets for £160 return, a ton cheaper than the other flight. We got on our plane with no grief, while all the other England fans had to put up with the hassle that was the norm when travelling to support your country. Only at a football match, by the way.

The flight had a free bar and we were well-oiled by the time we landed. One of the lads, Hodge, had forgotten to bring his mum and by the time we reached passport control had managed to lose his valuables, so we all had to wait in a lounge while the cleaners searched the plane for his pass-port and wallet. As we were waiting, the BA flight landed and the England contingent came through. They were look-ing miserable and were fewer than at the departure lounge. I went for a piss and one of them told me that about ten had been turned away at Manchester, the flight was dry and they were to be put on a coach straight to the ferry to Sardinia. The words cattle and herded sprang to mind.

When the cleaners brought Hodge the bad news that there was no sign of his passport and money, he sobered up and suddenly found them in his bag, so off we set. The Italians wanted us to join the other England fans on the cattle express to Sardinia, but tour agent Jacko, with his limited knowledge of the Italian language – he had watched Liverpool over there a few times – managed to convince the sweaty loser on immigration that we were over for a holiday and, as we had reservations in the seaside resort of Savona, it seemed plausible. The lads with me were actually not thugs and were after a bit of a football holiday with no hassle. How I was invited I don't know, in fact wasn't, I invited myself, and think that they thought, or hoped, that I would have been turned back at the airport. I was not, so they had the pleasure of my company for two weeks, if I lasted that long. Judging by my performances on past foreign excursions, hopes were not high.

As it was, for once everything went to plan, well nearly, and we had a great two weeks virtually trouble-free. We watched a few games, had a good laugh on the beach in the day and drank plenty at night with no lumber. At one stage I was actually enjoying being a normal football fan. Savona was a busy little seaside resort, and had the advantage of being central to four of the Italian World Cup venues: Milan, Turin, Sampdoria and Bologna. We went to the Germany v Colombia game in Milan, got some tickets from an Everton tout called Barto, and had a good day out. The San Siro stadium had just been built for AC and Inter to share, and was like nothing we had to offer back home; it made the notion of us sharing with Liverpool seem quite a good idea, when I was pissed in the hot Italian sun. We were going to stop the night but, as the Germans went on the rampage and all the bars got closed, we headed back to our seaside base. Six of us were no match for the hundreds of German thugs, well, not sober anyway.

A couple of days later we went to Turin to watch Scotland play Brazil and, after a few rows early on in the day with the anti-English brigade, got in with a sound group of Jocks. They sorted us out with tickets and we had a ball. One of the Jocks had brought his little brother with him; he was only seven and was dressed up in a kilt and all the other tartan cack. We took him everywhere and the locals loved him. As shop and bar owners had their pictures taken with him, we were having the places off and made a good day's profit from Wee Willie Wallace's presence.

As usual the Jocks got beat due to a goal-keeping error and they were out, which was a pity, as it was a good earner with them in town. We still did okay out of them, as they had foolishly bought tickets for the second stage and we got loads for the next game in Turin, which was now Argentina versus Brazil, not Scotland on the cheap. The money we made on them paid for our tickets, ale and hotel for a few days, so although it was a shame to see them go out, as a financial angle to proceedings Jim Leighton was our hero.

We had watched the England games in a bar in Savona and the locals had been pretty kind to us. One bar owner even put a buffet on for us for one game, such was his appreciation of the amount of ale we drank in the day. England qualified, just, so we decided to stay in Savona, go to Ireland v Romania in Sampdoria, have another day on the beach, then travel to Bologna for the England v Belgium game.

The Irish were very much like the Jocks and came covered from head to toe in green and white. We were having off souvenir stalls and then selling the clobber to the Paddies cheap. They would buy your snot if there was enough green in it, so once again we had a free day out. We had a laugh at the match. Like all the other games we went to, all the bars were open and the police presence was nil, leaving us to get bladdered at very little expense. We had tickets right behind the dugout and John Aldridge came off injured. He had scored against us in the Cup final the year before, so wasn't on my Christmas card list. As he walked past the fence in front of us, I shouted, "Aldo." He came over and, in his best Scouse accent shouted, "All right, lads?" His face was a picture when I replied, "I hope your leg's bust, you Red twat." Ireland won on penalties and the place went crazy after the match. The Paddies were all on two-day trips, as they must have thought they were going out, so loads of them put all their lire behind the bar for free ale. They were dead sound, apart from Aldo, and we had a good drink off them.

We went back to Savona for our last night and watched Italy win, I think against Yugoslavia. As was the trend over there after the game, they filled the streets with flags, set off fireworks and had a party. We had been up early so, after a few beers to be hospitable, we did one back to our hotel. The noise was dreadful as car horns were hooted into the early hours; Christ knows what it would have been like if they had won the World Cup. After a few sleepless hours, I was gagging for a drink, so threw on Hodge's England shirt and went back down to the hotel bar, only to find it was shut. I wandered up the street and walked into a bar full of Italians and asked for a big bottle of Coke. The place stopped dead; all you could hear was the television in the corner of the bar. It was eerie. All holiday everyone had been great with us but suddenly the place had turned moody. I knew we had skipped a few bar bills over the two weeks and robbed the odd bottle of wine but I was sure we hadn't upset this bar owner, so didn't know what he was ranting and raving about until I looked at the telly.

The thugs had landed. England fans were on the news dismantling Rimini and pictures of battered victims, smashed up bars and shops were being flashed across the screen. By the time I reached the door I had lost my thirst for a drink, as several just missed my head, and I had to run for my life. I knew my way to the hotel backwards after two weeks, so had easily escaped by the time the Italian hit squad had started their mopeds. I can honestly say I have never been so scared in my life, though. I got back to the room and nearly smacked Hodge when he started moaning that I hadn't brought him a drink back and complained that there was ale spilt on his England shirt. The next morning we were up and out early and the others could not understand my keenness to do one. No explanation was needed though, as I was as white as a ghost. My tan was still in that bar.

We got to Bologna and were glad this was the only England game we had decided to watch. You could not get a drink for love nor money and the atmosphere in the city stank. Okay, the English had gone for it in Rimini but the police were a disgrace. You got a baton over your head for stepping off the pavement. Anyone that looked a bit like a lad was escorted to a park where hundreds were queuing for match tickets. We had witnessed this for the Brazil game, but in Turin the tickets were on sale in plush hotels and you could get a drink and queue in comfort. Here there were two portable toilets and the tickets were on sale from an old caravan.

We managed to escape from the park – you could not just leave, you literally had to escape – and got tickets for a bit over the odds from an Italian tout. There was no chance of a beer, so I went in the ground two hours early for the first time in my life. The tickets were in the Belgian section but they didn't have many there, while we had a good 200 in the corner, so if it was to go off we would easily hold our own.

It was one of those matches you can remember little about except the goal. We had a bit of a scuffle at full-time as the gates were opened and a few Belgian hooligans came into the end but we scattered them down the seats. It was the first and last trouble inside a ground all tournament and of course had to involve the English, but the Belgians started it. Nobody cared about that and we got all the bad press again. The goal, when it came, was a belter. Gazza took a free kick and Platt scored with a top volley over his shoulder, which made him an overnight superstar and millions of pounds. He was an average player but that's all you need, one lucky break on the world stage and you're set for life. We steamed the Belgians again when they tried to have a go after the goal, but they were out of their league. The final whistle went with England dancing on the seats singing, "Let's all have a disco." I don't know where that one came from but have to admit I had a little bop myself just to wind the Belgians up. After the game was worse than before, and we were baton-charged all the way to the station.

We flew home the next day, having had a great holiday. Thirteen days of sun and fun as we watched the world's greatest football showpiece, and twenty-four hours of police brutality as we made the mistake of thinking the English would be treated the same as all the other fans visiting Italy.

it's coming home

One good thing about Euro 96 was that, being host nation, we didn't have to qualify. The other good thing was that we drew the Jocks and the Dutch. So the recipe for violence was there and all we needed was the ingredients. Although I was unsure about the Dutch showing, I was certain that the Jocks would not let us down. However after all the hype and scum paper reports that Euro 96 was going to be a bloodbath, off the pitch it was more like a scratched finger.

The marketing for the tournament was brilliant and Baddiel and Skinner's song perfect for the audience that the FA wanted for the games involving England. With a chance to stage a World Cup tournament a few years later, a massive police operation was set up and was a major success. I went to about ten games all over the country during the tournament, and saw less violence than I see in town on a Tuesday in April.

The first game I went to was Germany v Czechoslovakia at Old Trafford. There was supposed to be a mass turnout of the Germans but I saw about thirty skins all day and hooligan-wise it was a waste of time. It was a top earner though, as I met a tour rep from Czechoslovakia who had organised a trip but found that forty of his party were refused entry, as they had the wrong visas or papers. He was left with their tickets and I bought twenty-five for their next game against Italy at Anfield from him at a tenner each. Face value was £25 and I got £50 each on them from members of the Italian community, who are always a bit flush. A grand profit in a day, one of them a week and you could come off the dole!

I went down to Wembley for the Scotland game and that was on top. The stories of how England had a 2,000-strong mob and how the Jocks fronted them at Trafalgar Square have been told 100 times over and bore me. Yes, England had a massive mob, yes the Jocks had a pop, what do you expect? It was nothing major and the main violence I saw involved Cockneys battering Jocks in kilts who were out for a good day, and a few fights between different England mobs. For the record, my observations were that Boro had the best northern firm out that day and Tottenham were the best Cockney mob. Aberdeen were by far the tastiest Jock mob.

Quite a few of our lads went to the semi-final against the Germans and were had off by Carlisle, led by the charismatic Paul Dodd, who had replaced Mr Scarrott as "England's Number One". Number one blagger in my book. I never went, but by all accounts they were out of order and Paul admitted it when he used to come down to Everton during a brief spell when he did a bit of business down there. It also went off after when England had it with the police. As I said, I was not there and with my surname not being Brimson, I have no intention of trying to make money telling other people's stories.

With England losing the semi on penalties, the final was a non-event; apart from the money earned with the tickets it was a waste of time. In my eyes the whole tournament was marketed for the rich and their families; the real supporters were either priced out of it or banned from attending. It was a wise move though. Had the people I saw in the bars and pubs been able to attend, the chances of us ever staging a major football tournament would be the same as England's chances of ever winning one. Nil.

homeless

The sad demise of Wembley meant that, for the foreseeable future, England would have to play their home games at club grounds all over the country. For the northern fans in particular it was a dream, as many would get the chance to watch the national side in their backyard and on the cheap. For the authorities and the police, however, it was a nightmare, as it meant that the years of easy policing in the capital were over and for once they would have to earn their money. It did not need the flatcaps working for the hooligan intelligence unit in South London to suss out that whenever England played at a club ground, all the town's thugs would turn out to have a pop at the invading hordes.

The first game I went to while England were homeless was the World Cup qualifier against Finland at Anfield. It was the biggest police operation I have ever seen in the city and, although reasonably successful, was excessive and must have cost hundreds of thousands. I was in Lime Street waiting for a mate to drop off some tickets and was soon pulled by the Liverpool bizzies and searched. It was nine o'clock in the morning. By the time I had been sorted out with my tickets and tasted my first pint, I had been stopped and searched seven times. It was one major pain in the backside, and was set up to prevent people from having the time to even talk about football violence, never mind participate in any.

It made me realise how well known I was when two bizzies pulled me and introduced themselves as Derby County football intelligence officers. One said, "How many of your lads are out today Andy, are you teaming up with Liverpool?" They were so bad that I was embarrassed for them. There were words I would use to describe these whoppers and they rhymed with milly bunts. Intelligent they were not. Throughout the day I was also pulled by bizzies from Leeds, Manchester, Wigan and Leicester, as well as the locals, and in the end they gave me a sheet showing how many times I had been searched and photographed under some new law. It was like being in a police state. I suppose it worked though, as there was no way I would risk a kick-off when they had more pictures of me than my dear old mum possesses.

I went back to Lime Street to watch Man United come in, as they had told me they were firmed up, and firmed up they were. The bizzies closed the station down and escorted them out of the back doors. They were the only mob that day who had such VIP treatment. They were about 250-strong and before the game marched around Anfield ready to take on all comers. There were none.

The game was a major putdown for both Everton and Liverpool's mobs. We had about fifty in town who sat off and never went to the game. At night, when I met up with them, they'd had a bit of a torrid time and had been split up and had it with a large joint Midlands firm and later on with a mob of combined Mansfield and Villa. At least Everton had a mob though, as Liverpool had less than twenty out and had to watch Man United take the piss on their own patch all day singing, "Garry Neville is a Manc, he hates Scousers." They were all in the Main Stand and left at half-time. I walked back to town with a mob of Reds and, although small in numbers, they were up for it if they found the Mancs. They didn't look too hard though and I was not bothered in the slightest when nothing happened. It was a crap turnout.

Had they played England games at club grounds years ago, the Scousers United would have caused some damage. Neither Everton nor Liverpool are arsed about the national team, but they should have turned out in force to stop wannabe firms wandering around the city giving it the big one.

I also went to the final qualifier at Old Trafford, when Greece were the visitors. That was a top earner, as the World Cup bandwagon was out of control after the win in Munich and tickets were changing hands the week before for silly money. I had plenty and it was the best payday of the season for all the touts. I had to pick up a couple of tickets from a main Man United lad and he phoned to say which boozer they were in. I walked to meet him with my mate, who was a Kopite. As we approached the pub, a Manc bizzie recognized me and said, "Nicholls, if you're daft enough to go in there, we can't guarantee your safety." I told him I would be okay and in we went. It was full to the rafters of all the main United mob: they had the Cockney Reds with them, the Hibs contingent and all the other hangers-on. It was another mob they had rustled up that would have been untouchable on the day. My Kopite mate went as white as a ghost when Tony shouted across the bar, "All right, you Scouse bastards," before handing me the tickets and getting the ale in. Again they were sound and I knew I would be safe with these lads, as I was a guest of the cream of their mob. There were police outside on balconies taking pictures of us chatting and their heads must have been done in wondering what was going on.

Before long a spotter came in and the pub emptied. Stoke were in a boozer up the road and Man United marched down and kicked it off, resulting in a few getting nicked, including my contact.

It was nothing major and but for the non-existent but heavily hyped threat of hooliganism at the forthcoming World Cup in Japan, it was a charge that would have resulted in a decent fine on any other day.

The lad got three fucking years for his troubles.

I went up to the game and it was like being on a different planet. It was a carnival atmosphere and a million miles away from the city centre, which was moody to the extreme. It was a dream game for the Mancs, with their favourite son Beckham getting the injury time goal to send England to the World Cup Finals.

We spent the night in town with a mob of about ten Everton as a guest of another top United lad, Sam. It was a great night and, although I am no fan of the national team, I was made up for those who were. To me England nowadays are boring and I only go for the crack, but that day was special for thousands, and was an excuse for a good drink. I have been only once since and that was also to Old Trafford to see the Sweden game. It was a nightmare for the touts and loads lost good money. On and off the pitch the Greece game was strictly a one-off.

I heard it was a bit on top when Newcastle staged the game against Albania, with Boro fronting the show, but games at Villa, Derby and even Elland Road have passed off with relatively little trouble. You have to give the bizzies credit, as they do seem to have got it boxed off, and although it is a pain in the arse for the lads, all the stop-and-search stuff has proved to be a deterrent.

The World Cup in Japan came and went and was trouble-free. How many hooligans have got that sort of money to spend getting over to those games? Not many. I certainly wasn't there: I am banned and on the list with hundreds of others; it's no big deal to me. My days of sleeping on trains and being herded around like cattle have long gone too, but at the time it was the done thing, and I have had some good times and made some good friends watching England abroad.

I cringe now when I see the news footage of the Stone Island brigade from Wolves and Villa running the show abroad. Talk about missing the boat. These amateurs would have been slung overboard by the likes of West Ham or United during the Eighties, when you needed more than a £600 coat and a baseball cap to call yourself an England football hooligan. Being Everton I'm not sure how I made it watching England in the Eighties, as it was so on top for us, but I did and loved it large. Rule Britannia!

14 GOING DOWN?

HAD THIS CHAPTER been called "Wimbledon", there is a fair chance that half of the readers would have skipped it. Wimbledon have no lads, it's a boring place to go to and does not deserve a mention in any book other than one on lawn tennis. Most football purists hate them, as the way they booted their merry way to the then-First Division and then bullied their way to respectability in top-flight English football was frowned upon by many. Personally I have liked them ever since they beat Liverpool in the FA Cup at Wembley in 1988.

The reason I mention them now is through no fault of their fans though; it is all down to new Hollywood "star" Vincent Jones. Vinnie, as he is better known, was partly responsible for what could have ended up the most horrific incident involving players and fans our country has ever known.

On 29 April 1994, Everton Football Club were in the mire. Under the management of Mike Walker, we were in the bottom three and needed to win our last game of the season at Goodison, against Wimbledon, to avoid being relegated for the first time since 1953. It may not sound a big deal to many fans but Everton have been in the top flight longer than any other club and it is a record we don't ever want to lose. The week before, we had played Leeds away and lost 3–0. All the other results went against us and for the first time since I had followed Everton, we looked like we were going down, much to the delight of our Red rivals, who by now were pretty crap themselves and so were loving it large about our impending fate.

The Leeds game was a bad day all around. We lost and I

had four fights, losing two of them, including being battered by Liverpool fans in Church Street (see Chapter Five). We had a good firm at Leeds and ran them outside the ground before the match. Right on full-time we came straight out and a few of us got in with their mob following the Everton escort to town. Griff and all his lads were there and one said to me, "I hope these robbing bastards go down." I smiled and nutted him. The few of us were then legged up the road back towards our mob. It was worth it.

Back at the station, Leeds had a feeble mob. The lad I had butted was there with what looked like a big tomato on his eye. We had about forty who reached the station before the bizzies and we clashed with Leeds as soon as we came to the forecourt outside. They had only about twenty good lads in their mob but they were game and it was on top until our lot arrived and burst out of the escort. Leeds were overrated as a football firm. They were good wreckers but in my book never in the same league as Man United, Chelsea and West Ham once the casual era took over. In the days of donkey jackets and hobnail boots they were a nasty shower but once all the Pringle and Fila reached Yorkshire in the mid-Eighties they went downhill. I honestly believe it was because very few of the fat bastards could fit into any of the trendy gear. Instead their mob was full of pricks from all over Yorkshire who had latched onto the fashion yob scene.

Take the year they made it back into the top flight. They won promotion at Bournemouth and destroyed the place, making national news smashing beach huts and chasing kids on donkeys. They came to our place first game the next season and hid behind the bizzies before getting slightly braver after, when they did get out of the escort before meeting a massive Everton mob that steamed them back up Goodison Road. I was in the front with Mark Duvall and with Leeds coming towards us, a good 150. It was great, you could see they were nervous and more at home jumping on

sandcastles at the seaside than being slashed down a
dogshit-filled alley in the surroundings of Goodison. They
slowed down and we bounced into them. No punches were
thrown; they were off. Welcome back to the big time. A
brick hit Mark on the head and a few weeks later, when he
died, I really believe that had something to do with it, but
his brother still went down and took the full rap for it when
he hit him on the very same spot the brick had, killing him.

torched

So after the Leeds defeat we were, as I said, in deep trouble. Even if we beat Wimbledon, we would still go down if
the other results went against us. That season the old Park
End had been demolished, so we had a three-sided ground
and the place was like a morgue. All week was like waiting
to have your balls chopped off; hopes were not high that we
would stay up. We could not even sell all the tickets and
those unsold were going to be on sale on match day, which
is unbelievable. Even the lads in the mob weren't that bothered about going, as Wimbledon were probably the worst
London firm and there would be nobody to take out our
grief on.

Enter Vinnie.

On the Thursday night, Sky Television conducted an
interview featuring all the relegation teams and Vinnie was,
as usual, shouting his gob off and earning a few quid doing
what he does best, acting hard. They showed footage of
when the two Manchester teams had been relegated and the
subsequent trouble on the pitch. Asked if he was worried at
the prospect of sending Everton down on their own ground,
Jones made a bad error, and one that I believe kept Everton
up. Forget Hans Segars being "bribed" or Barry Horne's
wonder goal: the minute Vinnie said something like, "Nah,

it's easy up there, it's not as if were going to West Ham or somewhere nasty," Everton were safe.

All the next day, people were talking about the comments. The local papers made a big thing of it and there was a rallying cry to get behind the team. Most fans did – but we had our own way to deal with the Dons, and in particular Mr Jones, superstar, hard man, and gobshite. If Everton were going down there would be a massive pitch invasion, that was a cert. But something far more sinister was also planned. From I don't know where, it was decided that several smackheads would be given a good wage if, in the melee that was sure to follow, Vinnie was slashed. This might sound a bit far-fetched but we are talking people here who would rob the pension money from their granny's purse or mug an old man for £1 to feed their disgusting habit. So with a few thousand people around them, what was the risk of getting done for giving Vinnie a few stripes on his back as he was mobbed leaving the pitch? Word soon spread. Loads eventually knew about it and I can't believe it never got to the papers. But it was planned. I'm honestly glad we won and it never happened but, make no mistake, if we had been losing with a few minutes to go, it would have happened.

On the day of the game I was up early, and it seemed like a cup final. Town was bouncing and even Liverpool fans making their way to Villa wished us all the best. Lying bastards. The first lads I saw were pissing themselves and asked me had I heard the news. I thought it was out about the slash plot but was made up to read that the Wimbledon team coach had been torched outside their hotel and all their kit and boots were a bit singed. Nice and easy up at Everton, aye Vinnie? It was still six hours to kick-off.

It turned out that a car full of lads had been to a rave in Burnley and on their way back had passed the Daresbury Hotel, near Warrington. They had noticed the coach in the car park, continued the journey home, made a couple of petrol bombs, driven back and torched the bus. The Wimbledon players had been woken during the blaze and watched in horror as the bus blew up yards from their bedrooms.

the great escape

We made our way to the ground and were confident that if the players showed the same commitment as the arsonists, Everton would be safe. The ground was chocker, thanks again to Vinnie, and the only tickets left were for the 1,000 seats in the Upper Bullens Road Stand reserved for the travelling Wimbledon fans. We were getting chased around by bizzies on horses and it was getting nasty as soon as it was common knowledge that the thousands outside had no chance of getting in.

The police cocked up. Instead of letting Wimbledon fans pay into the section allocated for them, they made them queue for tickets in the old box office outside the Paddock. We were soon in with the whoppers, who were by now scared shitless. We simply took scarves and hats off them and joined the queue. Every so often we would be chased off by a bizzie that recognised us but most of them and the stewards were sound and turned a blind eye. They knew how big a game it was for Everton, plus it would be a lot easier to police a few hundred Wimbledon back to their buses than control us lot outside if things went wrong.

Before long we had bought about fifty tickets, and our little firm were all in the ground as the two teams took to the pitch. There were thousands outside and people in the trees in Stanley Park watching through the gap that was once the Park End. One mob broke in and put yellow hard-hats on and watched from the building site of the new stand without once being asked who they were.

As the Everton team was announced over the tannoy, the ground erupted. It came to the Wimbledon team: total silence until it reached Jones. Then the place went mental. He no longer looked like the hard man that had terrorised Steve McMahon in the '88 Cup final or who would smash people's heads in in *Lock, Stock and Two Smoking Barrels*. The few Wimbledon fans that were in the ground were told to sit down and shut up. There was not a single lad amongst them and nobody would get hurt if they did as they were told, not off the pitch anyway. For one individual on the pitch, that did not apply. I'm afraid Vinnie's fate was in the hands of the Everton players.

The game kicked off and after a few minutes Anders Limpar as good as caught the ball in our box and the referee had no option but to give Wimbledon a penalty. If there had been any doubt at all, I am sure the ref would have bottled it, but there wasn't, he didn't, and neither did Dean Holdsworth, who managed to just beat Southall and put Wimbledon one up. Half of the Cockneys clapped; the rest went whiter than white as we stared at them. Many got up and left. It was eight minutes into the game and they had seen enough. This was not about just football: relegation for Everton was a step closer and these fans had the sense to realise it was not the place to be when the inevitable happened.

A few minutes later, it got worse. A cross into the box caused chaos and Garry Ablett sliced the ball into the Gwladys Street End goal. It is hard to explain how you felt; apart from a close friend's death, it does not get any worse, and grown men had tears of despair and anger in their eyes. A couple of Wimbledon foolishly cheered and were set upon. It was turning nasty and it was only sixteen minutes past three. Things were not looking good for the Blues, but unbeknown to him they were looking a lot worse for Vinnie Jones. Another few Wimbledon asked to leave and I decided to go out with them. I had seen enough and wanted no part of what was to follow an hour later.

As I got outside, there were hundreds milling about. One lad had fifty people trying to listen to his pocket-sized Sony Walkman. I remember him shouting, "Bastards," and I thought that Wimbledon had scored again, but the reporter had gone to Villa Park and announced that Liverpool fans were doing a massive conga, having heard our score. As I got by the corner of the Bullens Road, a massive roar went up; we must have scored, but radiohead said Limpar had only won a penalty. As one we pushed the gates and were all in the lower section in time to see Graham Stuart put us back in the game with what turned out to be a ridiculous penalty award.

Half time, 2–1 down and, as it stood, relegated.

The second half got under way and soon the ball came into our section for a Wimbledon throw in. Up he came, chest out, "Give us the facking ball back."

Vinnie, you will never know how lucky you were. He stood at the touchline with stewards all around him, as he got the worst, vilest abuse I have ever witnessed at Everton. He was covered in spit from women and kids, not just the lads. The man was hated. Still, as the ball was thrown around the crowd to annoy Jones, people reminded the dickheads doing it that it was Everton's time they were wasting and one of the stewards, a mate of mine's brother called Garry, shouted for the ball to be passed to him.

He will go down in legend for what he did next. As Vinnie said, "Cheers," and held his hands out, Garry slung the ball into his knackers. It was worth millions, as from that moment there was no way we could lose. Jones was shocked, the other stewards laughed and within minutes Barry Horne hit a thirty-yarder that flew in and we were level. The pitch was invaded and although I was made up, I prayed nobody did anything daft, as we could win this game without Jones getting cut up.

Everton battered them after that but still needed another goal, as Blackburn, who were at the top, could not score against our closest rivals Ipswich. No surprise there, as Kenny Dalglish was manager and would have joined in the conga with his former fans for sure. Sheffield United were drawing at Chelsea so, although we didn't know it at the time, we were still down as the police tried to clear the pitch.

With minutes left, prayers were answered. Stuart got his second and our third to win us the game and ensure safety. A lot has been said about the goal and the so-called keeper's actions in trying to save it. Maybe he was bribed; I don't care. All I will say is that in that atmosphere I would have let one in for ten pence, as it was evil.

Word came that Sheffield had lost and, with seconds left, quite a few Wimbledon players were marking empty spaces near the dugout. To his credit Jones never hid and I was glad he came to no harm, as I admire him for achieving so much with so limited talent. As the whistle blew, the place virtually blew up and we were all on in seconds. John Fashanu must have got word something was about to go as he was seen on *Match Of The Day* screaming at his teammates to get off the pitch pronto. They all made it and we celebrated as if we had won the League, FA Cup and Champions League all at the same time, which is sad really for a club as big as Everton. Celebrating staying up, sad indeed.

That night in town was great. We took it over. The Reds came back from Villa gutted and we were all in Yates's, their boozer, singing "The Great Escape". They had planned to carry a coffin draped in blue around the city that night. In their dreams. It went off with the police in Mathew Street as we were just steaming into bars, we were out of control and at one stage we chased them back to their vans. Peter Mac was nicked and the car was attacked with bottles as the lads freed him, leaving the bizzies to drive off with the doors wide open.

15 DOGS OF WAR

big joe

The 1994/1995 season got off to a terrible start. Mike Walker was found out as a one-season wonder fit only for the likes of Norwich, not up to the pressures of managing one of the "Big Five" (soon to be one of the bottom five on a regular basis). He got the bullet as we went into December's derby with Liverpool. We were bottom of the League with just one win to our name. Joe Royle was given the job of saving us from relegation but things were looking so bad they might as well have given it to his distant cousin Jim Royle!

Big Joe got shot of Walker's signings – the likes of Vinny Samways were not going to get you out of the kind of mess we were in – and in came Ebbrell, Horne and Parkinson, who made up the midfield trio soon to be nicknamed "The Dogs Of War". We immediately beat Liverpool 2–0, with our midfield accused of kicking even a crisp bag that blew across the pitch. Duncan Ferguson scored in the first half and, with a minute to go, Paul Rideout got a second. It sparked a mini pitch invasion that saw me arrested for the seventeenth time. We won another couple of games and by the time the third-round FA Cup draw was made, things were looking a lot better, with Big Joe securing hero worship, for the time being anyway. I have never known a Cup run like it. It went off in every round right up to the final, and was actually responsible for the rebirth of Everton's hooligan firm.

lunatic fringe

We drew Derby County at home in round three. Derby have never impressed me. They are a small-time club famous for a muddy pitch and Brian Clough in the Seventies and, well, nothing else really. It had always been one of our best away games years ago, and we used to take the piss whenever we went there, so I was a bit surprised when one of the lads said he'd heard they were bringing a firm to Everton. But then the third round of the Cup is always a big day out, when even the least likely clubs should be able to muster up some kind of mob. At the time Everton had trouble getting a mob up unless one of the proper crews like Man Utd or Boro were in town, so very little interest was shown towards the so-called Derby Lunatic Fringe. They were certainly lunatics, thinking anyone gave two bob for them, so I suppose the name was fitting.

In fairness, they did bring a firm of sorts. Just before kick-off, I had finished doing a few tickets with a couple of Liverpool's touts when a dozen lads kitted out in the hooligan gear came down towards the main stand. Up they bounced, Stone Island coats making them seasoned campaigners in the world of football violence. Even outnumbered by three to one, the four of us stood, laughed and then lamped these arseholes back up the road.

I caught one lad plum on the button, and a few weeks later he met a mate of mine at some club and owned up to having made pricks of themselves. At least he deserves some credit for being honest. We won 1–0 and there was a bit of a skirmish after the game, nothing serious, but I can remember a big black Derby thug standing in the road giving it the big one, not knowing a little scally had set fire to his precious Stone Island jacket. Out of the Cup and your best coat ruined, bad day at the office.

back to the seventies

In the next round we drew Bristol City away. They had a bit of a reputation and had been having a ding-dong with Millwall for a few years, so they must have had some sort of a mob. I just hoped they didn't have a daft name like Derby. I had seen them in action once. I was working in Bristol and took a train to London to watch Everton, who were at Luton. On Temple Meads station, I noticed a good-sized mob but thought nothing of it and got aboard. I went down the carriage and was soon surrounded by young casuals asking where I was from and where I was going. They turned out to be all right. They steamed off the train at Reading and by all accounts smashed the place up. On the way home loads got back on who had been nicked, and told me their manager Terry Cooper had jacked in due to the amount of abuse he got when he tried to calm them down while they were wrecking the ground. They had also had a pop at Liverpool more recently, and a mob had gone into the King Harry pub looking for it, so we put the word out that we were coming down and had no trouble filling a coach, mainly with all the old boys who came out of retirement due to "Cup fever".

I had not long finished a spell working there again, so knew the city pretty well and also knew a few boozers they hung out in, mainly the Horn and Trumpet and the Pump House. Not being shy types, that was where we headed. There were no Bristol in sight. We had searched the city high and low and spent most of the day in the pub they were known to drink in. I began to get some stick, as a few of the lads even doubted that they had a firm, so we set off and walked up to the ground knowing things could only get better. And get better it did.

We had fight after fight from about half two till we

finally left at gone eight. We marched up to the ground and straight into a small mob by their end. They had a bit of a go but said that their main mob would be out after the game. I got talking to a few and they had been to Liverpool and didn't rate them but had heard we were the top firm in the city and reckoned that they were up for it. They couldn't believe that we had been in their pub all day and were well pissed off that we had taken liberties with a fifty-strong mob, albeit a mob with the average age of about thirty-five.

We won 1–0 with a goal in the last minute, when we should have lost 4–0. We were rubbish but they couldn't score, we did, and we were in the next round. Our name was on the Cup, someone said, but I think he was on drugs. When the goal went in, there was, as is the norm with Everton in the Cup, a massive pitch invasion, and a few of them came on as well. There was a fight on the pitch and a few Bristol jumped into our end. At the final whistle we piled out and went right into them across a car park. From that moment, we fought all the way to the coach park and another mile after that before the plod got sick of it and started nicking everyone. It was like a re-run of the Seventies, out of control, horses, dogs, vans, sirens blaring. Bristol were whacking everyone while we were just trying for their boys but in the end every man and his dog was at it, so anybody was fair game. They had blokes in their fifties getting out of cars to have a go and loads of old Scousers were ready to join in. At one stage the police lost control and it was a miracle how nobody was killed. "Fuckin' mental," shouted one of the Bristol. He was not wrong.

The police managed to get us back on the bus and we set off to the nick to wait for the lads that had been lifted. We parked up and went into a boozer which had the remains of their mob in. It was just one of those days. A few of them disappeared but we had already done the main lot, so the brave ones that stayed got a walkover. They could not believe we were still there. They were good lads who had given a good account of themselves but were honest enough to admit they had come second. The lads who'd been nicked were all bailed and we set off home at nine o'clock. What a day.

five-nil, respect nil

The draw was again kind, and even those not snorting the Devil's dandruff began to think it might be our year. With Man Utd and Newcastle left in the hat, to pull Norwich City at home was a right result. I have no doubt that there must be a few blokes in towns like Norwich and Ipswich who can have a go, but I don't think any of the big firms have ever had any respect for these two-bob clubs or any "hooligan" who believes that following them will gain him respect. Going to games at places like that was always a doddle. You would walk around as if you owned the place with little fear of comebacks from the local lads.

Oddly enough, we used to find that Cockneys tried to pull the same stunt *wherever* they went. They acted like they owned the place everywhere, not just in hick, outback villages. Many a time have they regretted walking up Scotty Road thinking they were in Brighton or Cambridge, but they never changed and would do the same thing the very next year. You have to hand it to them, they do believe they are the cream supreme.

We had been to Norwich once for a mid-week League Cup match, something to do on a Wednesday, and won 5–1. A few of them came in the seats we were in and I got a slap off one of them. We just went right through them: nil respect, twenty-odd of them running over the seats from six of us. The best they could do was the verbals. One fatty shouted, "I hope your car breaks down on the way home, you Scouse bastard," and his mate chipped in with, "I hope Liverpool knock you out in the next round." They should have had a £10 double because both came true.

To be fair to them, on the day of the Hillsborough Disaster we played Norwich in the other semi-final and they had a boss mob, many dressed in Davy Crockett hats on a boiling hot day. A good 200 of them had it with about fifty Everton before the game. They did well but it was a one-off game that the whole town had come out of the woodwork for and we doubted we would ever see them again.

So what happens? Norwich only go and bring a firm to Everton. The cheek and the nerve of it! It was a bad firm but still a firm of about thirty lads, all young and with the usual trademark clobber which amazingly makes some foolish pricks believe that the Stone Island badge or Lacoste crocodile will strike fear into blokes who had been smashing their ground up when they were still floating around in their dads' ballbags.

We were walking up to the ground as usual about five minutes after kick-off, only six of us, when we walked straight into this kiddie firm of Norwich's finest. They gave it, "Where's your boys?" and couldn't get their heads around the fact that we said, "We're here, you cheeky bastards," and steamed into them. It took a couple of the local plod to show up before they decided to have a go back. They must have had a bad journey home holding the inquest into how their busload of designer-laden psychos had backed off from six scruffy Everton lads who didn't have a single Stone Island jacket between them.

We won the game 5–0 and I was expecting them to have a bit of a show after the match. We managed to pull a firm together once everyone had stopped laughing that they had even had the cheek to front it earlier. But the reality of being out of their league as well as out of the Cup saw them skulk off into the distance without so much as a, "Goodbye, you

robbing Scouse bastards." Funnily enough, the manager
we'd had from them twelve months earlier had also ended up
back where he belonged for trying to fuck Everton about.

By now even the newspapers were tipping us for the Cup,
which usually means you get a nightmare draw in the next
round. We had been pretty lucky, so anyone at home would
do was the general feeling as the balls rattled and the quarter-final ties were drawn out of the bag.

lovable, loyal geordies

With Man Utd, Spurs and Newcastle still in the Cup, we
were hoping for Crystal Palace, but as one of the last two to
come out of the hat, it was good just to get a home draw. So
it was the lovable Geordies who would descend on
Goodison in their thousands and spend a day drinking with
us and generally having a good old day as friendly banter
was exchanged over the odd bottle of Newcastle Brown Ale.

Well, that's what the majority like to believe when
discussing the lovable, loyal Geordies. My arse. I felt sure
they would come to Everton taking the piss and would get
it in return. Sure as Kopites piss down their mate's legs, they
did come down *en masse*, they did take the piss, and they
did get it.

I have to confess an intense dislike of Newcastle that goes
back to the 1977/78 season. They had come to Goodison in
droves and at the end of the game the bizzies kept them in
for ages, which was very rare in those days; usually it was
one big mad free-for-all. Hundreds of Everton blocked the
road outside the ground and the Geordies were kept in for
their own safety. After about half an hour Everton's mob
split up, leaving mostly street urchins like myself hanging
around in the hope of catching a similar gang from the
North East and relieving them of their scarves, which was

the fashion in those days. The grubby items would then be worn to school on the Monday and exhibited like a top explorer would show off a lion's head on return from an overseas expedition; in fact a few years earlier when Millwall came up in the FA Cup, a few Lions almost had been decapitated, but that's another story.

The gates of the old Park End finally opened and out piled the biggest shower of horrible twats I had ever seen. Several hundred monsters in black and white chased us all up Priory and across Stanley Park. I think we stood for about ... well, it wasn't long. The turning point came when one young scally shouted "Fuckin' hell, la, they've got beards!" The end result was a good hiding for the few that got caught, though how the overweight brown ale guzzlers caught anyone is beyond me. There were no Newcastle scarves on show in double maths that Monday morning, just a few bruises.

Another reason I disliked them was the myth about them being "loyal" supporters. In the 1984/85 season we went up there with a tidy firm and didn't see any of them. The ground was comparatively empty – about 20,000, tops, and that included 3,000 Everton. All the Geordies were shouting to sack everyone, from the board to the players. I think they even wanted the tea lady on the dole, the fickle bastards. That was the time we came out of the ground and got stuck straight on a train that was bricked before we left the station. The brickers then ran into some rundown pub so some of our lads got off, climbed down the embankment, walked in, stabbed two of them, robbed some ale and got back on the train as if nothing had happened. You would end up getting a ten-stretch for that now with CCTV and the snide undercovers who spoil everything.

I think people have the perception that they are loyal because they wear very little except for black and white striped team shirts in the cold of December and January.

Loyal? In my book that is no more than stupidity. Loyalty is 35,000 every home game when you're in the bottom five every year, not 15,000 all season then 48,000 to watch Kevin Keegan's last game. They get 50,000 now, granted, but there will be a lot of empty seats in those flash new stands when the bubble bursts.

They turned up for the Cup quarter-final as if it was back to 1977; same shirts, same beards but with a few casuals now. We were in the Red Brick on County Road, a real good mob of 100 waiting for it to go but leaving the normals in the team shirts to do as they pleased. I can truthfully say it was always like that at Everton: 300 Arsenal or Chelsea could go in any pub decked out in the latest club fashions and wouldn't get a second glance, but come in a firm, step down the wrong side of the road and you would regret it.

The Geordies' mob, we were told, were in the Royal Oak. Although the Oak had loads of lads on match days, it was not really a "thug pub", as it was always camera'd up and had a police presence. It got so full that a few small gangs started to drift down towards the Brick and relationships became a bit strained. Then, as is usually the case, one loud-mouth got a bit clever and said the wrong thing to one of the lads in the bogs. Before he could finish his sentence, his head hit the urinal and off it went. It spilled into the bar, causing the Newcastle fans – who were still quite safe as long as they kept quiet – to panic and start running back to the Oak.

The Red Brick emptied and we made the short journey down County Road and steamed into the hordes of Newcastle who were all drinking outside on the pub forecourt. Kingy sparked the biggest one out and their arses just went. In two minutes it was carnage; they were all over the show, fighting each other to get away, falling over each other screaming for help. It didn't come, all that came was wave after wave of attacks and a lesson in keeping your trap shut.

I saw Kelly fighting with a couple who were trying to get up the side street to the ground, and gave one a left hook. He ducked and I connected with his skull, not jaw. I knew I was damaged when I felt a bad, bad pain shoot up my arm. I looked at my hand and it was obvious my wrist was snapped, mainly due to the pain but also because my hand was dangling at an angle.

The bizzies came, so we piled up to the ground as they were regrouping. We won the game with a Dave Watson header and drew Tottenham Hotspur in the semi. It could have been worse, as Man Utd had also won, getting Crystal Palace who, like us, were in the bottom four. The TV pundits and Joe Neutral were ejaculating in their armchairs at the prospect of a "dream final" between United and Spurs.

Newcastle never showed after the game, which I was glad about, as my hand had gone blue and was in need of some serious medical attention. Still we were on our way to Wembley, we shall not be moved, not until the pubs shut anyway. The next day, I went to casualty and made a lame excuse about falling over a kerb, in the hope of some compensation from the council. The doctor sussed that it was at least a day-old injury and all I got was a sicknote for six weeks as my arm was put in plaster. Still, the time off work would be nice.

the yids and jurgen

The semi-final was to be played at Elland Road, Leeds, which I couldn't make out. Usually they were played somewhere between the two clubs' venues. That was until the greedy blazers at the FA started to use Wembley for the semis as well as the final. Villa Park would have been the fairest location but Man Utd v Palace got the nod for that, so Leeds it was, and the advantage was Everton's. Although I ain't got a degree in geography, I was sure that it would take the Yids (as Tottenham's firm are know to one and all) a lot longer to get to Leeds from London than it would take us to get there from Lime Street, unless the flash bastards flew. Everton had a bad record at Elland Road but we'd had a bit of luck in the Cup so far, so off to Leeds we went to face Spurs for a place at Wembley. They were going well with a world-famous German striker in their side, Jurgen Klinsmann.

Some of my best moments watching Everton have come on FA Cup semi-final day: Southampton in '84, Luton '85, Sheffield Wednesday '86, Norwich '89, although the events at Hillsborough that day made celebrating another trip to Wembley a definite no-no. All these games Everton had won and all by the odd goal, and I would have settled for the same outcome as we boarded the first train out of Lime Street that Sunday morning. There was a good firm on the train, not massive but well over 100. Loads of the old boys were still on board after the Bristol game, so I felt quite happy we had enough to do any Spurs, Leeds, or both if we came across them.

We expected to be collared by the plod as soon as we got off at Leeds, but they let us out into the city centre, which seemed a bit iffy at first until we saw the place was deserted and all the bars were shut. The walk up to the ground took ages and we crossed a park and ruined a couple of Sunday League games before the plod picked us up and herded us all together. Our bizzie, Pat Cook, was telling the Yorkshire plod to open up a boozer so he could keep us in one place and stay with us, but they were having none of it. Now I don't like the police, as over the years they have succeeded to some degree in helping fuck my life up, but Paddy Cook was always fair to us and usually succeeded in getting us a drink – not least so he would know where we were. The Leeds police took no notice of him though, and herded us up to the ground, no pubs, no ale, no nothing – until a load of plod come running down the road telling us to get back. Turns out three coaches of Yids had arrived looking for us. Bingo, game on.

We got past the plod and up to The Peacock opposite the away end, but Spurs had been either split up or shoved in the ground, as the firm they had outside was not the best and offered only token resistance. A few of their old boys, big men in their forties, pulled me and said they would meet us at the same spot at full-time, that they had 200 and it was a proper firm. I've always rated Tottenham so had no doubt that these blokes were the genuine article.

Suddenly a big Rasta danced over with an even bigger chip on his shoulder: "Hey white trash, why you-all Everton scum hate us man? Racist bastards you-all, man." He sounded like Ali G but was about four foot taller. Off it went, and unluckily for him my Newcastle injury was still plastered, so he got a whack on his dreadlocks and the other blokes who were okay took a few slaps as well.

On the train we had been a bit bothered that all our tickets were for different sections: some in the Leeds home end, others in the old away end and loads in the Elland Road main stand. When we got inside, the mystery was solved. Everton had three sides to the ground and Spurs just the big new stand. The support we had was unreal and the atmosphere one of the best I had ever seen. The players came out to fireworks and the Waterboys' "Whole Of The Moon" playing. The noise was deafening.

We walked it, going one-up early on from a Matt Jackson header then netting a second when Ian Walker, son of Mike, dropped a clanger and Rideout scored. We were so much on top you could even enjoy the match, which is a rarity for such a high-pressure tie. Then the ref gave Spurs a dodgy penalty when Klinsmann, who else, dived. He took the kick, just beat Southall and it was game on again. There was then a fuck-up on the bench when Rideout took a knock and

Daniel Amokachi ran on by mistake to take his place. Joe Royle tried to get him off, as Rideout was okay, but the ref said he had been subbed, so Everton's answer to John Barnes (who was as much use as Des Barnes) had to stay on while we held on for what was becoming an unlikely victory.

Anyway, 2–1, hanging on and Everton break, Limpar crosses and who smashes it in? Amo. The ground explodes and Everton are all over the pitch. The good thing with a pitch invasion is that if you don't get nicked, which unfortunately I always do, you can all get back in the same section of the stand. That was the case here, as we had all sussed that, with us winning, no police – just stewards – around the pitch, and no fences, on ninety minutes we were all going on and if Tottenham would care to join us they were welcome.

A few Spurs came on after our third goal and a few more started smashing the advertising hoardings. The game was stopped when two Tottenham ran on and started swinging on the crossbar, which must have upset Amo because he scored again. Hundreds spilled on and seconds later the ref blew for full-time. The pitch filled with Everton and a few ran to Ian Walker who was crying on the turf. We picked him up, then started singing, "Ee aye addio, your dad's on the dole," in reference to his old feller getting the sack by us just before Christmas. Strangely he got a bit of a cob on so someone booted him up the arse.

We were having a ball when we spotted the Yids spilling over as the stewards half-heartedly tried to halt their progress. As we bounced over, the players were still trying to get off and Klinsmann pushed a little kid in his haste. I quite simply held my broken arm out at chest height and, through no fault of my own, the German striker ran straight into the heavy plaster protecting my injured limb. To say he went down like a sack of the proverbial would be an understatement and I can safely say he will remember that day for something other than his pathetic dive that put our place in football's greatest club showpiece in danger.

We fronted the Cockneys, and they had a bit of a go at staying put when we kicked off. I'm not sure if Spurs had their main boys at the front but there is a picture of the fight in this book, and all the Everton lads on it had been at it for years. Spurs fired some gas, then the police came on with horses and after a few minutes order was restored. Outside the ground it was obvious why there were so few police in the ground, as hundreds filled the road keeping us apart. A helicopter was out, the full hit. We walked back to the station and tried every route to get around the Spurs side but we had no chance. We got back to town and chased a few off the station but really there was little doing. A couple of lads had to walk past the Yids to get to their car and said they had a huge mob that would have taken some stopping. All I can say to that is that if we'd lost 4–1, with no police in the ground, and they had come on the pitch to celebrate, we would have done a lot more damage than swinging on the crossbar. And as for Klinsmann, he made a big song and dance about an Everton thug attacking him, and it made the back page of *The Sun*, but he knows what really happened and now so do you.

we shall not be moved

After the coverage the papers gave to the fighting on the pitch at the semi, some people were waiting for their doors to come in, but amazingly it never happened. There was always a chance though, so instead of staying in London the night before the final against Man United, we decided to book into the Hilton in Watford and meet up with the rest of the lads on the Saturday morning. The theory was that London, whether you like it or not, is a Man Utd stronghold on Cup final weekend. In 1985 the weekend had been piss-poor, so we thought that if we were out of the way we could have a trouble-free night out on the Friday, then if it went off on the match day, so be it. It was a sound idea in theory but in practice it was a disaster. We might as well have stayed in Salford and sung Munich songs all night.

We had met in one of the lads' houses on Oakfield Road the Thursday night before the match and the tone was set. KC was testing out a shark gun and, although we decided against taking it, we had a laugh trying to shoot his pet iguana with it. We left the Red Brick on the Friday morning with sixteen of us in a minibus, all booked into the Hilton, very respectable. Combined I think we had about fifty football-related offences between us, so yes, it was a tasty little mob. The minibus was like a Russian armoured car and I am surprised it got us there, such was the amount of weaponry on board. If we had been stopped and searched we would still be there now trying to explain why some of the items were needed for a weekend trip to the football. Sixteen men may not be that much of an army but given our pasts and with what we were carrying, we would take some stopping, even without the shark gun.

We got there without any hassle and had booked in by early evening. It was quiet and at first I thought we had made the right decision not going to London, as we had the run of the place. Then about six coaches of United turned up and our plan went out of the window. Although we blanked each other, they knew who we were, and as we set off to town it did not need Mastermind to work out that later on when a few beers and a bit of the dandruff had been consumed, something would happen.

In town we were knocked back everywhere so ended up in a bar near the hotel at last orders. It was jam-packed with United but they knew there was only a few of us and, although it was like a time-bomb waiting to explode, we managed to stop the fuse being lit. One of the lads' brothers lived in Watford and he joined us with an Arsenal lad, swelling our numbers to the dizzy heights of nearly twenty. It was added to when we robbed a big, stuffed bull's head from the bar, which we thought would be our lucky mascot, and headed off back to the Hilton.

Lucky it was not, and within minutes the bomb exploded. As soon as we got in the bar the predictable "you Scouse bastards" chants began and KC decked one of them. They were shocked that we hadn't gone to bed, given the numbers against us, but they did not realise that the mob was full of seasoned campaigners and, with not a mention of bed, we destroyed them.

It was carnage and the place was totalled. The fight spilled from the bar and into the lobby and one Manc was cut badly. They kept regrouping but Everton were not moving and blocked the stairs. If United wanted it, they would have to get up the stairs to have it, and that was not an easy option. Time and time again they tried and were forced back. Steve battered one, then threw him down the stairs, and his head made a hole in the plasterboard wall. It went on for about ten minutes before the police arrived and ten minutes is a long time for less than twenty to fight off 100. Yet by the time it had stopped, I swear there was not a cut or bruise on any of our lads, while an ambulance ferried quite a few casualties from their ranks to Watford General.

When the police arrived, Everton got a bit cocksure and ventured outside the hotel. It was a daft move and two got nicked. The funniest thing that happened was when a big bloke ran out and Franny dropped him, only to realise it was the hotel chef running to his taxi. How they never nicked everybody I don't know, and it was on top all night, with very little sleep taken. I got the bull's head and went to Franny's room and knocked his door. He looked through the spyhole thinking it was the bizzies and nearly passed out when he saw a massive furry head with horns, singing. Another lad said Simmo was seen scaling down the hotel wall, spooked but determined not to miss the game, and then had to climb back up when he realised it was a wind-up.

We were up early in the morning and made a swift exit. The place was crawling with CID and I thought we were all for the high jump. They were taking statements from all the Mancs but somehow we managed to get off before getting a pull. It was a scary time and I was flapping in case we got nicked and missed the match, as I really thought this was our year for the Cup and didn't want to be in a cell when we got revenge for the 1985 defeat.

We were lost at the first roundabout, with a minibus of Everton fans we knew behind us. They stopped to ask a taxi driver the way. It was a classic, and although not funny at the time, I always have a chuckle when I think of it now. One of the lads leant out of the window and said, "We're on our way to Wembley …" and before he could finish his sentence, the chirpy cabbie shouted, "… we shall not be moved," then sped off, laughing. We were desperate to get away and it was not one bit funny, but is now one of the legendary stories which always gets told after a few ales.

We finally reached the Twin Towers and met up with a good firm of lads, but United did not show until just before kick-off when most of us had been shoved in by the bizzies. They had a top firm though, as expected. None of them had been in the Hilton but they had heard about it. The game was a dream and we sneaked it 1–0 with a Rideout header after Stuart had hit the bar from a yard out. It was unbearable watching the last twenty minutes and we were getting hammered, but hung on. The whistle went and it was happy days, Dave Watson lifted the cup and the team showed the trophy to a half-empty stadium as all the United lot cleared off long before Waggy got his hands on it. It was great revenge for 1985, and the expected trouble after the game never happened. By the time we got back to our minibus they were on their way home and the only United we saw were in the services on the motorway. They had taken to banging a few nutty Evertonians who were not after a fight, and we were unopposed all the way home, which was just as well as we were still tooled up.

We got back to town and had a top night. The following day, I watched the team parade the trophy around the city. It had been a great run and I think that we deserved to win it that year. When Walker was sacked we were favourites for relegation, but Joe Royle's Dogs of War not only saved us from the drop but got us back into Europe. The chant that day was, "Going down, are we fuck, we stayed up and won the Cup." Never truer words spoken. Such had been the interest generated by our Cup run, both on and off the pitch, that it also brought Everton's hooligan following back together. Cheers Joe!

16 THE SNORTY FORTY

give us an e

After the mad Eighties, there was a dip in football violence, which was put down to many different reasons. The Government tried to take credit for it and Maggie Thatcher and her annoying sidekick Colin Moynihan patted each other on the back and enjoyed a pay rise, no doubt. They then foolishly sat back believing it was a job well done and the evil in our national sport was finally exorcised.

Anybody "in the know" will, however, agree that what really made lads from all over the country stop ripping each other's throats out every Saturday had little to do with the Government and jackshit to do with the dawn raids and heavy jail sentences. I copped a few heavy fines and got a short, sharp shock, as it was called, with my little trip to Brixton, but if you are a main player in this game it does not stop you doing it again. Believe me, football violence is an obsession and the only thing to stop you being bang at it is another obsession, the two most common being drugs and money.

I have never been into the drug scene and although I would obviously like to become a millionaire, I know my business limitations, so remained obsessed with the other. Many people who used to be bad hooligans got into the drugs and money. They left football and the violence that came with it and joined the rave craze, ending up either hooked on dancing daft and hugging everyone or making a fortune out of organising and supplying the events with whatever was wanted. That was the end of football violence for many, and they were mostly main players. Within twelve months my favourite pastime was as good as ruined! It never went away completely but was scaled down, and Merseyside, being an area with bad drug problems, was affected worse than most. By the early Nineties both Everton and Liverpool's firms went from being amongst the roughest in the county to arguably the most inactive.

I particularly remember one game when we played Newcastle at home and they brought about fifty lads. Half of then were allies from Shrewsbury and they came in the Oak and could not get a fight. A couple of years earlier there would have been serious casualties, but on this day not a punch was thrown even though they were gagging for it. I met their main lad, made a few excuses about the bizzies and said I would bring a mob up to The Arkles after the game and sort it out. As hard as I tried, I could not pull a mob to have a go at this combined Newcastle-Shrewsbury firm. It was an embarrassment and hurt worse than any hiding I ever received at the match.

Eventually we got about twenty lads and went up to Anfield in taxis. Me and Kingy went into the pub but had to do one as they were a decent mob and this twenty we had were not going to make any impression. I have never been one of the "better to show and have a go than not show at all" brigade, so I called it off. As we walked back to the Oak in the rain, a sorry and by now soaked little mob, even I was convinced that it was finished forever.

However, as the saying goes, every cloud has a silver lining, and that night in the pub a few of us agreed that it was not over and we had to get a mob together for Newcastle away and let them know we were still about. Luckily, before we played them we had a few decent games coming up. We got all the old lads up for a couple of the trips and had no trouble filling a coach, with the promise of a "proper" day out, just like the good old days. As I have already told, Middlesbrough and Bristol City were two of the first teams to cross swords with the newly formed "Snorty Forty". For obvious reasons I am unable to go into details of how this firm got its name; just use your imagination.

At the time they were great days and great battles but all the lads wanted was Newcastle. As chance had it, we played them on the Saturday before Christmas, so it was no problem increasing the Snorty Forty to the Snorty Fifty-six, and all seats were full for our festive away trip to Newcastle and later Whitley Bay. The season of good will to all mankind, however, was not on our itinerary.

happy christmas

In the early days of the Snorty Forty, we were known to the police but all the intelligence crap had not really taken hold. As we had been inactive for a few seasons, we were pretty much low key. After just a few skirmishes though, due to the nastiness of them and usual casualties, we were assigned with a couple of Merseyside's finest bizzies to keep a watchful eye on us, namely Paddy Cook and Frankie "Flatcap" Firth. At first they made no real impression and it was still easy getting coaches organised. They had no idea where we were going from and only stumbled across us when it had already gone off, leaving them to take a few photos and write a report or two for the files. Basically it was easy money for them – until Newcastle away.

We got there and were in the main pub outside the station by eleven. There were no Geordies about and we sat off for a couple of hours before going for a wander in the town centre. We knew they had a mob and it did not take long to find them; as we went through a small side street, a lad clocked us and scurried into a bar with huge plate windows. We got outside and it was full of them. We were about to steam it when one of theirs came out and told us to leave it, that the whole street was CCTV'd up and to move on up the hill, get in another pub and they would come to us. He was spot on, as when we scanned the place there were cameras everywhere and his advice saved us certain jail.

We got to the boozer he had directed us to and waited. It was not pleasant. I have always preferred the "bang, here it goes" and in you get. The wait for another mob to arrive sometimes gets people wary and battles can be won or lost in those few minutes of tension. In this case, however, that was not going to happen. This mob was not a kiddie firm or one like so many others, full of beauts clad in Stone Island who would be on their toes once the first punch was thrown. I scanned the pub: the average age of this mob was early thirties, with a few kids but they were there to make a name for themselves and were usually the ones with the blades. There were at least three lads who had been involved in armed robberies, several bouncers who were at it every week in one of the most violent cities in Britain and at least twenty of us who had been at this palaver for years. It was a tasty mob, and only the likes of Millwall, West Ham and Man United have similar mobs of that size that are as close-knit. Fifty-odd is not a lot but fifty-odd of this calibre is dangerous, make no mistake.

The wait this time was not long. Vic was on the door and came in with the shout we were waiting for: "They're here!" We piled out and were met with a hail of house bricks. All the usual bollocks from a mob could be heard from Newcastle: stand, stick together, come on. I have heard it all a hundred times before and counting, and was sick of it. Franny, Steve, Larry and all the usual suspects were not into shouting and walked into them, avoiding the bricks on the way.

To their credit they were quite a good mob, but were let down by younger lads who seemed to have dismantled a building site, judging by the amount of bricks landing around us. Some of our lot to the rear of the mob started throwing them back and, as is usually the case, a few Everton at the front were felled by friendly fire. We were screaming for them to stop but in the mayhem there was no chance and the street was soon like Beirut, with cars and shops being hit with misdirected, ale-fuelled shots from both sides. We backed them off as they ran out of missiles and a few were having it in the middle of the road as the rest of them regrouped. But for one lad with a flock haircut, who I had seen before, they would have been finished, but he kept at it and kept them together when they looked to be losing it badly.

A battle like that can turn in seconds and it happened here. We were so on top you could pick your target, when suddenly I felt a crack on the back of my head and not for the first time was counting the pebbles as boots rained into my earhole and kidneys. We had backed them off so far down the road that we had passed a pub full of locals who were not football lads but who had taken offence at us taking the piss on their manor. Now it was time to earn respect, as we had to fight front and back.

Luckily one of the lads had been having a line in the toilets when it first went off and, as he came into the street, he saw us down the road just as the Geordie barmies were piling out of the other boozer. He got to the door and gassed the pub, so as we turned to have it with them, many were coughing and spluttering, making it easy for us to finish them off. They were soon spanked back into the pub, leaving one last charge into the main mob, who had suddenly got a bit braver.

By now there was a cacophony of car alarms, as several no longer possessed windscreens. A shop was minus a few windows as well and it was not long before the familiar sound of police sirens added to the din. Newcastle had given it their best shot but it was not good enough. As we regrouped, although my ear was ringing and my kidneys were holding an inquest with each other to see why they had been punished so badly, I still managed a smile. I just hoped a few of the cheeky Shrewsbury bastards had been there to witness it.

We split into little mobs when the bizzies arrived and it was a dodgy walk to the ground. We had a few casualties and stood out among the crowds walking to the stadium. Had Newcastle come back as one we would have been in trouble but I never saw them until we got to the turnstiles. They were rabid. The local plod had followed them up and we were all filmed going into St James's plush new stands that were now full every week as the bandwagon was rocking and rolling. The lad with the flock hair was there and I told him he had done well but was with the wrong firm; he told us to go back to the same place after and said they were missing loads of their main boys. I could smell the bullshit and so could he; they were their main boys, they had all the advantages needed and they had been done. End of, and he knew it.

It is another game I have no idea what the score was, but didn't care if we lost 25–0, the smile on my face was not moving. At half-time, Paddy and Flatcap were not happy chappies and gave us pure grief. Once again the Merseyside Football Intelligence were not intelligent enough; they had failed the eleven-plus on this one and were sure to get lines or detention on return to base. On the final whistle we managed to give the bizzies the slip again and, after a walk that was, I admit, not one of my most confident, as every Geordie and his mother seemed to be out for us, we amazingly made it back into the boozer we had occupied earlier. We got a drink, manned the doors and began our second wait of the day. There was no way they were going to let this go and, judging by the look on the landlord's face, he knew that his pub was likely to be attacked at any minute.

A couple of idiots in shirts came in slagging us off. They had been gassed earlier. Soon Paddy and Flatcap arrived with a video camera and began to earn their day's pay. "Waste of tax-payers' money," one of the lads said, and a few grumbled until I reminded them that you do not get taxed on your giro! Frank told us to drink up and we were out of there. We argued that we were staying the weekend and planned to leave for Whitley Bay about nine. He laughed and told us we had five minutes to get on our coach, which had been brought right outside the boozer, or die. He was not joking. As we got outside and boarded the bus, further down the road were flashing lights and police vans. The riot squad, dogs, horses and every spare officer were attempting to hold back hundreds of irate Newcastle fans. Geordie shirtheads, casuals, sons, daughters, grandfathers, grandmothers, pet dogs and goldfish wanted our blood. We drove off laughing and singing the *Z Cars* tune as bricks and bottles were thrown at us.

The police followed us out of town and made sure we did not have the stupidity to go back. We were not likely to; we were mad and bad and, in one or two cases, evil, but we were not stupid and had done what we had set out to do. We did not make Whitley Bay, as the bizzies escorted us out of the county and before long we knew we had no chance, so headed for Blackpool. On the way I met for the first time my best mate Alfie. He had been off the scene for years but had been enticed back out of retirement like so many others. It was the start of a friendship I value highly.

Blackpool was shite. We had it with a few bouncers and a load of clubbers coming out of a huge club called the Palace, but it was not my scene and I was glad to get home. I slept well that night. The shame of Newcastle at home had been erased by the bucketful.

millwall

One of my best trips with the Snorty Forty was to Millwall
at the New Den. We have had a bad rivalry with Millwall
since the FA Cup game in the early Seventies but had played
them only the once at the old Den. I was banned at the time
and warned that if I got on the train I would be nicked; I
was sick but didn't fancy a week back in the nick, so I
skipped it. It was a bad call, as loads that were banned went,
got in and nobody got a pull. I still get stick now for missing it and it was over thirteen years ago. I don't brag about
things if I wasn't there but by all accounts Everton took
hundreds in the best firm we'd had since the Chelsea Friday
night game. It went off at the end of the match in the seats.
Everton say they steamed Millwall, Millwall say we never,
wasn't there, don't know, but I have been told by some
Cockney Reds who saw the firm we had at Euston that it
was seriously top drawer, and that will do for me.

To get Millwall in a cup draw was my idea of a good
time. They are undoubtedly one of the top hooligan mobs
in the country, and they had a couple of scores to settle with
us. It was the Littlewoods Cup, two legs, so there was no
hiding place for either side. We filled the coach easily. A
mate of mine had to work so another lad, Ray, who was not
a thug, took his place. He had not been to the New Den so
it was a day out and a bit of an eye-opener for him.

We got into London about five and straight away the lads
reckoned that the place was a lot less shady than the old
ground, and again I got a load of grief for not being able to
agree or disagree with their observations. The norm with
Everton is that, on seeing the floodlights, we always say,
"We're here, let's get off," and we always pile into the first
pub we see to sort ourselves out. It has backfired a few
times, the worst being at a quarter-final at West Ham when
we did the same thing and ended up being about three miles

from the ground, which looked a lot nearer in the darkness with the floodlights lighting up the sky. A walk that far in the East End is not for the faint-hearted.

The boozer was called The Barnaby and it gets a mention in the Millwall book *We Fear No Foe* by Colin Johnson. I don't know if he is a blagger but his recollection of what happened was spot on. We had a little nose in the pub and there was a mixture of lads and fans in there. I walked in and straight away the Cockneys knew we were there. A few stood up and a few made an exit through the fire door but I knew if we smashed this place up the bizzies would have us and this was hardly Millwall's finest. A few more went in and, as we were outside, a cab pulled up with a couple of lads in. In his book Johnson says it was him. If it was, he was lucky, as we were arguing amongst ourselves. Some were saying that we should do the ones in the pub while others, including my good self, thought otherwise and wanted their main lads, not a bunch of lads who would have it but did not want it. If these were Millwall's finest they would have been into us as soon as we parked up, but they weren't and in my eyes that gave them a walkover. As we were rowing, a couple of the lads in the cab went in. Seconds later, they back came out. Some of the lads thought they were fronting it and one of the Urchins was ready to cut them. We stopped him and asked these lads where we would find the main mob and they happily directed us up the road.

We had got only a few hundred yards when what seemed like half of London's police force arrived and pulled us up near a work yard. We were searched from head to toe, and to do the fifty-odd of us must have taken half an hour. A few managed to ditch blades and the bizzies were even checking our notes for forgeries. The workers in the morning would have been made up as the yard was littered with blades and half-gram bags of charlie.

Our escort to the ground was soon shadowed by a mob

of Millwall; no major numbers but they were old school and looked the part. As soon as we got by the ground we split into two smaller mobs and tried to go in the seats in the Paddock. Millwall came straight into us and there was a tidy little off before order was restored and we were forced into our own seats in the upper section behind the goal. They had a bit of a moody firm to the left of us but nowhere near the numbers I thought they would have. The game was goalless and the best incident in the whole ninety minutes was when a lad kept jumping up in front of Alfie trying to get everybody to join in a daft chant about Bakayoko, our new African striker, who was crap. In the end Alf's very short fuse blew and he banged the lad out, getting ejected for his efforts. It is not the best place to be out on your own, so a couple of the lads went out with him and stayed in the pub nearest the ground. Two Cockneys came in and were sound, saying if we wanted it after the game to head for The Tropics. They even walked one of the lads up to find it and said they would be waiting.

After the game we were herded behind the ground in a massive pen. The London cops said Millwall had hundreds outside that needed shifting before we could get to the coaches. I didn't believe them. After what seemed ages, they began to walk us up the road. Most of the fans then did a left but we had been told where The Tropics was and went right. It was a bit of a suicide mission if all that had been said about Millwall was to be believed, as we were only forty-strong, but we had come for it and it was worth giving it a whirl. Nothing ventured, nothing gained and all that.

We had been walking for a few minutes when we spotted the pub and, as we got level, a few of their lads at the door ran in. I thought we were in serious trouble, as this was by all accounts their main boozer and there was not a bizzie in sight. Yet instead of steaming out, the lads shoved a huge sandwich board into the doorway to stop us getting in. It turned out they were well outnumbered even by our small firm. This was a surprise given the enmity between our two hooligan gangs. In Johnson's book, he says:

> The hatred many Millwall fans feel for Everton stems from the 1974 clash when many Millwall supporters were stabbed in skirmishes inside and outside Goodison Park. We are brought up never to forget and rest assured whenever Millwall play Everton there will be a very real possibility of serious disorder.

Well Colin, we played you that night and you all must have forgotten, because it was one of the biggest letdowns of my hooligan career. Sometimes it happens, but I was shocked at how few the Lions had out. I will never call them because I know they are as good as you can get, but that night they were not showing and that is the truth.

We made an attempt of sorts to get in The Tropics and a couple, including Bruce, made it. Millwall went out the back exit and police baton-charged us across the road and escorted us back to our coach. I was also surprised at how quickly the police had got there, until we got on the bus, when my mate Ray told me what had happened. Not looking for a fight, he had stayed with the main escort and stood with the drivers as the fans got onto their respective coaches. After five minutes, a police sergeant asked the first driver, "How many did you have on?"

"Fifty-six."

"Any missing."

"No."

Second driver. Same question, same answer.

Our driver. Same question, answer a bit different though.

"I had fifty-three on."

"How many missing?"

"All of them."

The copper's face dropped and he radioed all officers to look for us. Paddy Cook then went up and asked him the location of the nearest Millwall boozer where we would get a fight. He was told The Tropics. He informed his London counterpart that we would be on our way there, hence their speedy arrival. I later asked Pat why he had left us and he said the local intelligence had been following us and filming everything and told him to stay out of the way. He saw the film and told us that it was a load of bollocks, that the light wasn't working and the pictures were too dark to identify anybody. Intelligence, my arse.

We had a top firm of over 100 for the second leg but Millwall didn't come in any numbers, which again Johnson admits in his book. Fair play, he is an honest lad. We lost 4–2 after being two up and after the match a few Cockneys took a slap. The best fight was when a mob of Everton's younger lads attacked a few Millwall walking back to their car. They picked on the wrong blokes and these five monsters chased about twenty Everton back up the road. A few of us joined in and in the end they sped off in a Mercedes, nearly running everyone over. They were mental and made a show of those Urchins on their own (another honest football hooligan author!).

leicester city

The Baby Squad hardly have a frightening nickname but I have respect for the Leicester firm, as they brought a tidy mob to Goodison the first year they were promoted and always have a few knocking about at home. It is usually the case when a club gets promoted; they always seem to have a good turnout in their first season against the top clubs. Most of the so-called bigger sides in the Nationwide have allegedly got tasty mobs nowadays, though apart from the old favourites like Millwall and Cardiff, who have always been bang at it, I find it difficult to give the others much respect. It is easy now to pose and look hard with all the surveillance but where were they in the late Seventies and early Eighties when it was a free-for-all? I'm sure your West Broms and Stokes will argue the toss but when it mattered they simply were not there and they and all the main players around at that time know it.

But as I said, Leicester were a bit tasty at home, although like so many others they had never shown at Goodison. It was a bit of a surprise, then, the first year they came back up, when a lad told me by the ground that they had a proper mob in town. It was too late to go down and have a look, so a few of us waited for them to be brought up to the ground. They duly arrived and had the lot: casuals, a load of blacks, which always makes a mob look better for some reason, beer monsters, who although they look a sight can knock you out, and loads of older lads who had the Seventies dress and tattoos to match. Combined, it was one of the best firms I had seen at Everton for several years.

We waited for them to start queuing by the Bullens Road, then fronted them. They seemed wary. They would have bounced the small firm we had hastily assembled but, as is so often the case at both Goodison and Anfield, very few mobs stray too far, for the fear of being cut up is always in their minds. Yet we had no more than thirty and were showing for the sake of it really. Steve and I walked into the queue and it took them seconds to start nervously shuffling about. One shouted, "Here's their boys." They stood off and soon realised we were a very small firm but still not a dig was thrown.

The brief commotion alerted Flatcap and we were soon chased back to the Park End. In the ground they looked impressive and you could see row after row of lads. In the Upper Bullens Stand was another block full of them. They could have done some damage if they'd wanted, but they didn't; after the game they got in the escort, disappeared to town and have never been seen since. I will give them credit for turning out such an impressive mob, particularly when things were a bit quiet on the hooligan front, but they did nothing with it. It's like having a Porsche convertible and keeping it in the garage all summer. If I had one I would be out in it from dawn to dusk and if I'd had their firm that day, the place would have been in disarray.

There was no way we could match that for the away game, so the trusty Forty set off on an invitation-only tour. It was likely to be no place for the weak-kneed, so only those we knew best were allowed along and the rest could please themselves. Leicester, and particularly the area around Filbert Street, is a bit of a dive and the ground is a disgrace – only Fulham is worse – and I am glad they have been relegated. We got there and tried to get in a boozer but had no chance, so wandered around the ground. It was early, there were no lads about and the day looked, like so many before, to be a waste of time. It was not like that for long.

We were hanging around by the Main Stand when a black tout fronted us, telling us to stay put and he would go and get a firm together. He was okay but soon started going on about us being too early, why weren't we in town, why didn't you phone, and so on. So Joe drop-kicked him and chased him down the road. He lost his tickets and from a distance shouted something like, "Wankers. Don't move."

The ground was still locked and we were arguing with ourselves – for a change – about whether to walk into town or not. A couple of lads were getting a burger and I saw a bit of a scuffle. I thought the burger bloke had been liberated of his takings but a few Leicester barmies had fronted Kelly. One of them threw a punch then darted into the car park where I was standing. He had a big grin on his face and must have thought we were easy pickings. He shot towards me and threw a haymaker, missing by a mile. As he fell towards me, I threw my head right into his grinning, lager-bloated face. He was grinning no more. It was an impressive header, on a par with anything Bob Latchford or Andy Gray had conjured up in the famous royal blue jersey, and Billy Bloat was away with the fairies.

A bit of a roar went up and his mates were scattered. I stepped over him and walked casually into the Leicester club shop while the commotion died down. It was a bit scary, as when I came out he was still flat out and had a bird's fur coat over him while paramedics tried to bring him round. It was his own fault but he looked in a bad way. He was loaded into the ambulance and I'm sure was no worse off for it by the time he came around, which judging by the look of him was a couple of weeks later. I had a small cut on my head and headaches for a few weeks, so went to the doctor's and he cut a piece of tooth out of my head. That took some explaining.

It wasn't long before the ticketless tout surfaced, bouncing up the road with a little mob of their main lads. We were now all over the show and a few of us got backed off to another burger stall near the away end. Because we had split up, it was touch and go as to whether we ran. A Jock who said he was Celtic was their mouthpiece; for such a little gobshite he was a major mouth and I gave him a few digs for his cheek. A few Everton blokes got stuck in and the potential disaster was averted, just.

As Paul was fighting with two Leicester, I was backed off into the burger stand again by a couple of them, but once the blokes flew in they were off. I couldn't resist grabbing the tomato sauce bottle from the counter and firing it at one of the lads Paul was sparring with. He had a white Stone Island coat on and was covered in ketchup. When the bizzies came and it stopped, he walked off, then began shouting that he had been slashed. He looked terrified and the plod believed him. I only stopped when I took a bang in the back of the head. I turned to front it and stood facing a big fat burger bird who obviously worked on the basis of sell one, eat one. It was the best dig I took all season. I handed back the offensive weapon and the police searched us and even had a laugh when the slash victim tasted the claret and realised it was HP's finest. I was released, as "saucing" someone has not been made a criminal offence yet, and went into the ground still chuckling.

The game was just as mad as the commotion outside: we were 2–0 up, then had two players sent off and Leicester ended up getting a draw. All game we were pelted with coins but we were buzzing. Little fights broke out in the home seats as Everton were sussed out, and it was a bit of a throwback to the Eighties. When they scored their second, a seat just missed my head and a woman passed it back to me. I went for double top, the Leicester section, but was a better shot with a sauce bottle and the seat hit treble three, which was a bloke sitting about six rows in front of me. It was time to go and a few of us got by the exit but Leicester had mobbed up and were already attacking a few Everton fans that were leaving early. The mouthy Jock was at the front and pulled a blade. He was a wretched little twat and, as lads and normal fans backed off, I ran through and booted him in the bollocks. He crumbled and was nicked as the bizzies got sight of his blade. They also grabbed me but the crowd turned on them, as I had saved a couple from a possible slashing, and they were great, pulling me free. I was pushed to the back but in the melee lost my favourite jacket, which was worth about four ton.

Outside it was going off all around and there were running battles across the road as Everton piled out and Leicester regrouped, though the bizzies were soon in control. I got a coat from Kelly and made my way out and back to the coaches. As I was sitting there, I spotted a bloke walking past wearing my coat. I soon reclaimed it and waved a merry farewell to Filbert Street. We still had time to ransack an off licence before we hit the motorway, and it was a jolly trip home with the sauce-slashing story being told long into the night.

style and fists

Before long we were finding it very difficult to get transport to games. The Football Intelligence had been back to school and had us sussed. Every time we went somewhere we were followed, and it turned out every coach company in the Merseyside area had to inform the police if a coach was hired for an Everton match. The train was a waste of time; as soon as we got on it we were searched, pestered and followed. We went to Barnsley and Steve, Kelly and myself were told to sit in the station bar while everybody else went to the pub. If we moved, we were nicked. We then started hiring minibuses, but after the Boro sketch they were told not to take us, so for a grand finale to the season we decided to splash out: the Snorty Forty became twenty and we booked stretch limousines for the game at Blackburn.

It was a legendary day from start to finish, though I wish we had been playing somebody else, as Blackburn are a joke. We had battered them once at a service station after playing them at Wembley in the worst Charity Shield game ever, the year they bought the League with Jack Walker's millions. All the proceeds from the game go to charity but they'd have been better off raffling a bottle of whisky, as there were less than 30,000 there, with no more than 5,000 Blackburn. I took a coach but was followed all day by both the Scouse and Cockney Intelligence. It wasn't even a hooligan bus, just full of lads, most on a jolly. The cops spoiled my day and it was the first time I really sussed how badly they were on my case. I was searched about four times before the game and ended up miles away in Swiss Cottage, just three of us having a beer outside a wine bar. It was boiling and there was not a fight in sight, not that we wanted one. Two blokes drove past, parked on double yellow lines and a bizzie in uniform told them to move on. They had a word and he left it, so I kept an eye on them as they sat across the road in another bar. Sure enough, when I went to leave they were over. "Where you going now, Nicholls?" and another five minutes wasted while they fiddled with my underwear for non-existent weapons or drugs. I asked for a search slip in the end; every time I was stopped, I had to show it and was supposed to be sent on my way, but still got frisked another five times before we set off home. I could have understood it had we been playing Chelsea but a few lads on a day out against Blackburn was hardly terrorist activity. Still, on the way home we pulled in the services and the bus with all the lads on had just battered Blackburn everywhere. The plastic Mancs had got a bit clever with their numbers by all accounts and been hammered out of sight by seasoned campaigners.

So when, the season after, we went in the limos, we thought they might be out for revenge, but I never saw a Blackburn skin all day and don't think I have since. We stopped off in Preston on the way and it was a scream. People were looking at us thinking we were famous whereas in truth we were a nasty bunch of bastards taking the piss out of the Intelligence for stopping our coach trips. We arrived in Blackburn and told the driver to head for the main entrance, and it was a delight to see all the police stop traffic while we were waved in to the directors' parking zone. The best was when Paddy Cook opened the gates for us, only to frantically fumble to set up his video camera when he realised who we were.

After the game we were given an escort out of town, as

they did not see the funny side of it, and before long we were back in Preston. We ended up in a club and were having a ball until there was trouble at the doors between the bouncers and a gang of locals. There was about thirty of us by now, as a few on the train had met up with us. We let the bouncers get on with their job, as it had nothing to do with us. Then they asked us to leave; they said Preston's mob was outside and was trying to force their way in to get at us, having returned from some away game and been told we had been in their town all day.

It was a major error on their part. As they tried to force their way in a second time, a few of their mates inside the club got a bit brave and were soon slapped about. Steve and I could see what was coming and agreed this needed nipping in the bud. Witty was fighting with a lad and ended up losing about £500-worth of gold as his watch and chain flew across the dancefloor, so Steve knocked the lad clean out and we made our way to the door. They were outside telling us to come out but were not in the same league as the firm we had. As soon as we piled out they were scampering around looking for a hero in their ranks, but none existed. Steve knocked another out and as I followed up he said, "Don't bother." He knew the connection was enough to send Preston Boy to slumberland and we set off after the rest.

We walked along a row of bars, all packed, but there were no takers. Preston were finished and it ended up going off with the bouncers as they tried to stop us getting through the doors to the mice inside who thought it was clever to throw glasses and bottles from safety. One of the younger lads put a load of windows in with a sandwich board, which brought the local police out in force, and we were rounded up and escorted to our limousines. We drove off with "Land of Hope and Glory" blasting out of the CD player.

We had a few more good days out after that, the main one being the weekend in Aberdeen, which for me turned into a long weekend. But soon it was impossible to go anywhere without the Intelligence spoiling, or saving, the day, depending on which way you look at it. Paddy Cook was replaced by a WPC who seemed to take our antics personally. Paddy made his job a success because he knew how we worked and knew what made us tick. He would get us in boozers and could tell if we were on a jolly or on a mission. Loads thought we had a grass in the camp but I didn't, I just think he was good at his job and but for him, some of the scrapes we got into would have been a lot worse. We did bring it on top for ourselves with the knife business, but that could not be controlled by any individual.

In the end, a bit of jail here and there and a few banning orders caused the break-up of the mob. For every one that left, there were young, game lads ready to replace them, but for me it wasn't the same. Although Everton can pull similar, if not bigger, numbers today, in my book it will never be what it was. Some disagree; it's a free country. In some of the lads' eyes, we never got the terrace credit or became the force we could have been, as we were as always leaderless and lacked organisation. But that is typical Everton. One thing is for sure though, if you did bump into the Snorty Forty on a bad day you would remember it. Out of all the years I played up – as I prefer to call it – at the match, those few seasons were my favourite. We were all mates and, as well as the lumber, we had a good laugh. Only a small, tight-knit firm will ever understand what I am talking about, and the one we had I would put up against the same numbers from any club anywhere.

I saw Everton get done at plenty of grounds when we were all young in the Seventies. In the Eighties, it happened occasionally. But that little firm, when the forty of us were together, did not get turned over once. That is the truth, and only a blagger will say otherwise. The Snorty Forty were unbeatable and I am proud to have been one of them.

17 HOME AND AWAY

THROUGHOUT THIS BOOK I have tried to give as honest an account as possible about my time as a football hooligan. It will obviously have a slant or bias to Everton and the firms I was involved with, but I have tried to keep it real and, where needed, researched in libraries to back up certain stories. That is important, as who would believe a mob of Scallies would be able to turn a ship around in the middle of the Irish Sea to go and pick up a few of the lads? Not many, but I have the newspaper reports that prove we did. The same goes for the Wimbledon coach being torched; you could ask Vinnie Jones but there is no need, as I have the pictures and report. The England subs' bench and line-up sketch is another that is almost impossible to do today. It all happened. If I read such stories myself, I would find them far-fetched.

What annoys me about some of the hoolie books on the market is that they lack back-up and may be fiction for all anyone knows. The Chelsea and West Ham books are amazing: is there a Cockney on this planet who has ever taken a hiding or been run at the match? If you can't admit when you took a kicking, you're not worth a toss and if you have never been put on your toes you are a liar or come from London. If I was going to make stories up I would not admit to running for my life at QPR or being put on my fat arse by the likes of Oxford and Stockport. Wherever possible I have also tried to tell only my own stories. There are times when you need to use other people's views and experiences, but I have kept it to a minimum.

No doubt many of you are asking by now, "Who is this Nicholls fella?" I have not had the press coverage that my old mate Mr Dodd had on his crusade to become England's number one, or even that of his mentor, the late Paul Scarrott. Both when at the height of their hooligan activities were publicity freaks and would sell their arse at Euston if it got them in the papers and a few quid to boot. That carry-on does leave you liable to a touch of jail. Personally I have turned down many reporters' offers of a good few quid for a picture and a story. I have had the chance to go on TV and talk about my favourite subject but thought better of it; the timing was never right. It is now.

You don't need to be like Doddy or the late Mr Scarrott to have respect up and down the country. Take Cardiff, Manchester United, Middlesbrough and Aberdeen: they don't come much bigger than those four on their day. I can go to any of those places and drink with the top lads from their firms and not have to buy a round all day – apart from in Aberdeen, but you know what the Jocks are like. You cannot do that without having earned respect. I believe I have, and lads from other firms can come to Everton under the same rules, because like me they are old school. Some of the pricks that run around today would not have lived in the days when the Swallows, O'Neills and Chellews ruled the terrace world in the Eighties. So now you can all put a name to the face you have seen at your grounds, that is if you bothered to stand and have a go. To be honest there are not many who did. I have been to over seventy grounds all over the country and fought at the vast majority of them.

At the time of writing the first edition of this book, a table had been published of how many so-called hooligans from each club had been banned from attending the World Cup Finals in Japan and South Korea. Why do they bother? It's pointless (although it has helped me to go through all the clubs and has jogged my memory of the strength of certain hooligan followings). The table was a factual guide of how many people are banned from attending the World Cup but no doubt bell-ends up and down the country were on the Internet bragging that they had a better firm than their rivals.

Perfect examples: West Ham, thirteen banned, Shrewsbury, fourteen banned. Does that mean a trip to Gay Meadow is worse than a day out in East London? Birmingham sixteen, Derby thirty-seven; the DLF more active than the Zulu Army? Everton six, Liverpool five, fewer hooligans combined than Lincoln City. Give it a rest. Poor old Brentford, Bournemouth, Kidderminster, Macclesfield Town, Southend, Torquay and Wycombe have no banned fans. Does that mean they have no hooligans at all? More like their bizzies are lazy, as every club in the country has hooligans.

I would like to have seen a similar "table of shame" before the World Cup in 1982 if we'd had the police surveillance and courts of today. It would have read something like West Ham, 1,597 banned, Everton, 1,364, Liverpool, 1,196, Manchester United, 1,845 and so on. They would have needed floating prisons in the Irish Sea to keep us all on; believe me, the prison population would have been fifty per cent football hooligans. Most of those big clubs have had plenty of coverage so this chapter is for all the other clubs who I have not yet mentioned. It is not because I don't particularly rate a firm: it may be that Everton have never played you, or that we have never really crossed swords. The likes of Birmingham, Cardiff, Portsmouth and Millwall have some of the tastiest mobs in the country but I can't help it if they have crap teams and have been in the lower divisions for years.

There are two sides to every story, unless you come from the capital, and I hope that when reading these short tales from around the country, you may also remember them. I hope some of you will have a laugh about it when you think, *that was the bastard who nutted me!* Or on the odd occasion, *that was the bastard we had off.* I can certainly laugh about it now, the good and the bad, because shit happens in all walks of life. In thirty years of being a hooligan there are plenty of bad days to go with the good ones and I believe they are all equally important. I have named this final chapter "Home and Away". Unlike some of the other hooligan books though, one thing is certain: it ain't no soap opera.

aston villa

Over the years we have had a load of trouble with the so-called Villa Youth. As a firm, I rate them mid-table with the likes of Coventry and Derby – they are certainly no better. Which amazes me. Birmingham is a huge city, and in other big cities with two major clubs, such as Liverpool, Manchester and Glasgow, there has never been much difference in the size of mobs both clubs could pull. But Villa, despite their huge gates, can't pull fifty lads week in, week out, whereas their Birmingham Zulu rivals have had hundreds for years.

I first had it with Villa the year they won the League in 1981. They have always brought a good following to Everton, you cannot fault them on that score, and that year they brought thousands and filled the Park End, which left loads looking for somewhere else to go. A bit of a mob went in the Lower Bullens Stand, a crazy move. All our lads used to go in the Paddock below and it was easy to climb into the stand in those days. When we went 3–1 down, we all went in. Villa were trapped in the stand and were wasted. It was a bit naughty, as there were loads of fans with them and some of them ended up getting it when they tried to help the lads. It was a lesson learned; in those days you had to stay where you had safety in numbers or get filled in, pure and simple. They fared no better after either.

A couple of years later, we played them in the last game of the season at their place and took a top mob in the Witton Lane Stand. A few minutes before the end, a few from behind the goal came in and told us there were loads of Villa mobbing up outside. They had a good mob and loads of blacks, which is not the case now, as Villa are a bit of an NF mob. We went out and it went off all the way back to the station. I think we shaded it but it was the best I had seen from them. We took a casualty when our best-known fan from Wigan was thrown through a shop window and ended up in a bad way. He got a top payout so in the end we all had a good result.

By far the worst violence we had with Villa was when we played them in a Milk Cup semi in 1984. They brought one of the biggest away followings we had seen in the Eighties and had hundreds of lads. They got in the Blue House early and when we steamed it, it was carnage. The battle lasted ages and it took our best shot with all the top lads of the time to do them. About ten were slashed, according to the *Liverpool Echo*, and that included a couple of Everton. The Blue House was a dangerous place if you got stuck inside; it has a massive lounge and a small bar and we used to split into two mobs and go through the bar and the lounge at the same time. It was chaos when it went off and if you were caught in one side you could struggle to get to the other. That night the place was smashed to bits and a Villa lad was stabbed, then thrown out of the window into the street. It was one of the worst nights on record at Everton, for arrests, for injuries and for pure violence.

The goings on at the second leg I have already written about, when about seventy of us were nicked. It was not as bad there as at Everton, and I missed it all after, but the firm and amount of lads we had in our 16,000 away following was awesome, and Villa Park was taken. They had another good turnout years later when, under Graham Taylor, they had a chance of winning the League in 1990. Again they filled the Park End and loads were put in the top balcony. It was a nightmare to police and before the game they were wandering around lost in small mobs and were easy pickings. After the game they were just as clueless. We were all outside the Red Brick a good hour after it had finished when a coach-full drove down County Road. I don't know if they were looking for it or not, but it was a stupid move and within seconds we ambushed them. They did try to get off, which makes me think it was a bit of a firm, but the bus was totalled and only a passing OSD van stumbling on it by accident saved them. They really were that lucky.

Villa knocked us out of the FA Cup a couple of seasons ago and again they were crap on the streets. We collared a couple of lads and they were given a walkover and ended up on the ale with us all night and still keep in touch. They are as baffled as I am as to why they can't raise the same numbers as Birmingham City. We went to meet them at Villa and they took us to a couple of boozers. Villa's main mouthpiece, Fowler, got wind and was apparently going to come down and sort it. He never turned up but a load of nasty bizzies did and we were sent packing pronto. They have the nastiest bizzies in the country.

One of them said to me, "You were arrested here in 1984, weren't you Nicholls?"

"Yes boss, were you on duty?"

"No, I was in fucking primary school. Isn't it time you grew up?"

For once I was speechless; he had a point, though.

When England played at Anfield, Villa jumped a main Everton lad in town and again Fowler was the mouthpiece. He has a reputation at England games as a bit of a bully and this was confirmed when I bumped into him and his mob in The Crown outside Lime Street. I was going to a wedding do, so got off straight after the game and went into The Crown for a quick beer before getting the train. It was a bad move, as about forty Villa were in there, including the bloat Fowler himself and his chief sidekick. I ordered a beer and straight away one of them clocked me.

"Are you Kelly, mate?" he asked.

"No, mate."

"Bruce?"

"No."

"What's your name then, mate? I've seen you about."

"Nicholls, mate."

"Yeah, we've heard of you. Where's your mob today?"

"Don't turn out for the small clubs, mate."

It was not the answer he wanted and off went my newest "mate" to tell his fat leader the news. They gathered around and told me they didn't want any trouble with Everton and that they were waiting for Huddersfield to come back from Tranmere, but I should not take the piss and if I wanted a go, to get a mob down. Allegedly, they were all banned from the match and had been on the ale all day. By the look of Fowler he had been on the ale since he was nine, but who am I to talk?

I was ready to get off but spotted Kelly outside with his wife, so went and told him Villa were on his case and to do one, as the mood by now was not improving. He went down to Spoons and I said I would meet him there once I had phoned a few of the lads and warned them not to go into The Crown unless they were mobbed up. As it stood, I could see this sly lot turning on any group of more than two or three. As I was outside on the phone, a cab pulled up and five of the lads got out and walked straight into the boozer before I had a chance to warn them. By the time I got in there it had already gone off, and indeed I was right that Villa were a sly little gang who would attack a mob of five.

Now, the incident was investigated by the police, and I believe a couple of lads were later convicted. I don't know what was said in court, but this is my version of what happened. When I got back in, there was a fight at the bar and about ten Villa were onto two Everton lads. Villa were tooled up with chairs, glasses and bottles and were peppering the place with missiles. They saw me coming in and I was bombarded, so picked up a table to protect myself from the onslaught. I forced my way to the bar, grabbed one of the lads, who had been cut, and tried to get him back to the door.

One of their lads shouted for Villa to stop throwing stuff and I thought it was because they realised we were not mobbed up. I put the table down. They roared again and one shouted, "Aim for his legs." With that we were pelted again. I was picking glass out of my body for days. We got to the door and were nearly out when a lad put a glass in my mate's face and opened his cheek up. Another one of ours fell by the door and was kicked unconscious. Now, had we had another ten lads I would not have a problem with any of that, as it is a risk you take and comes with the territory. My point is that the lads that got done in were not looking for trouble and were left in a bad way. One needed over 160 stitches in his face. It spilled outside and only a couple of Villa came out. The OSD turned up and gassed Everton and we had to get into the Yankee Bar to escape.

About two minutes later three taxis turned up with all the lads in and Villa needed an escort to the train. They will never have an ounce of respect from me after such a sly attack. The bizzies were asking lads to give evidence but nobody did, and the lad that was cut up bad could not claim a penny because of it. I'm not sure that in the melee many of them knew what was going on anyway. Everton's intelligence bizzie pulled me at the next game and said they had a film of me outside The Crown and that I was in the shit. I told him to give me a look at it and I would be prepared to go to court. I had hoped there was not a jury in the land who would convict me for trying to help two innocent people out of a pub as they were attacked by forty lads with glasses, bottles and chairs. I was wrong, as over a year later CCTV footage of the incident was used by the prosecution which helped Merseyside police secure another worldwide banning order against me!

barnsley

One of the best rows we had came at Oakwell after an FA Cup fifth-round tie in 1989. The lads will remember that day for the battle but thousands of other fans will also remember it for a crush on the terraces that nearly became a disaster. The away end was crammed and obviously over-full. There was only one way in and people were getting crushed at the front with no way out, as the fences were still up. Luckily there was a bit of a no man's land between our end and the stand and everybody spilled into the empty terrace before major damage was caused. It was on the local radio for days after about the potential for a disaster. The FA were supposed to have investigated the incident but I doubt if they ever did.

Just weeks later, a few miles up the road, a similar thing happened at another FA Cup tie. This time there was no spare terrace for the fans to spill into and football as we knew it would never be the same again. Everybody blamed each other but the truth is Hillsborough had been waiting to happen for years. It took the deaths of ninety-six fans to convince the FA and authorities that crumbling terraces and twelve-foot-high spiked fences had no place in the game. I believe that if urgent action had been taken after the incident at Barnsley, it could have been prevented.

We won the game and, when we came out, were not mobbed up as we headed for the station. As we got out of the big car park on the hill and came onto the road, Barnsley went for it in numbers and for a few minutes we were getting had off. Luckily loads of lads and blokes were parked up on the same road and before long we got it together. Barnsley did not care for the bizzies or us and were having a right pop. It went on up and down the road for minutes and ended about even. After their performance that day they will always have the respect of Everton's mob. We had most of our lads out and they took us to the limit; no other Yorkshire club has done that since Leeds in the Seventies.

A few years later they got promoted and we took a tidy little mob there. They had spotters in Wakefield and assured us they would be waiting for us. After the game they pulled tidy numbers down the same street we'd had it with them in before. As we approached we could see it was a bit of a kiddie firm and sensed they were wary of us. They were all pretty young and made no attempt to come at us. We fronted them a couple of times but they kept moving when they could have stood, as our police escort was nothing major. That day I finally realised that the football casual fashion had gone too far; one of their lads wore a leather flying hat with built-in goggles. I ripped him about it and all he could shout back was, "It's fashion."

We hung back at the station for ages after and we could see they still had a mob milling about, but no old heads were evident and we dismissed them as the kiddie firm that had followed us from the ground. Maybe it was just me and the lads getting old, but there was no way they could have bothered us that day. Still, that first time at Oakwell will never be forgotten, and I will always rate them after it.

birmingham city

Having just spent around fifteen years in the lower divisions, Birmingham missed the boat in terms of the kind of opposition that could match them. It was a major surprise though that on their return to the top flight their mob had disappeared into thin air. Many people thought they would cause havoc but for whatever reason it has not happened and by all accounts even Villa have started to gain the upper hand in England's second city – and that is taking the piss!

We played them a few times in the Eighties, the first major clash coming at the first game of the season after the summer Toxteth riots. Nobody gave a toss for the bizzies in the aftermath of Tocky and after the game we had hundreds out trying to get at a relatively small mob of Brummies. One bizzie who everybody thought was in plain clothes tracking us was put in hospital for weeks when he was set upon and battered. Other officers in uniform and on horses were attacked as we made our way back to the station in the hope of getting at Birmingham. The Zulus did come out of the ground a bit early and have a front with us outside the Paddock but didn't stay long and made no attempt to get out of their escort to the station. I could not blame them, given the mood and evilness of the Scousers that day. Toxteth was fresh in everybody's minds and respect for the law was nil. Soon the bobby on the beat was phased out and replaced with the gentle souls of the Operational Support Division. It is safe to say that the OSD have got even with us on many occasions.

St Andrews was not a ground we ever did that well at off the pitch. It was a nasty place and as dangerous at times as West Ham. We took mobs there but never really had it with them on the scale we did at other places and my own experiences were bad ones. I got picked off outside once, had to do a swift one and ended up blagging a ticket in the Main Stand. I was sussed in minutes and was slung out for my own safety. I did not object. The only other time I went there was on a coach for a midweek game. There was no sign of them before the game but after, a few of us were legged all the way back to the coach.

The last year they were in the top flight (until their recent return) they brought a cracking mob to us. We were all mobbed up by the Blue House and a police van went flying down towards The Abbey. We knew they were on their way up. Suddenly they appeared in front of us, led by a huge black lad wearing a Burberry deerstalker hat. They looked the business and there was a massive stand-off before the police forced them into the ground.

A couple of seasons ago, they came in the Cup and brought a full firm. I went into town and they were everywhere. A few of them were told that Everton would be up by the ground and nothing would go in the city centre with all the CCTV. They made their way up eventually but made no attempt to get out of the escort until they were right outside the ground. We went into them as they were going in and they had a top mob out, with virtually every one of them in the queue wanting to have a go. One nutcase was running at a police horse and butting it, he was demented. But after the game they not once came out of the escort, which we fronted a few times on the way to town. They had the numbers but were a lot quieter than I had expected, and the day's police operation was hailed a massive success

It was a different story when they played Liverpool in the FA Cup. At St Andrews, a couple of coaches with all Liverpool's lads on had been ambushed in a pub, and for the replay every face from Liverpool and Everton was out. The Brums came early and holed up in a pub called Sam Dodd's, near Anfield. There were also small mobs of them everywhere and a lot were cut up. One Everton lad had slashed four of them and gassed a van by The Arkles and was back at home having his tea at six o'clock, watching the news about the trouble at Anfield. After the game there were running battles all over Anfield as Birmingham took a beating. They came again in the 2001/02 season and did a bit better, smashing up a load of Everton boozers before the game, which was clever, as we were all at Stoke. One of my mates told me they brought a mob around to the Kop and got spanked, which proves the Reds can still pull a mob together for teams other than Man United.

bolton wanderers

These are another mob who are rated on the England scene but we don't even bother to take a firm there any more. In the Seventies they played us in a League Cup semi-final and brought thousands. They had it all the way back down Priory Road and did as well as any firm I had seen in those days. They had mobs everywhere and were not hiding but looking for it.

When we next went there in the FA Cup years later, I was expecting it to be rough, and we took a good mob and had it with them up at the ground. Their so-called casuals were getting had off all around the place until a load of beer monsters baled them out with a bit of a show. After the game, a huge mob followed us to the station but when it went off, so did they.

At the replay they were worse. They had a little mob outside the Park End and as I walked past them I was hit across the face with a traffic cone, which bust my nose. I "lost it" and ran into them on my own. I was fighting the main lad and ripped the hood off his ski coat before I was nicked. He was pleading with me to give his hood back, so I slung it over a wall. The sad bastard was in tears. I got a caution, got my beak fixed and was back at it with them after the game. Again they did not want to know.

That new ground of theirs is a joke too. It should be in Greece or Cyprus; as soon as it rains you get piss-wet through. You would have thought, given the climate they have in Greater Manchester, that someone would have sorted out the roof. We were the first side to play at the Reebok and should have lost when they scored but it was not given. No major fuss was made, as it was September, but they were well pissed off when we stayed up and they went down on goal difference the following May.

We nearly had it with a few of their lads more recently at Goodison. We were in the Lounge at the ground having a drink when I got a call that they were getting a bit lippy with some of our kids in the Oak. We went down and arrived as the bizzies were getting them out. One of them said, "Who the fuck are you lot, the cavalry?" They do not know how close they came to being hurt.

Bolton isn't all bad though. I met a bloke from there, Big Shaun, and now do very well out of him. He's a top bloke and invites me into the executive box every time we play them with the promise of free ale all day, no expense spared. He's not daft – he knows I'm even banned from the posh bits!

bristol rovers

When I worked in Bristol, I took to Rovers, and regard them as my favourite Nationwide League club. They had a good little mob and after a dodgy start I got on well with them and made some good mates. Stroudey, Mayo and a lad Colin, who also went with West Ham, were great with me and I was always made welcome when I went to watch them.

It was not always that way. I took a bad caning there the first time I ventured out. Bristol is a violent place and the rivalry between City and Rovers is severe. When I worked there it was really bad and there had been a spate of tit-for-tat attacks in various pubs across the city. I was living in Filton which, along with Patchway and Kingswood, was a Rovers stronghold. I went out to meet a lad in a boozer called The Britannia in Patchway and did not know of all the hassle, nor that it was not a place you went in unless you knew everybody in there. I walked in to meet my mate and a bird was singing "I Will Survive" on the karaoke. When I went to the bar, she stopped and the whole pub went quiet. I thought it was a wind-up and ordered a pint of Guinness.

The barman said, "Half a Guinness."

"No, a pint please mate."

"Half a Guinness."

"A fucking pint please, what's up, haven't you got any pint glasses?"

"You won't have time to drink a pint."

I turned around and saw a meathead behind me taking off a scruffy leather. I scanned the boozer and it was full. There were birds with pitbull terriers, and some of the dogs were better looking than the women. The meathead walked over and said, "Have you come for the karaoke or for something else? If you want something else, you're in the right place."

I knew he was not messing so went for bust and chinned him. It wasn't a bad shot but a bad idea and the place erupted. I got ragged out of the door but there was that many of them they could not cause any real damage. I was lucky not to get cut up and managed to escape outside and get a taxi to another boozer. It was a close call and the bird singing on the stage had picked the right song.

I met my mate in the other boozer and asked him where he had been. He told me he had walked in and a load of lads were sniffing glue at the bar, so he had walked right back out. I went to the bogs to clean myself up and a couple of lads came in and asked me if I was City. I thought, *fuck this, it's too on top, I'm off home*, but when I told them I was Everton and working down there they were sound. They were Rovers and told me about the attacks between them and City and showed me a newspaper cutting about a Rovers lad who had been beaten with a baseball bat full of nails a few weeks before. Because of this, any strange face in their pubs was greeted with extreme caution, and I could understand why.

It turned out that I was very lucky in The Britannia; a week earlier, a Pakistani had gone in there after his car broke down and they had set him on fire. The place was full of the dregs of Bristol and the Rovers lads had a laugh that I had been in there and come out alive. I stayed on the ale with them and ended up watching Rovers with them a few times; they were top "kiddies", as they like to call themselves.

At the time they were playing their games at Twerton Park in Bath and it was a bit of a pain to get to but they had Big Malcolm Allison as manager and got half-decent crowds. The best game I went to was when they beat City 4–0. I was made up for the lads, as City were supposed to be top dogs and yet were annihilated by Rovers. We met up in a moody club in Kingswood and made our way to Bath in cars. Rovers had a tidy little firm and were looking all over for City, but they came in late. After the game I was with the main Rovers mob but apart from a few minor skirmishes there was little trouble. City get all the news down there but from what I saw Rovers were capable of giving as good as they got.

I was a bit pissed off when I had to leave Bristol and it came after a fight in town. A big black City "kiddie" was fronting everybody outside a chippy and I had a go with him. He picked up one of those metal rods that the council stick in roadworks to tape around, so I got one and we were like fencers while a massive crowd watched. He was too strong for me and, when I dropped my mock sword, the bastard put his right across my forehead. He missed my eye by an inch and I still have the dent where he cracked my skull. I was finished and got pulled into the chippy by a crowd but the bloke went mental, picked up a full paving slab and threw it through the window. He got nicked and it turned out he was on angel dust, which explained his power.

I was not too clever and had a spell off work and lost my job, which was a pity, as I loved it down there. Bristol is a rough place but if you are in with the right crowd it is a top night out. As Chris Brown wrote in his excellent book *Bovver,* "Goodnight Irene." It was goodnight for me after the metal pole attack, but I will always have good memories of the Rovers lads. I lost touch with them when I left and have not been back apart from when Everton played City a couple of times. We played Rovers a couple of seasons ago in the Worthington Cup and they brought loads. I had a lookout for any lads I knew but it was a bit moody with the bizzies. If any of them read this, they will always be welcome at Everton.

cardiff city

The Soul Crew are now one of the most famous football firms in the country, no doubt partly thanks to: the recent pitch invasion and coin throwing against Leeds (that is all that happened, by the way); the behaviour of their nutty chairman Sam Hammam; and the recently published book named *Soul Crew,* written by David Jones and Tony Rivers. I am not qualified to assess them as I have been there only once and that was many years ago, but I have seen a video that has been doing the rounds and the numbers they had out against Millwall and Stoke were unbelievable. But are they as good as they make out?

Having seen the 2002 TV documentary focusing on Cardiff, there is no doubt that they can pull a firm to take on anybody. That is unquestionable. They are a bit of a rent-a-mob at times though, the Chelsea or Man United of Wales. When they have a big match, it seems the whole of the country turns out for them, bar Swansea and Wrexham. I know this is a fact as I have mates in Bangor and they go to about six games a year and I bet there are hundreds of lads in the Valleys who do the same. Good luck to them. But for those six games, there are another forty when they may have just a few dozen lads. Believe me, they have been to places with a handful of boys, just like the rest of us. So the hype about them and their 2,000-strong mobs every week is just that, hype.

I know one of Cardiff's top lads, and he is called that in the *Soul Crew* book. He has been a guest at Everton a few times and is a great fella, and I have yet to meet a more genuine lad. He would have written a different story, because some of the stuff DJ Dai (Jones) and Lakey (Rivers) have put down about us is, let's say, highly disputable. By their own admission one of them is a closet Kopite so I shouldn't be too surprised. I met Lakey when he was on the panel at an event about hooligan books in Liverpool and we had a good chat about our differences, and have also met Dave; both are good lads but maths is not their strong point!

Take the first time we played there in 1977. One of their mates describes the game: he has 4,000 Evertonians in mohair jumpers coming on two trains (long trains in those days!) and being wasted before running back to the station by twenty past four. Yes Everton got had off, before the game especially, but keep it real, we were never on a train before the match ended, and if that is the biggest walkover you have ever had, they must have had some serious battles over the years.

Their story of the day Everton played in the Cup at Newport, of how they were at home to Millwall on the same day but the game was called off so both mobs turned up at our match and there were three segregated areas in the away end, gets off to a cracking start – then they spoil it by claiming Everton asked Millwall to team up with them to have a go at Cardiff. It is like saying Cardiff asked Swansea to team up with them to have a pop at Flint Town United. Anyone aware of the bad blood between Everton and Millwall, after seven Londoners were stabbed at our place in the Seventies, knows they wouldn't piss on us if we were on fire.

Still, that does not take away the fact that Cardiff are among the best firms in the country, and the documentary about them only enhanced their mob's reputation – though considering they are supposed to be "untouchable" at home, the Mancs appeared to be taking a few liberties down there and I heard that Spurs gave them a welcome to remember recently. I also witnessed them getting a bit of a caning in Russia before a Wales game when a large number of so-called lads watched from the safety of the hotel bar when the going got tough.

They do have the potential to be a massive club though and I hope they make it into the Premiership some day in the near future. And I would love Sam Hammam to take over Everton: he is off his barnet and would do a great job for us and would maybe let me back into my beloved Goodison!

coventry city

Highfield Road will always have a place in my heart, as it was the first ground I was ever arrested at. Joking apart, it is not the soft touch some people think. They recently showed this against Man City in the Cup and made the headlines with their televised battle at home against Portsmouth. In the Eighties, true, we would take thousands there and it was one of the easiest places to go in the Midlands, though I jibbed into the Main Stand one year and was had off by a load of punks. My prospects looked bleak until a few old Everton blokes bailed me out. The walk back to the station was a good one and they always had a go as you walked across the park at the bottom of Highfield Road.

One of our lads, Kenny, got jail once after a game there

and it was the biggest laugh we have ever had in court. We had been on our way home on the train and a load of kids raided the buffet bar. At Crewe, about twenty transport bizzies got on and began searching everyone for evidence, of which most had been eaten. Kenny picked up an empty sandwich case, taking the mickey, and asked a bizzie if that was what twenty of them had stopped the train for. They did not see the funny side of it and nicked him for handling stolen property!

Kenny would not plead guilty on principle and the case ended up in crown court. In the end the jury found him guilty. It was hilarious. The next courtroom had a murder case going on – a policeman had been charged with killing his wife and faking a car crash to cover it up and all the national papers and TV were there. Kenny's case was so funny that they all came in to see him sentenced. The judge went on about this eighty-seven-pence sandwich costing the taxpayer seventy grand, and gave Kenny three months. The whole courtroom was in bulk apart from Kenny, who was taken down shouting obscenities about British justice.

The worst time I had at Coventry was when a couple of lads did that old chestnut, the ticket scam. At every ground we would ask the girl at the desk if there were any tickets to collect for Mr Young, and then would clock a few names on the envelopes as she went through them. A lad spotted the name Quinn, and after a few goes somebody ended up with a load of tickets and Players' Lounge passes after guessing the first name. It turned out they belonged to the brother of Mickey, the Scouser who played for Coventry, who was not a man to be crossed. Minutes later, Quinn's brother turned up with a load of mates and nearly put his head through the window when the bird said somebody had already had them away. Word was passed around and I think he got them back; I'm not sure, as I was in the Everton end as soon as I heard who they belonged to.

Coventry nearly sent us down a few years ago, and their support that day was great. We needed a win to stay up. They filled the away end, equalised with a minute to go and were going mad. Everybody piled down the front to get on the pitch when a massive roar went up: Bolton had lost and a draw was enough for us. It would have been nasty if we had lost, but Coventry didn't seem to give a toss; they were either very brave or plain stupid.

It is strange how the tide turns. In 1985 we had been to Coventry as Champions and they needed to beat us to stay up. We had won the League weeks earlier but the team turned in a disgraceful performance and were beaten 4–1, meaning Coventry stayed up and Norwich were relegated. If that happened now there would be an inquiry, we were that bad. After the game, thousands of Coventry went on the pitch and all the Everton fans were singing, "Champions." I wondered how many of them would have sung it if we had won and sent Coventry down.

grimsby town

We played Grimsby home and away in the late Seventies and early Eighties and they had a good go at both games. In fact when we were arguably at our best, they were the best firm from the lower divisions to come to Everton. At their place, we lost in the League Cup and it mattered in those days, as it was a trophy worth winning. Just before the match finished we took a firm into their end and thought it would be a walkover. It wasn't, and we were fighting like fury before the bizzies restored order. Outside was a bit iffy as well and we had a battle on the way back to the coaches. They did not budge an inch at home.

In 1985 they came to us in the same competition and got in the Blue House early, as lots of mobs did. Villa, Boro,

Newcastle and Sunderland had all pulled the same stunt, but Grimsby took more shifting than all of them. We went in there again and again and, as was the norm at the time, a few were slashed. Yet they were right up for it, and although they were not a casual mob as such, they had loads of good big lads who did themselves credit. They beat us again on the pitch, and after the game they even put a bit of a front up when they came out. It was a big match for them and the whole town must have turned out, but in my eyes they were as game as anybody who came to Everton that season, and we saw all the top firms that year.

hull city

These are the only firm I will mention that I have not crossed swords with. I saw them a couple of seasons ago in Manchester and they were an impressive sight. They had a good 200 and looked the business. They are called the Silver Cod Squad after the boozer they drink in, and their main lad is still at it in his forties.

My man in Cardiff told me that Hull had a bit of a result down there and also at Swansea. At home they can pull over 300 for a big game and all the bouncers turn out with them.

They had a bit of a do with Boro pre-season and a few got jailed. Their man who wrote *City Psychos* got in touch when they were doing a benefit night for the lads' families. I sent a few bits up to auction that Owen and Rooney had signed and the day after a couple of them phoned thanking me and invited me to a game, which was a nice touch. Once my ban is up I will take them up on their kind offer but make sure I take plenty of coin, as I have worked with loads of lads from there and they could all have a fight but were tight bastards!

ipswich town

I cannot believe we turned out for these muppets two years
running, but after we went there once and had a bit of hassle,
we felt obliged to go again. It was a case of having to really,
just in case they thought they were something. They are not,
and we should not have bothered. All it did was bring it on
top with the bizzies, who wanted to nick me for organising
violence. Jail for having it with the Mancs or Cockneys is an
occupational hazard, jail for the likes of Ipswich is pure
stupidity, and I swear I will not go there again.

We went on a jolly as an excuse to wet the baby's head,
as one of the lads had just become a dad and as it was
planned as a bit of a bender we had a full turnout. We got
to a big boozer by the station early, and for once trouble was
the last thing on our minds. After about an hour, a baldy
knobhead came in and told us he was a Colchester hooligan
– the mind boggles – and that Ipswich were on his mobile
and wanted to sort it with us. He passed over his phone and
the lad on the other end backed up Colchester's finest,
saying that if we walked towards the town they would meet
us halfway. It was a daft idea but we decided to go and have
a look; personally I thought it was either a wind-up or,
worse still, a set-up.

We got by a huge roundabout and Ipswich were indeed
on their way towards us. They had about thirty, which soon
halved and by the time we met had melted in the hot sun
to about six. I was going to give them a walkover and ask
the lad to come back later when his mates had found their
bollocks, and introduced myself very politely to him.

"Good afternoon mate, I'm Nicholls, and if you want it
after, tell us where. If not, stop pissing us off or we will have
to fuck you."

He had his chance but instead threw a dig, mumbling
something about me carrying a few pounds – he was not as

polite as me either. So I dropped him with a cracking right and he was pleading not to be slashed. He wasn't, but a young lad took his Stone Island badge from his coat to teach him a lesson. He was not a fast learner and jumped up and shouted something about my sexual habits involving my right hand, so I booted him in the bollocks and he jumped over a wall into the subway. I heard a crash and looked over the wall: it was at least a twenty-foot drop and the Ipswich lad was in a heap. His mates got a few slaps before we were pulled by the bizzies and herded to the ground.

We got out early and headed back to the boozer about twenty minutes before the end of the game and waited for a good hour after. We never had a sniff of them, so off we set. Four of our lads were on the train, and as soon as we left, Ipswich battered them. Their mob had been in the station all the time, waiting for a couple of stragglers. It was tough on the lads, and Terry had a busted nose, but they should have been on the coach with us, and not showing off on the train. It did mean that we would have to go back the next season though. I heard they were on the Internet the next day whining that forty Everton had battered five of them and that two were in hospital. That was their fault, not ours.

We filled a coach easily the following season and were there by twelve. We went into town and never saw a lad until about seven at night, when we went into a boozer and the Ipswich bizzies had to get ten lads out before they burst into tears. By now we had been pissing off the bizzies all day and they were sick of us. I got a pull and told that the coach was being brought up to the boozer and I had fifteen minutes to get everybody on it or I would be locked up until court on Monday. It was not a hard decision and we set off home, without a punch being thrown.

Their mouthpiece to this day is still on the hoolie sites calling me a shithouse and even claims I was not there when he was KO'd. Well if he would care to let me have his address I will gladly send him back the Stone Island badge that fell from his jumper as he was getting ragged and which I kept for a souvenir.

leeds united

The Leeds Service Crew, or the Yorkshire Republican Army, are one of the most feared firms in the country, well in Bournemouth anyway. I rated them very highly in the Seventies, when they would always look for it up Priory Road. At home they were a nasty shower, and the walk to and from the ground was dangerous. It did not matter if you were only a kid in those days, unless you were draped from head to toe in white and yellow, you were fair game.

Since the casual scene hit Yorkshire though, a few years after it reached Manchester and a decade after we discovered it, I have never particularly rated the masses from Elland Road. They have taken large firms to the capital and have a good name at Chelsea, but in Manchester and Merseyside I know they are not that well thought of. They have hit the headlines on many occasions but usually it has involved mass vandalism; I reckon they never recovered from the Miners' Strike riots and thought they could get away with it for years after. Take the time they went ballistic in Bournemouth. It is hardly a result on a national scale setting fire to a few deckchairs and slinging donkey dung at holidaymakers.

Since the Seventies, they have never brought it to Everton the way they used to before they swapped their scarves and three-star jumpers for cap sleeves and cords. There has been trouble but they were not the same mob once they turned casual and loads of their fighters were left behind, as there was nothing trendy that would fit them.

The best battle we had at their place was in the FA Cup in 1985. They were doing well in the Second Division, on and off the pitch, and we were top of the first. We had 500 on the ordinary and were locked in the station on arrival to await special buses to take us to the ground. I jumped across the track and saw that the mail area led out into the street, so shouted for everybody to get over the platform. Very few bothered, so I yelled, "Only the wankers get on the buses, what the fuck have we come here for?"

Within seconds, we had about 300 out in the street and straight away bumped into a mob of Leeds. They could not have realised we were Everton and stood until it was too late. I butted one, his head smashed a shop window and the rest scattered. The bizzies were on our case and soon the 300 were less than 100 as many were forced back to the station. We carried on regardless and soon were surrounded by hundreds of Leeds. As we went under the big tunnel near the station, they were mixed in with us, with mobs in front and behind us. The was a deafening chant of, "Leeds, Leeds, Leeds," and we were seconds away from being legged or killed. The first option was my preference, by the way. All around me was chaos. It was dark and horrible, nobody knew who was who and all around lads were getting punched. Leeds stopped in the front, blocked the road and I thought it was the end, but Mark pulled a machete out of his coat and said, "Anybody goes past me gets this."

It saved us from humiliation. As one, we charged into the Leeds at the front and they scattered. As they went, we turned and went back into the mob behind us and they backed off, leaving us to walk unopposed into the town. The bizzies appeared and forced us up onto the steps of some civic building and Leeds looked amazed at how few we had. There was a massive row going on in their ranks as they realised that eighty Everton had chased two massive mobs.

I shouted to one lad, "You have just been had off by eighty of us."

He replied, "Fuck off, we have just been had off by ourselves."

He was spot on: the lads at the front thought the entire mob in the tunnel was Everton, while the Leeds behind thought that, when we turned, the Leeds at the front were Everton too. So in fact Leeds had legged Leeds with the help of eighty Everton. Well, it was not our fault that the thick bastards didn't know who their mates were.

We were given a massive escort to the ground and were dumped into a crappy stand above the paddock. Leeds were packed into the stand across from the old Kop and were all standing on the seats. Rozzer had a flare gun and fired it at the masses behind the goal but he was a bit short and it ended up in the net. The bizzies had to put it out before the goal caught fire. The next shot was a direct hit and the Leeds were like dominoes falling backwards and knocking each other over.

We won the game and that made Leeds worse: we had shamed them in the town, shot them in the ground and knocked them out of the Cup. It had been a bad day at the office for them and was sure to be interesting when we got out amongst them. We were kept in for ages and from the back of the stand could see them mobbing up on a big bank outside. It was too good an opportunity to miss and another couple of flares were fired into them. They were direct hits and we could see them sliding down the muddy bank on their arses. The bizzies piled in and nicked a lad for firing the flare; it wasn't him but when he went to court the forensic had found traces of the flare on his coat and the poor lad got nine months for standing too near the real marksman. The bizzies tried to put us on buses but we all walked and there was a few hundred of us. They took us the long way around, as Leeds were after revenge. Nothing happened on the way back until we got on the station and chased a small mob off the platform. It was a great night for Everton and saw the best mob we ever took to Leeds. They could not live with us.

After that experience, I thought they would have a go back when they next came to Goodison, but when we played them first game of the season after the Bournemouth riots, they came in numbers but never ventured very far out of the escort. They were a let-down after all the hype. It is easy to smash up small towns when you are full of ale, and that is what Leeds do best.

manchester city

The City mob were called the Guvnors, but Guvnors of where? Not Manchester in the eyes of many Scousers, that is for certain. Whereas United came year in year out and had a go at both our place and Anfield, City made only the odd show and at times in the League did not even fill half the away end. As Mickey Francis reports in his book, called *Guvnors*, they did come mob-handed for a couple of Cup games and fared as well as anybody, but they ended up cut up on both occasions. The quarter-final game was the best and they did have a great mob but we had hundreds. The walk to and from Lime Street took them hours.

At their place, we went in the Platt Lane Stand two years running and had a mixed reception. The first year, we got in just before kick-off and City came in behind us and were battling outside the turnstiles to get in with us. It was too late and as soon as we mobbed up we went for it and chased them all over the seats. The bizzies put us on the pitch and threw us into the Kippax. The year after, we got in a bit early and the police stopped the main mob going in. Only about sixty made it, and in those days it was not enough.

Everton got steamed in there. I suppose you could call it a score draw.

The best crack I had at City was when a small mob of us went in the new Umbro Stand. We planned to keep quiet until half-time, then do them in the bar, but we scored in the first minute and by two minutes past three there was uproar. We backed them off and the bizzies took us into the Main Stand. City had a massive mob blocking the exit so the bizzies made us wait while they were cleared. As we were waiting we scored again and it caused murder in the stand. We were lucky to get put back in the Everton end and not get nicked.

At half-time, I was pointed out by one of the Manc cops and they threw me out. It was moody outside and a few City faces knew me, so I paid into the Kippax and watched the second half with my gob shut. We went 4–2 up and, with a couple of minutes to go, I went out and got back into our section to get the lads together. In the last minute we scored again, and I bet not many people have done what I did that day: I saw my team score from every side of the ground. At the end of the game, we were kept in the seats. We had some thunder flashes from a lad in the army. A steward sat with his back to us on a milk crate and I landed one right behind him. Everybody could see it fizzing and we started a countdown; the flash went off and blew him off the crate and the whole Everton end was in bulk.

Afterwards, we went up to Piccadilly Gardens and ended up attacking the Dry Bar, which was owned by the people behind Factory Records and the famous Hacienda club. It was a bad move, taking liberties at that time of the evening. We marched in and a few City were there flapping, no great numbers, so we had a wander further up the road. On our way back, we noticed a few large lads in the window, so we tried to force our way in, but the doors were bolted. Some bounced bins off the windows and doors but these blokes inside just laughed. Something didn't seem right to me – they clearly didn't give a fuck for us, and one or two seemed to be slipping things onto their hands. The next minute the doors flew open and they piled out – tooled up and as horrible a bunch of gorillas as you will ever see. Turns out they were Manchester's main door firm, meeting up in the Dry Bar at the start of the night before heading off to their various pubs and clubs.

It was a top ambush by them. Not only did we have these roid-heads chasing us with extendable truncheons, chains, coshes and knuckledusters, but at every pub we retreated past, the doormen had been radioed and came out to wade in. With a few City joining in with a missile bombardment, we had to back off down to the Gardens, and were lucky to get away with damage limitation. Still, shit happens, and it didn't spoil a top day.

One incident you won't read about in the *Guvnors* book is the Battle of Hilton Park (see Chapter Four), the day they slashed an Everton lad in London only to suffer frightening retribution at a service station later that day. Still, I am glad City are back up with the elite, as they are a massive club, have strong local support and are a bit like Everton; they too have to put up with the rich-neighbour shit and all the international fans crap.

I always rated United as the main Manc firm, but have it on very good authority that the city centre has seen a slight swing in ownership recently and United have to be on their guard following a couple of defeats on returning home from away games. I went to a pre-season game at City's new ground and it is an impressive arena, certainly a lot kinder on the eye than Maine Road. I cringe when I think of that place with all the back streets and alleyways on a Tuesday night in November, because I kid you not it was frightening.

oldham athletic

Of all the smaller Manc clubs, I have had the worst trouble at Oldham. They never brought a mob to Everton but a couple of times when I went there I found it to be a place where, if you wanted lumber, you would get it. They still have a firm at home now and one of their lads, Martin, who was featured on a hooligan documentary on TV and is heavily into the right-wing Combat 18, comes to Everton for the odd game.

We played them in the FA Cup in the early Nineties and, after two uneventful draws, we went back there for the second replay. At the first game, a couple of lads in a car had been battered when they went into a boozer near the ground, so we arranged to pay it a visit and see if they were as keen to have a go against a busload of us. I went in and got a drink before the lads turned up. Through the bar I could see all their lads were packed in the far corner. A few of our lot then came in and I went to the toilet before the inevitable kick-off. I had to pass them all to get to the bogs but, as I had kept a low one, I felt pretty safe as I emptied my bladder. It was not one of my better decisions; as I was doing what comes naturally, I heard the windows go through in the main room. I came out and Everton had the door blocked from the street, all the windows were in and they were screaming at Oldham to come out. Oldham were cowering behind each other and I thought I could push my way through and get on the right side before I was attacked by my own mob.

As I went for it, a Manc saw what was going on and put a stool over my head. I managed to stumble outside but was not too clever and can't remember much of the ensuing battle. Oldham eventually got out and, as we were fighting in the street, an Asian lad came from the side of me and nutted me in the face. I was well pissed off, with a nasty cut across my forehead and one eye shut, and I'd been in the place only ten minutes. I had concussion from the stool and don't remember any of the match; although I was there in body, I was missing in mind and it took me days to get my head together.

The next time I went there, I had a fight in the paddock but was let down badly by a lad I won't name and shame. The Everton end was a sell-out, so I bunked in the Oldham paddock and tried to keep a low one, which is something I have never been a master at. Tony Cottee scored for Everton and a lad near the front jumped up and was set upon by a load of Mancs. I thought it was my mate Kenny, so I piled in and pushed him onto the track by the side of the pitch. They then started on me but I was in front of them by a crush barrier and, as they came under, I was volleying them back. A circle opened up but none of them could get behind me. I was in my element.

I turned to Kenny to get him to pull me out but he had gone. Then, to the left of me, I saw another Everton lad who was watching the fight and did not help. I backed off to the wall and a steward shouted for me to pack it in. Pack what in, taking on a full end of Oldham on my own? He got his mate and came in and they put me in a headlock and pulled me backwards over the wall. As I was on my knees, a Manc leant over and smashed my nose. I was led out and was given a top cheer from the Everton end.

Outside I saw the lad I'd thought was Kenny – and it wasn't him. He was boasting that "we did this" and "we did that" and I had to warn him that there was no "we", it was just me, and that if he carried on he would get a bit of what Oldham had had. My nose was broken again and I was that angry that just before full-time I went back in there to have some more, but was spotted by the stewards and chased out. I then asked the Everton lad why he never helped me and he said I was doing well without him! Like I said, I won't name him but he knows who he is and he also knows he let me down that day. In fact I don't know how IRISH JOHN can sleep at night after that.

oxford united

If I could tell just one whopping lie in this book, it would be that I never got chased and hammered at Oxford, but it happened and is a story that needs telling, as I can now see the funny side of it. It also proves that if you don't show respect, you can get hurt wherever you go. At Oxford we showed none and were sorry for it.

It was a Milk Cup quarter-final in 1984 and we went there in a Transit van. Everton should have lost the game. Oxford were in the old Third Division but were winning until Kevin Brock played a short back-pass to his keeper, Adrian Heath nipped in to score, and weeks later we were at Wembley. We went from being rubbish to champions in two years. I was with a few mates and mates of mates and never really trusted some of them. They were a bit clever for their own good and talked a good fight but rarely performed. They helped fill the van and paid for the petrol, so they just about got my nod to come with us, but they had bluffers written all over them, and it turned out I was a good judge of character.

We parked in the town centre. As we were getting out of the van, a couple of Everton fans ran past mumbling about being chased by a mob of black lads. We should have left it, but the bluffers thought they were hard and so we all headed in the direction of the trouble. We walked straight into a good-sized mob of Oxford, and they were all black. It went straight off and Ian belted one over the head with a cider bottle, but it was plastic and he got done in for his troubles. In less than a minute, we were being chased all over town and I had lost a training shoe and had a lip as big as the lads chasing me. I ran into a massive department store and came across a few Everton lads in there on the rob. They helped me out and we blocked the doors with a rail full of clothes, but Oxford all piled in and off we went again. It was no time to be a hero, there was loads of them and a couple were tooled up and shouting to cut us.

I made it into a DIY shop and picked up a brush handle. Seconds later, a big black bloke came in and I broke the stick over his head. Behind him came his missus and she started screaming for me to leave him, yelling that they were only after some paint. He had nothing to do with the mob. Sorry about that. I made it outside and saw a white lad across the road so walked over and asked him the way to the ground. He smiled and booted me in the bollocks, shouting to all his black mates that I was there. I saw a bloke on a bike and ran over, pushed him off and pedalled into the distance. I didn't stop for about two miles, when I saw the floodlights and threw the bike over a fence and walked the rest of the way.

After the match, we took a mob into town with all the proper lads and never had a sniff of them. At the replay we ambushed two buses and there was not a single lad on them either. So I don't think that the mob we bumped into were a football mob, but they did us in and that is that. I will never get revenge for that beating and it still bugs me today. I bet the poor fella who was out buying a tin of paint feels the same too! You could ask 99.9 per cent of Evertonians what they remember about Oxford United and they will mention the Kevin Brock back-pass. I am the 0.1 per cent that would say a plastic cider bottle, a brush handle and a ten-speed racer.

port vale

We went to Port Vale in 1980 for a pre-season friendly and they had a bit of a mob in the stand to the side of us. After the game, we bumped into them. They were hopelessly outnumbered but stood and took their punishment. I have seen bigger numbers get on their toes. The other highlight of that night was when we were walking up to the ground past a river or canal. There was a load of blokes fishing and they kept telling us to be quiet and all got lashed into the water for their troubles.

It was obvious that when they came to Goodison in the FA Cup in 1996, they would bring a firm, and they did not disappoint. Before the game they had loads walking around the ground giving it the large one, not really in a mob as such, but you could sense they would have a go so we pulled a tidy firm together and blocked Goodison Road at full-time. I was expecting them to go left and up to the coaches when they saw us, but they got it together and turned right and there was a brief skirmish before the bizzies stormed us and put Vale into an escort.

I thought that was the end of it and we all ended up in the boozer thinking they had been put on a bus to Lime Street. After about half an hour, one of the lads phoned and said he had seen a crowd walking down Scotty Road with no escort and that they must be Port Vale. We jumped a load of taxis, met in Wetherspoons and made our way to St George's Hall, which they would have to pass on their way to the station.

We had a good fifty but had no idea how many they had. I loved it when it was like that. One of the authors of the Cardiff City book *Soul Crew* wrote that there is no better buzz in the world than being with 1,000 lads and knowing you are untouchable. I disagree; when you are in a mob that big and know you are unbeatable, you may as well be doing a spot of gardening, as you are not going to get a fight. The biggest buzz is being with a small crew and not knowing what is coming to meet you. That is when the adrenaline really pumps.

It was a freezing night and the ground was thick with snow. Apart from the traffic, there was a deadly hush and we were all silent, waiting, half-thinking it was a bluff and half-hoping it wasn't. Next minute you could hear a crunching noise as feet broke the icy carpet and, unless there was a Greenpeace march around St George's Hall, it had to be Vale. Indeed it was, about sixty of them. All the lads from the little kick-off on Goodison Road were on show. There was a brief stand-off as we sized them up, while they seemed shocked that at nearly seven o'clock we were still around and had found them. Their main lad gave them a rallying call, put his hand down his pants and pulled out a pathetic-looking blade. I screamed for one of our younger lads to pass me a machete that we may or may not have had; it mattered not, they did not like the sound of it, crumbled in seconds and were off. It was like a scene out of a cartoon as they tried to run off and we tried to chase them: with the floor like a skating rink, nobody moved an inch. They finally got into gear and we ran them all the way to Lime Street where, among the safety of the station police, they fronted it to save a bit of face.

Vale had given the bizzies the slip and made it to town for a battle, had done all the hard work … and then blown it, like a golfer who gets on the green in one and then five-putts.

sheffield united

A few of our lads are good mates with the Blades boys. We always get a good reception when we go there and are well looked after. They are top blokes and, from what I have seen, rule the Steel City with relative ease. I first met them when they turned up at our place a few years ago. I was not aware that they had been invited and it was a bit of an uneasy afternoon. They were mobbed up in our boozer and it looked like they were taking the piss.

Years later, now that I know them and respect them, I know that was not the case and they are welcome to do the same anytime. Not that they get the chance as, since Hans Segars slung one in for us against Wimbledon in the last game of the season and Sheffield were relegated instead of us, we have never played them. Incidentally, the book *Blades Business Crew* by Steve Cowens claims that we were legged at Bramall Lane once. I cannot remember it and neither can any of the other lads. Mr Cowens must have mixed us up with Liverpool!

southampton

It may surprise a lot of people but Southampton will always have respect from us after a crazy three or four years when, every time we played them, it was bedlam.

The first time was after an FA Cup match at The Dell in 1983. At the end we all piled onto the pitch, as we had secured an unlikely replay. They had a load of whoppers giving it the big one in the paddock and we bounced in and cleared the whole section in a minute and a half. The morning of the game we had been in Lillywhites sports shop in London and a load of Yids mobbed up outside, so we got tooled up with golf clubs and cricket bats and steamed them all over the road; they lasted less time than Southampton.

The following year brought one of the all-time great riots when, after the FA Cup semi-final at Highbury, there was fighting on the pitch for over half an hour. Adrian Heath scored our winning goal in the last minute of extra time and thousands invaded the pitch to celebrate. It took minutes to restart the game and seconds later we were on again as the referee blew for full-time. There were no fences at Highbury and within seconds we were joined by a couple of hundred angry Saints. We were all casuals, while most of them were still in scarves and bobble hats. Yet when it first went off, loads of Everton ended up getting legged back from the Clock End, which was full of Southampton. We soon surged back though and mounted officers on the pitch were simply ignored. We fought for ages. I put one lad on his arse and as I was going to finish him off a young bizzie went to hit me over the head with his truncheon, so I blocked it with my arm and ended up with a dislocated elbow. I had never known pain like it.

Had that battle happened today, it would have been made into a film. There were over 100 arrests, seventy-odd in hospital and ten stabbed or slashed. At the time it hardly got a mention on the national news, but there are some incredible news photographs of it and it had to be seen to be believed. Winning the game in the last minute of extra time, then having a proper riot on the pitch after, was as good as it got for us, like winning the Pools and the Lottery on the same day. It even went off again in the streets after, as mobs of Arsenal teamed up with Southampton to have another go at us. I looked a right soft twat all the way home with my dislocated arm stuck in the air, as the first aid crews would not help me at the ground – they were overrun with casualties.

The following season, we went there for a crucial League game and took thousands. We had loads locked out and forced the gates, ending up in the home section next to the Everton fans. There was about 200 of us on a little strip of terrace above the Southampton fans and when we went 2–0 up they had a bit of a charge at us. We had the numbers and the advantage of being above them and it was not much of a fight. However, as it calmed down, a lad pointed out that my arm was bleeding; I had been slashed in the skirmish. Some shady bastard had striped me, and it had cut through my leather and just broken my skin. I had to go to the first aid room to be bandaged and was taken past the Everton bench. The sub, who I won't name, gave me a wink as if to say well done. That was what it was like at Everton that year: on and off the pitch, we were the best and were as one.

The following season we had them again in the FA Cup and beat them 2–1 at our place. They didn't bring many and there was no sign of them around the ground before or after the game, so we all went to the Oak on the ale. After half an hour, a lad in a green flying jacket came in and announced that he was Southampton and that his firm was outside. Only West Ham and Middlesbrough had ever done that before and we were stunned.

Everton steamed out and sure enough there was a tidy mob of lads all waiting for us. They were the real thing and fought well. We backed them off and eventually they tried to jump into the two vans they had come in. The traffic on County Road had reached a standstill and it was murder; by now we were ragging them and the vans were getting wrecked as they tried to flee. They escaped in the end but it was a close call and the casualties they received were minor compared with what might have been had we been prepared for them. But they had given us a shock. Bruce and I met a few of them in Stuttgart during Euro 88 and we had a drink and a laugh about it. They seemed completely unconcerned about it and thought they had put up a good show. For a few minutes they did, but they also agreed they were lucky to get home alive.

stoke city

On 6 December 1980, I celebrated my eighteenth birthday in style: a day out on the "ordinary" with 300 Scallies running amok in Stoke. The ordinary was legendary with the Scousers; it was the scheduled or ordinary rail service, as opposed to the club-organised "special" trains. It took other firms years to suss out why we called it the ordinary – and they call us thick. Stoke was a grim place and the people looked on in amazement as we marched out of the station all dressed in Lacoste jumpers, Lois jeans, white Stan Smiths and wedged haircuts, to the last man and boy. The police later described us as a plague of locusts. Nothing was left unturned and nothing that was not worth a quid remained in its rightful place. There were no Stoke around to fight with; they had a crew in their half-empty end singing crap songs but Stoke away in those days was like a school trip without your teachers. We drew the game after leading twice, and the crowd was just over 15,000, well above their average gate. They call Stoke a sleeping giant but they hardly brought any fans, never mind lads, to Everton, though that was no disgrace, as very few clubs did. We took over 6,000 to that game, more they have ever brought in their history to Everton and it's only an hour away.

A few years later, we played them in a FA Cup third round tie. It has since become a famous game for Everton as, had we lost, it was rumoured that manager Howard Kendall would have been sacked. We won 2–0, and Kendall reported that his team talk consisted of opening the dressing room window and telling the players to listen to the thousands of fans singing. The rest, as they say, is history: we went on to win the Cup that year for the first time since 1966. After the game, the only difference was that the Stoke had swapped their donkey jackets for gear that had been trendy four years before in Liverpool.

The following season, we went there with the biggest away following I have ever seen Everton take to a League game, apart from when we walk across the park and enter the cesspool. An estimated 16,000 took the ground and the few Stoke in there had to watch us celebrate another victory that took us a step closer to our first Championship for fifteen years, while they were relegated, never to be seen in the top flight again. Give them credit though, earlier that season they did show with a small, game firm at our place and had a bit of a go on their way back to their coach on Priory Road. Off the pitch it seemed they were getting better.

In 2002, after twenty-two years, numerous arrests, a jail sentence and more fights than I can remember, I was back in Stoke to see Everton in the FA Cup third round again. Things had changed from that day when on my eighteenth birthday we went there unopposed. I was now in my fortieth year, and not even the oldest lad in a firm that had swelled to over 200 as we pulled out of Lime Street. The numbers we had were relatively the same as in 1980 but Stoke were now rated as on of the tastiest mobs in the country. We were firmed up not because we were going to take the piss, but because we had to be. The day, by all accounts, was to be no school outing.

We got off at Crewe in the hope of meeting Birmingham, who were on their way to Anfield, but already it was on top with the bizzies and we were penned in on the platform. The Everton bizzies turned up and were even accompanied by "Will Carling", Liverpool's top police spotter, which was strange, as I thought the Zulus would have been his priority for the day. He told us it was not so, that no trouble was expected there, this was the main one, and it was the biggest police operation in the history of Stoke City FC. A massive compliment to us, one lad boasted. I doubted it; I reckoned it was due to all the bullshit that had been posted for weeks on the hooligan websites. But there was not a single "cyber warrior" on the train that pulled out of Crewe.

We got a call from some lads who had arrived on the earlier train and decided to get off a couple of stops before

Stoke, as the place was heaving with bizzies. The game of cat and mouse had begun and it was only twelve o'clock. We should have gone straight there and taken our chances of breaking the escort, or leaving it to Stoke to get at us, which by all accounts they were ready to do. As is usually the case, however, we had too many chiefs, not enough Indians, and ended up in a boozer in the middle of nowhere, which within minutes was surrounded by riot vans.

It was the biggest police presence I had ever witnessed. After an hour, we were forced out of the pub, and for half an hour were searched and photographed. We were then made to get on buses taking us to within feet of the turnstiles at the impressive Britannia Stadium. We filled a double-decker, a coach and two minibuses, which still left about twenty to travel in police vans. It was a tasty 200, the full hit, with guest appearances from lads previously not seen in years. It was indeed 2002, with "techno hooliganism" at its height, and the mobile phone was like the proverbial hot potato as Stoke tried to sort it with us. Yet inside the ground seemed pretty mellow: when you go to the so-called "hard case" grounds it can be hostile, but Stoke seemed quite friendly. It has a lot to do with the new stadiums that are springing up all over the country, though the New Den is still a bit tasty.

We had been instructed by Stoke over the phone to do a right afterwards outside the ground but there was no chance, as a huge gate was locked. A few of them were milling about but nothing major, so we moved through the coach park and made it to the top of the road without a bizzie in sight. It looked like game on: we were on Stoke's patch with a top firm, all we needed now was some opposition. It turned out to be another fuck-up. The blind had been leading the blind and we ended up on some waste ground. Suddenly the lights went on and we were ambushed by 100 bizzies in full riot gear. A helicopter hovered above. The biggest police operation in the history of football in Staffordshire was a success. It must have cost tens of thousands but in the eyes of the police was worth it. I had my doubts. For the sake of letting two groups of hooligans have a fight on some waste ground for a few minutes, the money could have been put to better use than paying a load of bizzies double time to help pay off their Christmas overdrafts.

It was indeed a top operation. They had huge spotlights all over the place giving them the required light to film and take pictures of us all. We were pushed towards some buses and made to get on them. The firm was too big really. Two hundred lads look a bit conspicuous walking in the opposite direction to all the other fans – but they still praise the police intelligence for finding us. One of the bus drivers said they were going straight to Crewe station, so we got off. We didn't get far before the officer in charge of the operation – who was also in charge of the loudhailer – pulled me. He said if we did not get back on, we were nicked, but I argued that they were going to Crewe and loads of us had cars and vans parked at Stoke station. It was a blag but the top bizzie in charge of intelligence believed me. He turned his speaker on and announced that two of the buses would go to Crewe and one into Stoke, and everybody in cars and vans should get off the first two buses. Suddenly over 200 decided they were in cars and vans, and nobody had come by train. The boss cop could not get his head around it.

He began to get the hump when the Everton bizzie took over and told him the score. He then agreed that one bus could go into Stoke, and pointed at the buses while bellowing through his loudhailer, "Crewe, Crewe, Stoke." Unfortunately the loudhailer was not switched on, so he tried again. After he had yelled, "Crewe, Crewe …" I couldn't resist shouting, "Barney Magroo," which had everyone in bits, even the Everton bizzie, but the Stoke cop snapped and hit me over the head with his loudhailer. We were forced back on the buses and I was bitten on the head by a police horse, which was a new one on me.

At Stoke station, the first bus had already parked up and a small mob had tried to walk across the road towards a boozer full of Stoke lads. The bizzies let a dog loose and an innocent Everton lad was so badly bitten that he needed several skin grafts and was in hospital for a week. To make matters worse, he was nicked as well. We were surrounded and could not move until a train came. We got off at Crewe, still entertaining hopes of a fight with Birmingham if we could get across the platform, but the station was like a prison, with hundreds more bizzies.

For days after, the local papers and radio stations were full of people complaining of being attacked at Stoke, including parents walking their kids back to the cars. We were the mob they should have been after, but instead some of their so-called hooligans apparently wasted normal football fans out for a day at the match. I know this happens and am sure the main Stoke lads frowned upon it as much as we did, and rightly so. We had three double-decker loads of the best mob I had seen Everton take away for years, full of lads my age and a few older and younger lads who would cut you as soon as look at you, but I can't say they sought us out. A lot of firms bull up Stoke, and maybe they are as good as some claim, but those who beat up blokes with their kids and fans wearing club shirts will never have respect and let their mob down badly that day.

stockport county

These were another shower who were given a chance to make a name for themselves thanks to a kind FA Cup draw. Like so many others, they failed miserably. They came to

Goodison the same season as Port Vale and after the game, which they got a draw out of, Paul and me spotted a little mob of them on Goodison Road. We went over to tell them to keep walking in the same direction, as they seemed to be getting a bit nervy. In situations like that you can usually approach a few lads and point them in the right direction. I walked over and just said, "Okay lads, keep going past the boozer and you'll get it down there."

Instead of giving me a yes or no, the shady bastards gave me a bit of a kicking. Not the first or the last I will get, but it was out of order, as I was only helping them on their way. I took a punch in the side of the head followed by a few more for good measure. I found my bearings and saw a few of them onto Paul, so went over to help him and this time got put on my arse in one. They were big bastards and could hit hard, and I was glad they were not blade merchants, as for half a minute my head was somewhere in space and I was at their mercy.

I dusted myself down and saw that they were now surrounded by a mob of ours who, as far as I was concerned, were two minutes too late in showing. Still, it put the Mancs in a right flap. They were shouting for the bizzies to help them and fortunately for them got an escort to their minibuses. We kept an eye on them and apparently they had lost their driver, so when the main group of bizzies moved off we went and fronted them again. They were all lads but now they didn't want to know. There is no shame in taking a slap or having to get on your toes occasionally, and they had certainly given me a few good ones, but they did not fancy getting one or two back. I suppose there is the fear of the blades and I don't blame them for that; Everton in the dark is a nasty, evil place, but Stockport just kept bleating for the bizzies to help them and eventually they were all put in taxis and taken home.

At the replay they had a load of lads out but we had mobs everywhere and pretty much took over the town. We scored in the last minute and were all on the pitch – as usual – when a few fights broke out and I was nicked. It was a bummer really as Everton took a massive mob into town after and went on a mad one and I missed it all.

A couple of years later, I was on a train coming home from Barnsley with a lad who went to loads of England games and knew everybody. A moody little firm got on and they were Stockport. I thought I was going to get slung off when a couple recognised him and soon they were all around us on the train. They turned out to be all right and were full of praise for the mob we had taken there in the Cup. I knew a lad called China through a Man City mate of mine and he was with them and we had a beer. They all got off at Piccadilly and went into Manchester to look for United. They asked me to join them but I declined; I'd had enough hassle with United when I was with Everton without looking for it with another mob. The Stockport looked a game little firm but I doubt if United would have bothered their arses with them.

sunderland

In the late Seventies, if there was a ground more on top than Roker Park, then I never went to it. Unless you were draped head to toe in red and white – which we never were, obviously – then you were a target. It did not matter if you were not even old enough to shave, you were fair game, and until I was about twenty I used to hate going there.

The first time was in August 1979, first game of the season and T-shirt weather. I was chased for miles within seconds of arriving at the ground. When we were queuing up to go in, we were jam-packed against a load of Tyne Tees

Television vans and there was a little gap between all of them that these fat bastards were trying to squeeze through to get at us. It was impossible and so they were slinging ale and piss at us. I was looking at them and thinking, *These are as old as me dad, for fuck's sake.*

A few years later, they brought a casual mob to Everton for the first time and got steamed out of the Blue House on Boxing Day. It was a tidy little battle and I rated them better than Newcastle by a mile. Many years later they brought a boss mob and loads didn't go to the match. I heard they had been making a nuisance of themselves in town and handing slaps out to Joe Public, so went into the Blue House for a nose. There was about thirty of them in there and their main lad was a sound bloke. I can't remember his name but he was a stocky bastard and had a brown Lacoste woollen hat on. They really did love the wool up there.

We arranged that they would clear off up to Anfield and we would meet there after all the bizzies clocked off at half six. I knew we would do this mob, as a lot of them were looking a bit wary and asking me how many we would have and did we all have blades. Once you start that caper, you are on a loser. We kept our part of the bargain and I made sure they got on their way out of the boozer unscathed, as a few of the Everton lads were into doing them straight after the game. It could wait – what's an hour and a half if it means no chance of getting nicked? A lad went up to Anfield in a taxi and came back with a positive, they were all in The Arkles, so we got eighty together, split into two mobs and went through different sides of Stanley Park. We came out at the same time on both sides of the pub – and nothing. They had disappeared into thin air. I don't know how they got away so quickly or, more importantly, why?

In 2001, word was that they were all staying overnight as

it was the last game of the season, and one of the lads said they were at it again, pissed up in Williamson Square swilling ale over everybody. A couple of us went down and they were there, about fifty and all lads, acting the goat kicking shoppers up the arse and lashing ale at birds in their going-out gear.

We walked back, mobbed up in The Crown and a couple of us walked down to Wetherspoons to see what they were up to, as by now they had made their way up there. Their behaviour had not improved and they were kicking off on a load of lads on a stag night who were not even football fans. Within a minute it blew up and we got together and steamed them. They were battered and chased from Spoons all the way around the square to the Adelphi, and took a few casualties for their cheek.

Everton were crackers; the whole area was CCTV'd up and yet we still went for it, which turned out to be a stupid move. There were lads getting done in all over the road and I was amazed that, when the doors came in, only about three Everton lads were nicked. One of their lads, Daz, lost his phone and I met him and gave it back. He stayed with us all night and admitted we were too strong a mob for them. The big disappointment was that when a few of ours got nicked off the CCTV coverage, the Sunderland lads gave evidence in court, and at the time one lad got sent down for it. It is hard enough to stay out of jail these days without fellow hooligans helping to put you there. We put it to bed and thought it was over but two years later lads are still getting pulled for it and one has just been jailed for an attack with a pool ball in a sock, which was caught on film. If ever there was a case to sit up and realise that it's over, that game was the one. In the old days if you were not nicked on the spot you were free to kick off again two minutes later; today every knock on the door is a potential jail sentence.

tranmere rovers

We used to play Rovers every pre-season and for a few years always took a firm there. One of our lads got six years for allegedly slashing a Birkenheader a few years ago and it was yet another bad call, as it was the wrong lad who did the jail. After that, it was always on top with the police over there and no-one even bothers going in a mob now. They chased a few Everton lads a couple of years ago and claim a result but in reality they are insignificant and not worthy of a real mention.

We played them in the Cup a couple of seasons ago and they were full of it in the run up to the game: 500 lads on the ferry, 200 on the tube, 300 through a new tunnel, but it was no surprise when they turned up with about sixty and hid in a boozer at Central Station. We were all in Spoons and, for a rare one, had bothered to turn up in town, such was the concern that they would bounce out of the underground and claim a result having chased a couple of blokes selling the *Echo* on Lime Street. I saw a couple of lads come in the side door scouting and asked one was he Tranmere. He said, "Yeah," and looked like he was fronting it, so I went to have it and the two of them ran out into the street. We thought it was to get us out and followed but they scampered back to the boozer and all stood huddled by the door behind a load of bizzies.

They were nowhere before the game at the ground and must have got a bus straight back to their smack-ridden town, as we never saw one after the game. We had loads in town but they were back in Birkenhead by quarter past five. At ten o'clock they phoned us and said they had a mob in their town and wanted us to go over. Though it was a stupid idea, we decided to go, but the OSD got onto us outside The Hanover and we had to abandon it.

They all sing, "You can keep your cathedral and your

Pier Head, we are not Scousers, we're from Birkenhead." Is right, fucking stay there.

wigan athletic

Although I have never been to Wigan with Everton, I had a classic meeting with them in Manchester. We were there for a pre-arranged kick-off with Oldham after we had been away at Sheffield Wednesday. We searched for Oldham for about an hour, even though they had been on the phone and reckoned to have an imaginary 100 looking for us. On our final trawl we went to Oxford Road. I went into the station with a mate and saw a mob of about thirty in the buffet bar, so walked in. I knew a few Oldham lads and none were there, so I went to walk out when a lad stood up and said, "What's your fucking problem?"

"Looking for Oldham, mate. You seen them?"

"You're no fucking mate of mine but you've found Wigan and you have got a problem with us now."

I could not believe my luck. I smiled at the prick and picked my words. "You're the one with the problem now, dickhead, as I've got eighty lads outside, and here they come, mate."

He looked out and I swear he changed colour as he saw our mob coming towards the bar. I continued, "If you say sorry, very quickly, by the way, I may, just may, not tell them what you have just said."

He whimpered an apology and quickly sat down. I managed to contain myself and keep my part of the bargain, waving our lads away. The dickhead's mates had been no problem and did not deserve a kicking, so we left it at that. As I walked out I turned and told him to have a nice weekend but I knew his world was shattered and his mates were even smirking as I left. When I told our lot about it, they wanted to go back in but nothing could have bettered the humiliation that laddo suffered.

My mate who went with England at the time asked a couple of Wigan heads about the incident and they told it as it was and agreed their man had been made an idiot of. He apparently has promised to have me if ever we cross paths again. No comment.

wrexham

I am mates with quite a few of the Wrexham lads and ended up watching them a few times when I was banned from Goodison for my conviction at Arsenal. I had a go at doing the ninety-two League grounds and ended up having some boss days out with the least famous Frontline, as Boro like to remind them. They don't have great numbers but always like to put on a little show and had a few creditable results over the years.

One of the best rows I saw them have was after a play-off game at Orient. The year earlier I had been nicked down there and foolishly went back for more. Wrexham lost and had a top mob out and it went off on the way back to the Tube station. They were backing the Cockneys off all the way until they got it together and started giving it the ICF chant. After that it was about even. When they thought the mob was all Orient, they were on top, but the West Ham presence (or bluff?) seemed to turn it.

Another time I went to Shrewsbury with them and they fronted the home boozer, I think it was called the Elephant and Castle. Shrewsbury would not come out so a load of us walked off. A few minutes later they piled out and badly filled in a couple of the lads I knew. It was strange going to these small grounds and seeing how it was. If I had been there with Everton I would not have given most of them a minute of my time. We would have caned them in seconds, but with the smaller clubs and their numbers you could end up getting hurt, and that is what made it interesting for me.

The best laugh I had watching them came when we went to Northampton to see them get promoted. They took a few thousand and I was locked out. Northampton had a small mob and fronted us, so I butted this lad who thought he was the cream of the Nationwide, and Wrexham had the rest off. I then saw a load of stewards entering the ground and walked in behind them. Minutes later, I was in a yellow jacket and was in charge of the Wrexham end. My brief was to keep them off the pitch and point out any potential troublemakers to the police. When Wrexham scored, I let them all on the pitch and a lad later sent me a picture from the local paper that showed them all steaming on and me laughing.

At half-time, I went over to the Northampton firm, told them where to meet us after and wound them up that they were going to get cut. There were fans looking at me like I was from another planet; they clearly thought one of their stewards had gone mad. Eventually I got fed up, went to the boozer and kept the jacket. I still have it, just in case Everton ever play there.

I did the tickets at Wrexham a few times and came unstuck. Once was when Cardiff were going up and brought thousands. I sold a few of them tickets for the Wrexham stand and it went off in minutes. They were slung out and I was still outside and had to do a swift one, as they were not a happy little firm and wanted a refund. Another time, Wrexham got Man United in the Cup Winners Cup and I got grief from both sets of fans. The Mancs tried to have me off for being Everton and a load of Wrexham came out of the woodwork for the big game and had the hump that I wanted to make a few quid. It was a dodgy night; I took about ten slaps and never made a bean.

It was inevitable that we would play them, and we ended up getting them in the Littlewoods Cup home and away. I tried to keep a low one, as the likes of Neil, Stan, Chaz and a few of the others were good mates of mine, but it was impossible. All the Everton lads wanted to have it with them so I tried to sort it and not get involved myself, and just about pulled it off.

The first game was at the Racecourse and we won 5–0. Before the game, a moody mob of them pulled a blade on a couple of our lads. I smoothed it over and saved a Wrexham lad's arse. After the game, I took Everton down all the back streets and we came out behind McDonald's, where they all used to meet. I left them to it. Everton fired a flare into them and they were off, that was the end of it. My man there still says it never happened and said it must have been a load of kids waiting for their Happy Meals. It was ten o'clock at night.

At Goodison I arrived late and went into The Winslow on Goodison Road for a pint; it was thirty minutes into the game and I just could not be arsed with it all. I saw a load of lads walking past the boozer, so went out and it was about forty Wrexham.

"Where's your boys, Nicholls?" shouted one.

"In the ground knobhead, it's nearly half-time."

"Oh, yeah."

They had walked from Lime Street, got lost and were looking for Everton at eight o'clock. God loves a trier. They left the game twenty minutes before the end and took a bus back to Lime Street. I was glad. I did not want to fall out with a few mates over a nothing game, but some of them still have the hump with me to this day over the flare gun incident.

I hadn't been there for years until we played them in the summer of 2002, pre-season, but still kept in touch with Neil, the one Cardiff call the baldy ginger lad. He is seriously obsessed with football hooliganism. If you need to know anything about what happened at any ground in the country on a Saturday, he is the man in the know. My psychiatrist would make millions if he could get into his head and sort it out.

It went pear-shaped at a pre-season game when I had a call from some of our lads who had opted to stay in Chester on the ale rather than join us in Wrexham. A few young lads went into the home end and got a load of shit from the Wrexham Stone Island brigade. Four of us left the boozer and paid in and soon saw the culprits, who sloped off into the middle of their crumbling kop. It was a quality sketch: we went into the middle of them and, as the whole area parted like the Red Sea, we offered them all out. About a dozen of them stood there and looked down at their snide Rockports without so much as a whimper. We laughed and were then thrown out by the Wrexham bizzies, who had witnessed their lads' most embarrassing moment.

My man was soon on the phone and I agreed to go and meet him for a drink and to argue the toss as to who was out of order. We walked into town and as I made it to the to the pub with a few mates, a moody little mob of them thought we were looking for it and it went off briefly. I ended up taking a bottle over the head and needed a few stitches. It was a fuck-all incident but typical of some of the knobheads who play the hooligan game today, someone was claiming on the Internet that Wrexham had put Everton's top lad in hospital. In their fucking dreams.

I was dismayed when we drew them in the cup later that season, as I knew that Everton would rightly not be arsed with them and was also aware that they would be banging on the drums recruiting every lad for miles who owned a fake Burberry cap. I was not wrong. What happened that night still pisses me off to this day and the respect I had for many of them has gone for good. Amazingly, I had the sense for about the first time in my life to stay away, as in fairness to my mate over there he had tipped me off that the little skirmish a few weeks previous was still under investigation and I was likely to get nicked if I went anywhere near. It still didn't stop them phoning me every half hour for an update on our mob's whereabouts. They would not believe that Everton did not take the mighty Frontline seriously and bombarded me all afternoon for numbers and locations which did not exist.

After the umpteenth call I snapped, belled our lads and was told that sixty of them were staying in Chester till about seven, as the bizzies were swarming around the station. I told the Wrexham lot but instead of waiting for the lads they should have been fighting, they took it to pubs full of ordinary fans and families and claimed a major result.

Our lads came in at twenty past seven, scattered what was left of their rent-a-mob and watched Rooney score his first goals for Everton, unaware that earlier Wrexham had taken to kicking the shit out of football fans. It was that bad that a senior police officer from Merseyside told the Everton lads he would let them out early and turn a blind eye for a few minutes to allow a bit of payback. Not much happened after the match but a few weeks later a load of Wrexham were nicked for the assault and I heard a few got jailed. Everton bizzies viewed the CCTV and spotters' video and not one Everton lad was nicked, which proves that they were not there when Wrexham took up the sport of attacking people who were not there for the fighting. There was outrage when one young lad was glassed and I had to stop a firm going through a couple of Wrexham lads' doors. They were not the ones responsible; had I known who the cowards were I would have let them take the punishment.

After their night of shame they put a bit of a run together and I've heard they have a load of young lads with them now who are lawless. Lawless they may be but they are thick with it, as there is not a month goes by without doors going in and lads getting jailed for a bit of brick throwing with Port Vale or a spot of synchronised dancing with Chester.

I still get on with some of their main lads, but as is the case when a big club with a reputation comes to the town of a smaller club, the rules go out the window and innocents are hurt. That shit happens and always will but bragging about it months later is poor – and that is what loads of their hangers-on did.

the jocks

As well as Aberdeen, we have had it with both Celtic and Rangers at Goodison and I have seen us play both of them in Glasgow. I also went to the Scottish Cup final between the Old Firm in 1980, when it went off on the pitch. That was a frightening battle and neither side budged an inch. It was pure hatred and went on for ages. Of the two, I prefer Rangers. I was in their end and there were literally thousands going at it. I knew no-one there and kept my gob shut. We had gone in a van to that game and, as we were getting onto the East Lancs Road heading for the motorway, a Liverpool fan asked us for a lift, thinking we were going to the English Cup final. We all kept quiet and he was well pissed off when we let him out near Carlisle.

The Old Firm both came down for testimonials at Goodison, Celtic for Neville Southall's and Rangers for Dave Watson's. Of the two, Rangers had the most lads but Celtic had the numbers. We kicked off with Celtic when they put a huge IRA flag up outside the Oak and were playing Republican music on a ghetto blaster. Loads of people think the Jocks are a great laugh but I think they are twisted for using religion as an excuse to play up. When it kicked off some Everton fans were shouting, "Leave them alone."

But what did they expect when they promote terrorism at our ground a year or so after a young Evertonian, Tim Parry, was blown to bits by an IRA bomb in Warrington?

At least when Rangers came they were a football mob and were looking for trouble with hooligans. It went off before the game and they had a load of Chelsea with them but although there were about 150 arrested, it was as a preventive measure or for basic public order and not major violence. Most of our lads were locked up and released uncharged after the pubs shut. The only loser was Dave Watson, who had to foot the bill for the hundreds of bizzies on overtime at his testimonial.

We went to Ibrox in the Eighties for Colin Jackson's testimonial and it was well iffy. We had only a couple of hundred and were all over the place. Had we stayed together, there is no doubt we would have been killed. At the time they had Everton down as Celtic-lovers and we were not made welcome up there. In fact Everton are no great lovers of Celtic or Rangers; personally, after the games at Goodison, I hate the pair of them. We went to Celtic Park a couple of years ago for a pre-season friendly and in fairness they were sound with us. That pissed me off too, as we took a load of lads and were looking for it. They can't win really!

Having fought with the three main mobs up there, and knowing the Hibs lads well, I doubt if the others will have much joy with Celtic and Rangers, as the numbers they have are frightening. Aberdeen and Hibs are not big enough to make a real impact. I am certain that if the "Big Two" are allowed to play in England, initially in the Nationwide, you would see football hooliganism return to a scale not seen since the Eighties. Millwall v Rangers: the mind boggles.

18 EXTRA TIME: ANDERLECHT

WHEN I COMPLETED the previous chapter, I thought I had simply to write a short epilogue and, bingo, it was next stop the printers. I bargained without Everton's pre-season trip to Anderlecht. It was our first major jaunt abroad since 1995, and I bet everyone behind the polished oak doors at the Goodison boardroom wishes we had stayed at home and played the likes of Preston. The scale of violence and the size of Everton's mob that night were beyond even my wildest expectations. Apart from about twenty lads, every single hooligan who has fought for us over the past thirty years turned up in Brussels. I can say, hand on heart, that it was the biggest and maddest mob I have ever seen Everton turn out.

The week before the game, the fixture was in doubt, as the Belgian authorities were not too keen to accommodate us. Had they known what was coming, they would have pulled the plug immediately. Forget England slinging plastic chairs and playing up in Euro 2000; that was like the Chelsea Flower Show compared to what unfolded on 6 August 2002. It was as bad as I have seen, and believe me, over the years I have witnessed just about the lot.

I travelled on the Monday to Amsterdam, figuring that if I took a direct flight to Brussels I would be on the first available plane back; since 1995, when I was deported from Iceland, I have been banned from travelling abroad to watch Everton. I should not have worried, as not one single individual was turned away, and there were people there who I would not let loose in my backyard. The Dam was its usual seedy self, but the introduction of the euro has also made it an almighty rip-off. A beer used to cost three guilders, so in theory should now be about two euros. As if. They have just changed the letter, not the number, so a beer is 3E, not 3G. As one lad said when haggling outside one of the windows, "Thirty nicker for a suck, fuck off, I'd rather have a wank and ten ales."

We got to Brussels and mobbed up in O'Reilly's, the infamous English haunt. It was pissing down, which is always a bummer and spoils a good drink. An Anderlecht lad showed and told us to be ready, assuring us that they would have 400 out later. He was told they would need it, as we had that already and there were several planes still due to land. He also confirmed that both Chelsea and Man United had seen the Belgians in action and neither had fared very well. I was dabbling with the tickets when they played at Old Trafford and indeed they had given a good account of themselves, so I had no reason to doubt him.

At half six, we made a move to the underground. I walked with a good 150 lads. Why didn't we have numbers like that every week? Never mind Easyjet, it's a lot cheaper to get to Boro than it is to Brussels, end of chat. We stopped on the way at an obscure station, where the bizzie in charge made the mistake of telling the lads not to get off as this was where the Anderlecht hooligans congregated. You can imagine the response. As one, we piled off the train, leaving a red-faced Belgian bizzie pondering if his English was that bad or if we were crackers, as we had done exactly the opposite of what he had ordered. His English was perfect.

We made our way up a hill and came across a huge barrier that the police had erected to prevent the locals attacking us. We removed it in seconds and marched towards a couple of street bars that were by now emptying their contents, which were Anderlecht's lads. The riot bizzies were in front of them in force but were in disarray; we had not read their script. They had dropped an almighty bollock by letting us get up this street and the look of panic on their faces was a giveaway that things were not going to plan. They drew riot sticks and started banging them against their shields; all it did was excite the Belgian mob, which was impressive. I looked behind me and although a few had gone AWOL, we still had a firm three times larger than usual and it was ready to rock.

All hell broke loose as we reached the bizzies. Anderlecht bounced down towards us, a sight I have seen hundreds of times that rarely comes to anything. The usual sketch is that the bizzies nick the few brave ones at the front while a gang of wankers at the back sling a few bricks and bottles and the bluffers shout, "Stand," before running. Then comes the inquest as to why they never went through us. This time it was different. We panned out in the road and I told everyone to let them come, as we were going up the hill and that is a big disadvantage in a gang battle. Those coming down can force you back or, if numbers get behind you, you're equally in trouble. Stay put, let them come and if those at the front stand it's a battle of the fittest. Those at the front of our mob were going nowhere. So either Anderlecht wanted it or it was all a show.

This was no show. They piled straight into the riot bizzies, opening a gap, and Everton forced through it. The locals did not give a fuck for the bizzies and fights broke out all over the road. At first we were all wary of getting nicked, but it was not going to happen as the bizzies just whacked everyone in sight and tried to force us back down the hill. Loads of their lads were wielding brollies, and glasses and bottles smashed all around us. By now we had sussed no one was going to get nicked, Everton broke through the descending thin blue line and briefly it went off big time.

The bizzies were forced to fire a massive gas bomb into the middle of our mob. I had never seen anything like it; it shot out of a huge gun the size of a fire extinguisher and landed by us in the shape of a big red balloon before exploding. It was an unbelievable contraption, but 100 per cent effective. I have been gassed by opposing fans and by police at home and abroad but this stuff was lethal. As well as blinding you, leaving you unable to breathe and causing you to spew up, it burnt your skin.

As the red mist evaporated, the Anderlecht mob had regrouped and were having another go at getting at us. You have to give them credit, they were a game mob and as good as anything I have seen at home for years. They treated us and the bizzies with contempt. We had one more charge with them but there were gassed lads spewing up on both sides and the riot bizzies finally got it under wraps. I stood yards from them and the Belgians were loving it, going mental. There were lads taking their shirts off and showing off huge "Anderlecht" and "West Side" tattoos; the latter, I assumed, was the name of their end.

We were forced back down the hill, escorted through a park and made it to the ground unopposed. The police then dropped another bollock, however, and let fifty of us wander off looking for the West Side. We found it and forced our way in past the lone ticket collector, occupying a mass of empty seats in the opposite corner to the rest of the lads. There were a few Belgians in there looking worried; they had missed the battle and seemed shocked that we had managed to get into their end. For good measure we gave it an "EV-ER-TON" and the Scousers at the other end applauded, whilst the players warming up looked across and cringed at us.

A steward came over and said to me, "Please go in the other end, soon there will be hooligans in here."

I smiled and replied, "Fuck off, the hooligans are already in here, mate."

He took note but soon we were swarmed with the riot bizzies and taken to the Everton section. It was worth a try.

At half-time, all the talk was of the battle and I was

amazed that they were still selling us ale. The mob leaders emphasised that if before the game was anything to go by, there was little chance of getting nicked, so to make an impression on the Anderlecht mob we had to play by the same rules: Fuck the bizzies. Everyone was told to come out early and get off before all the normal fans got mixed up with us. This was no place for amateurs and, judging by what I had seen before, we needed to be mobbed up big time, as Anderlecht would be back for more.

With about ten minutes to go, I wandered out and could not believe my eyes. Around 1,500 Everton supporters had made the trip and about two-thirds of them were outside ready to go for it. A good mate of mine, Barry, who must be touching fifty, was there. He's been everywhere and done the lot: Kenny High Street, the Den, never misses a game. He was standing there like a kid on Christmas morning. He grabbed me and was shaking me, going, "It makes you proud." I am sure the club and the authorities will disagree but I knew exactly what he meant.

A couple of vanloads of bizzies were waiting for us and had erected another barrier to stop us getting away from the ground. They looked a frightened shower and I thought to myself, *it's not going to take much for this to go*. It didn't. A few blokes with kids asked to get past and we made way for them, but they were forced back by the twitchy bizzies. There was a bit of pushing and shoving, nothing major, but then one of them lost it and fired another gas bomb right into the middle of us. These bombs are indiscriminate, and everybody copped some: kids, lads, dads, women, normal fans and hooligans alike.

The bizzie with the gas gun has a lot to answer for. Pure and simple, Everton as one – not the Snorty Forty, or the old lads, or the young wannabes – but about 1,000 lads, retired from the Seventies and Eighties and with all the usual suspects, as *one* put the Belgian riot police on their toes. It was a sight that will live with me forever. As the bizzies were getting ready to tackle us, putting on their gloves and helmets, Everton steamed right into them. They were punched, kicked, relieved of their batons and helmets and forced to run – not back off, fucking run – down the road as Everton waded in.

They regrouped by another fleet of vans as reinforcements tried to back them up. Riot helmets flew through the air into them and another makeshift barrier was dismantled and dropped on them. One lad said it was like the Miners' Strike. I disagreed. Fuck your "Coal not Dole", this was Everton. All the old chants came out and "We Are Evil" filled the air as yet another twenty-foot section of railing was used a battering ram and the bizzies were off again. One lad started singing "Rule Britannia". I told him to shut up; we were Everton, not England.

Time and time again the bizzies tried to save face but there was no chance. Everton were having none of it and as one mob was gassed, another regiment of troops piled through the mist and were back into the Battle of Brussels. I saw lads wearing riot gear, the full lot, and some Everton fans thought they were undercover bizzies tooled up; in fact they were Everton lads wearing what had been left behind by the police.

As a last resort, two huge tanks drove up and fired gallons of freezing water into us. It had been pissing down all day and we were soaked through anyway, so who gave a fuck? They gave up, reversed to their mates and had another go with the gas bombs, but were forced to give up and let us through in the search for Anderlecht. They were nowhere to be seen. We passed one bar and the doors were locked up, with the lads inside looking through the windows in amazement at the size of our mob. None ventured out; it was no place for heroes and the night belonged to Everton and Everton alone.

Back in O'Reilly's it was buzzing. The place was full to the rafters of lads and the other two bars nearby were the same. Lads who had not been seen for years were shaking hands and hugging each other. It turned sour a little when, as usual, some Turks started to gather and little mobs of them began to sling bottle and glasses at us. A few retaliated and there were brief skirmishes. I could not be bothered with the shady bastards and a few of us went back to the hotel for a late drink. The bizzies were now filming it all and had the full city police force on standby. We found a little seedy bar that was open until six so in we went. It was no surprise to see three of the first-team players in there; some things never change. No need to name names, they bought us ale and were sound.

We flew home the next day. The earlier flights had been met by reporters looking for a story of the night's violence. A few obliged and I later read reports that blamed everything on the police. Whoever told them that must have been on another planet. In total, twenty-four Everton fans were nicked, mostly for the skirmishes with the Turks. Had the bizzies been arsed, or brave enough, they could have nicked ten times that amount, bang to rights. At one stage I had even felt sorry for the local bizzies, until another gas bomb landed by my feet. Of the arrested, only two were charged and in fact very little was made of it by the media: it had a brief slot on the TV news and a small column in *The Sun*. Had it been in England it would have been headline news, front page of the tabloids and Kate Adie reporting, now back to Peter Sissons in the studio.

I'm no lover of flying, and always think the worst the minute my arse leaves the ground. They say that just before you die your whole life flashes before you, well I'll tell you what: if the pilot on our flight home had informed us that both wings had fallen off and that we were going down, I would have had flashes of Kevin Ratcliffe lifting the Cup

EPILOGUE:
FULL-TIME OR DO TIME

THE TRIP TO Anderlecht was proof that although football hooliganism was not as widespread as in the manic Seventies and evil Eighties, it was still a popular pastime for masses of fans given the right ingredients. I say masses and although the fools who think they are experts on the subject would disagree and call us the minority, they are talking bollocks. Eighty per cent of Evertonians at the match that night were bang at it. The peaceful passing of the 2002 World Cup once again prompted the authorities and these dickhead experts to kid themselves into thinking that they have got the problem under control. They do so at their peril.

There was never going to be major trouble in Japan. The banning orders were a success of sorts, although how many of the banned lads had the coin to go anyway is debatable. I suspect it will be a different story in 2006 when Germany host the Finals. Even the European Championships in Portugal will be in disarray if certain countries' hooligans bump into each other, as it is a lot cheaper and easier to get to the Algarve than to the other side of the world, and England's following in Portugal will be nastier than the brass band and replica shirt brigade that joined in the carnival atmosphere in Japan.

I predicted nearly two years ago that the qualifying rounds could even see deaths. I kid you not, the same thing could happen at the finals. England v Turkey could have been a bloodbath, home and away. There would have been serious disorder without the major operation to keep England fans from travelling to Turkey. I and others believe the blanket ban on travelling fans saved lives. But it will be a lot harder to keep the thugs apart in the holiday resorts of the Algarve and indeed all over the country. It is a very difficult task but one I believe the authorities must have a crack at unless they want to be attending funerals. I sincerely hope I am wrong – it is a frightening thought.

From a personal point of view, my days are over. I knew there was a conspiracy at Goodison to stitch me up for anything bad that happened on a match day even before I wrote this book, and watching Everton became a risky pastime for yours truly. For instance, in one season I was pulled in for alleged "racism", ticket scams and violence. I was not charged with and was indeed not guilty of any of the allegations, but the Merseyside bizzies were letting me know I was in their sights. Writing this book gave them the ammunition to pull the trigger and, fuck me, did they pull it.

Once the local press got onto *Scally* my days of going to the match and even into town with the lads were numbered. The week before the book came out I agreed to do a bit of a piece for the *Liverpool Echo*, as they say no publicity is bad publicity. I expected a couple of columns and a little bit of fuss. No chance: I got a front-page full colour picture under the headline "STOP THIS THUG NOW!" Inside was a three-page spread and the silly bastards even called for MPs to ban the book – which no-one at that time had read – and had a phone poll which surprisingly was against me selling said tome.

Well, when people are told not to buy something they often do the opposite and thanks to my friends at the *Echo* the book's first run sold out in a couple of weeks. The police also got involved and tried to stop me having a launch party: they had their usual success rate when taking on the lads and after a game of hide-and-seek we had a blinding turnout in a club one of the lads runs, while the bizzies were parked up in town by the vanload waiting at a bluff venue we had printed tickets for!

Everton went a step further, and in a week when they were in deep talks over the proposed multi-million-pound move to Kings Dock, they actually held a board meeting about me and the book and banned me from Goodison Park for life. No doubt the disruption of the release of this book got to them as they fucked the ground move up with ease. The thing with a club ban though, is that unlike a court banning order, you can still go and if you get caught you only get slung out or at the very worst fined for trespassing. So that's what I did, with varying degrees of success. Every game I was spotted at was a nightmare and in the end I gave it up and stayed in the boozer near the ground. Believe me, you look a right soft bastard in August with a hat, scarf and overcoat to go with your sunglasses!

The other thing is, you get a bit paranoid. I went to a game against Newcastle and as I got up into the stand, a Tannoy announcement asked all police and stewards to "commence Operation Goodison". Thirty stewards and bizzies started heading in my direction and I ended up legging it down the stairs and bunking over the turnstiles back into the street. Later a steward told me that it was an exercise planned for evacuating the ground in the event of a bomb scare!

The Merseyside derby is a game I never miss so I got a decent disguise together and went in. Within minutes a senior bizzie came up to me and asked me to leave.

"Why?"

"Andy, you're banned lad, now do us all a favour and piss off out of here."

"My name's Dave, officer, don't know what you're on about."

"Okay Dave, you're nicked until you prove that you're not Andy, now stop pissing me about. Are you still Dave?"

"I'm Andy, sarge, see you later!"

At least he had a sense of humour. I have taken a few sly slaps from the OSD who aren't happy about the things I say about them in the book. After the derby we went into town and a decent mob of about 100 walked from The Crown to Wetherspoons and fronted the Red mob across the road. I took a stick across the back and was filmed for the rest of the night. At half one in the morning a van full of bizzies pulled up and booted me up the arse, hoping for a response that was never going to come. One of them searched me and then threw one of my shoes in the middle of the road and told me if I went across for it he would nick me for endangering road traffic. I laughed and told the sad bastard that the book was doing well and I had bought plenty of pairs of Prada shoes with the profits. I got another smack but it was worth it. That night was to be my downfall though, as the little confrontation in town with the lovable Reds was filmed and the noose tightened.

Everton were playing a friendly in Holland and I was nicked at the airport and locked up before I had the chance to get to the duty free shops. There are all sorts of laws out now that can stop you leaving the country, which should be used to stop people getting in. Fuck me, there would be enough jobs and houses to go around twice if it was as difficult for the refugees to get in as it is for a British hooligan to get out of our beloved country. Within days I was in court and the police applied for a banning order, which after a few weeks of contesting I had to accept. Basically they had film of me still "involved" since the release of the book and with what I had owned up to in *Scally*, it did not give me a leg to stand up on. In court the defence brief had the prosecution file and it was unbelievable: 300-odd pages of surveillance and shite. Most of it was nothing but it was a wake-up call, as there were times when I was not even at the match and the bastards were on my case and taking snaps of me. Things like on a Tuesday afternoon going for a Chinese with Alfie, Wednesday night at Anfield dropping tickets off – it was over the top but did the job. I received a two-year ban from all grounds and am not allowed in any town or city Everton are playing in on a match day. I cannot enter any area within ten miles of Everton on a match day and can't even have a pint with the lads. In fairness, in the battle to prevent football disorder I have found it pretty fucking effective!

After the court banned me the press were back on my case and Ian Millar, the Everton top bizzie, was on TV and radio taking great delight in telling all and sundry how a dangerous thug had been brought to justice after months of continuous undercover police work. The soft bastards only had to go to Waterstone's and buy the book and it was all there for them. Still, I suppose it keeps them in a job. I told Radio City exactly that and to their credit my interview was broadcast during primetime news. That day a nail bomb was thrown through a nightclub window and a Liverpool reserve player was shot in the arse, yet I still made the five o'clock headlines. It's barmy.

As well as Everton, I am banned from watching any Football Association fixture abroad. I made a big mistake and broke that one. I thought it only covered England matches so went with some mates to watch Wales play in Russia. A week after I got home the doors came in and I ended up looking at six months for breaching the banning order. I got fined £750 in the end because they believed my defence that I had misunderstood the details of the banning order. They were not wrong there as Rumpole of the Bailey would have to sit down with you for a week to explain it. It is a hideous document and a recipe for disaster if you don't read it carefully. Basically if you're on holiday and two birds on the beach start kicking a ball about, get off your sunlounger and get home sharpish – if the bizzies see you you're going to jail.

In fairness I never intended to be one of the typical "hooligan authors" who makes a few quid and pretends he has changed and is a hooligan no more. I cannot change. I am addicted to it and have sought professional help to try to get to the bottom of my problem. Because that is what it is – a mental problem that needs addressing. Had I been a flasher, an alcoholic or a drug addict, the courts would have got me counselling or medical treatment. As a football hooligan, they just want to lock you up. I would rather do what I have done on Saturday afternoons – thump lads similar to myself – than stand in the woods in a long overcoat, flashing my bits at passing kids, yet those perverts get help. It's a mad world. By seeking help from a psychiatrist, I hope that I will be able to pack it in. And there are literally thousands of people like me all over the country. I will be forty later this year and know I should have grown out of it. It does worry me, big time.

Since the age of sixteen, I have been arrested over twenty times, spent weeks in court, been jailed, paid thousands of pounds in fines, been battered, cut up, had failed relationships and a broken marriage, and lost well-paid jobs, all because of football violence. I've been at it for a quarter of a century and have seen hundreds of lads come and go. In that time I have seen some bad things happen, very bad things like Heysel and Hillsborough. I have seen people with horrific injuries, and on several occasions – usually the day after I've been locked up – I have sworn to myself that I will pack it in, knowing full well that at the next high-profile hooligan game, I will be in the thick of it, just like the wino who swears never to have another drink, only to find himself waiting for the offy to open at half ten in the morning. It's an addiction: drink, drugs and football thugs, all the same.

As for Everton, we don't have a top mob any more and will never see the numbers we had in the Eighties on a regular basis. However, there are plenty of young lads who will make sure we always show. Then we have so called "big games", like Stoke in the cup and the trips abroad, that prove what we are still capable of. Forget what the kids and pricks on the Internet lied about; we had a boss mob that day and there were not many kids with us, which proves that when it matters, Everton can take it to anybody. I was regarded as one of the main lads at Everton and had been for years. We never went for this "top lad" crap; there were about a dozen of us who could pull a tidy mob together in a matter of hours if need be. The drawback was obviously the attention I got from the bizzies and I knew that it was only a matter of time before I came unstuck because of who I was. Writing this book just helped speed the process up.

So was it worth it? Is right it was. I have had a great time over the years and writing brought the memories flooding back. The *Echo* wrote in an editorial that I should "bask in my 15 minutes of fame". Well thanks to those idiots I have done slightly better than that. This is the fourth print, the book having sold many more copies than I could have dreamt of. I am soon bringing out my second book, am doing some writing for TV, whilst *Scally* is in the hands of some American film producers who are toying with the idea of *Scally The Movie*. Although I am unsure who they want to play me, favourite at the bookies is Paul Usher *aka* Barry Grant for the early years and Ricky Tomlinson for now! I also do a bit of hooligan expert analysis for Sky TV and have had no end of spin offs. The one downside is it has brought an end to my off-field activities, as I now prefer to call them. But that is not such a bad thing.

You might think it's crazy, but even after we went to Anderlecht I had every intention of going to St Andrew's on Boxing Day and "enjoying a fun day out" at Old Trafford, Maine Road and the Riverside. I thought I would be there with Everton's mob looking for people just like me: football hooligans who love it and will always love it, who know they should call it a day but can't, because when it goes off there is simply not a better buzz in the world.

Anderlecht should have changed all that. For a start,

nothing any firm could throw at us would top the events that day. Secondly, I knew I was heading down a one-way street if I kept attending matches. So I said, "That's it for me. I'm finished with it." Retired at the top, if you like. But I was kidding myself. I could not stop going and but for getting nicked on the way to Holland I would still have been at it over there, and that is God's honest truth – I was an addict and hooliganism was my drug.

Two things changed it for me. While writing this book, my father died after a short illness. He was eighty and had a good innings and all that, but as I sat by his bedside and watched him leave us I could not help thinking of all the pain and sadness my life must have caused him. He was a tough man but a gentleman and never once in my life did he or my mother raise a hand to me – maybe they should have! I will always be sad that he passed away knowing I was still bang at it and was bringing trouble home with me.

Secondly, at the grand old age of forty I became a father and that was the one that made me have a long hard look at myself. I have been to jail and without sounding blasé it did not bother me a great deal, as I lost a bit of weight and brushed up on my reading, but now the thought of not being able to see my little girl grow up will keep me out of trouble for a long time.

So that's it, it's over for me and I'm finished with it. But before Merseyside Police, NCIS and the courts slap each other on the back, let me tell you, it's nothing to do with the stupid rules and bans, sly beatings and bullying tactics you throw at me. It's down to finally having something which replaces the buzz of a full-scale kick-off.

Maci Olivia Nicholls, "You make me happy when skies are grey."

End of chat, no back answers.